Peace and Plenty

Peace and Plenty

Finding Your Path to
Financial Serenity

Sarah Ban Breathnach

GC

GRAND CENTRAL
PUBLISHING

NEW YORK   BOSTON

I would like to gratefully acknowledge all the writers I have quoted for their wisdom, comfort, and inspiration. An exhaustive search was undertaken to determine whether previously published material included in this book required permission to reprint or be quoted. If there has been an error, I deeply apologize and a correction will be made in subsequent editions.

The legal and moral rights of Sarah Ban Breathnach to be identified as the author of this work and the creator of the intellectual property concepts contained within, including Simple Abundance®, "Gratitude Journal," "Illustrated Discovery Journal," *The Peace and Plenty Journal of Well-Spent Moments*™, *The Peace and Plenty Comfort Companion*™, and The Thrill of Thrift™ has been asserted.

Simple Abundance® is a registered trademark of Simple Abundance, Inc., and used by Grand Central Publishing and Hachette Book Group with permission.

Peace and Plenty acorn illustration by Patrick Munger, © Simple Abundance, Inc., 2010.

Grand Central Publishing
Hachette Book Group
237 Park Avenue
New York, NY 10017
www.HachetteBookGroup.com

Printed in the United States of America

10 9 8 7 6 5 4 3 2 1

Grand Central Publishing is a division of Hachette Book Group, Inc. The Grand Central Publishing name and logo is a trademark of Hachette Book Group, Inc.

Library of Congress Cataloging-in-Publication Data
Ban Breathnach, Sarah.
    Peace and plenty : finding your path to financial serenity / Sarah Ban Breathnach.—1st ed.
        p. cm.
    ISBN 978-0-446-56174-7 (regular edition)—ISBN 978-0-446-57370-2 (large print edition) 1. Women—Conduct of life. 2. Women—Finance, Personal. 3. Spirituality. 4. Meditations. I. Title.
    BJ1610.B358 2010
    332.0240082—dc22
                                2010025832

A ministering angel shall my sister be...

—WILLIAM SHAKESPEARE,
HAMLET, ACT 5, SCENE 1

She was.
She is.
For my cherished Sister,
Maureen Rose Crean,
With dearest love and deepest gratitude.

Helping one another is part of the
religion of sisterhood.

—LOUISA MAY ALCOTT

In a time lacking in truth and certainty and filled with
anguish and despair, no woman should be shamefaced in
attempting to give back to the world, through her work, a
portion of its lost heart.

—LOUISE BOGAN

Contents

Part Three: You Might as Well Live

Part Four: Down for the Count

Part Five: All About Eve

Part Six: To Begin Again:
Creating a Life of Contentment

Upon Reading This Book

When money is plenty this is a man's world. When money is scarce it is a woman's world. When all else seems to have failed the woman's instinct comes in. She gets the job. That is the reason why in spite of all that happens, we continue to have a world.

Once more the job of managing the households is up to the women. To many the job seems utterly impossible. They find themselves working against strange, unseen forces that relentlessly destroy.

The old rules — the rules that were set to jazz by the stock sellers and the politicians — simply do not fit... Everyone has lost something in terms of money, and a few have lost everything. It makes no difference if the income came from investments or from a job. For those who have lost everything, there is nothing but a fresh start needed.

— *LADIES' HOME JOURNAL*, OCTOBER 1932

Welcome to *Peace and Plenty: Finding Your Path to Financial Serenity*. A fresh start for all of us: living well, spending less, and appreciating more. In between the lines of this book, you'll find sublime moments of unexpected serenity, cozy contentment, a shared smile of recognition, and, if you need it, a friend to pass the vintage hankie. In

1995 I wrote *Simple Abundance,* a book based on the transformative practice of Gratitude, Simplicity, Order, Harmony, Beauty, and Joy to change your life. It worked for
me and millions of others around the world. We found the
sacred in the ordinary and felt better able to cope with the
changes in our world. We're going to rediscover the *Simple
Abundance* promise and payoff in *Peace and Plenty*: affirming
the luxury of enough by counting our blessings as well as
our cents and celebrating the feminine art form that I call
"the thrill of thrift."

Unless, of course, you'd like to continue flailing in
the relentless downward economic spiral we've all found
ourselves trapped in—gnashing our teeth, wringing our
hands, and frantically tossing and turning all
night—worrying ourselves sick over too little, too late,
spilled milk, wide-open barn doors, and foxes smacking
their chops in the henhouse. Who's afraid of the Big Bad
Wolf? We all are, and boy, he can smell our fear. Why else
do you think he's huffing and puffing, ready to blow our
house down?

We've worked ourselves into quite a frenzy. It's been
hard to avoid, with economic doom and gloom around every corner. With every "breaking news" alert on television,
we're joining a bread line, pushing a shopping cart on the
street, or packing our imaginations in a rickety old jalopy
crammed full with threadbare blankets, grimy mattresses,
battered tin pots, plates, and every ratty dish towel we've
ever owned. Next, we're pitching a tent on the outskirts of
every town from Oklahoma to California, forever on the
lam and blowing out the kerosene lantern when the sher-
iff's pack of dogs starts yapping.

But we don't solve this or any problems by running
scared. No, we're going to have to solve this as only
women can—we're going to sit down and have a frank
feminine heart-to-heart. *Now*—take a deep breath—we're
going to talk about money. Not yours—at least, not at first.
We'll start with mine or the lack thereof. In an ironic way,

many people thought *Simple Abundance* was about money. But *Simple Abundance* was about finding out what's important to you, cherishing it, and giving thanks for it every day. It struck a chord in millions of women and earned me quite a lot of money quickly. I just wish I'd known then what I've learned the hard way now.

Yes, I'll come clean: All the money's gone. But when it's back—and it will be—I'll know better, and so will you. That's why you're going to love this book as much as I do.

Peace and Plenty is about women and money. It's an emotionally volatile relationship for most of us. It's also the most complicated relationship we have—and the one that most controls our lives, because we let it. Acknowledging that money is important to you, cherishing and respecting your ability to create and maintain a sustainable flow in your life, handling it wisely so that it can serve you and yours well, and giving thanks for this gift every day during these perilous economic times may seem impossible. I agree with John D. Rockefeller, however, who believed that "the ability to make money is a gift from God." Even more important, the ability to *keep* the money and learn to be a good steward of your resources is a Providential promise if we seek wisdom and ask for discernment. But did you realize that these blessings are Divine Gifts you need to *ask* Heaven for directly in prayer? Don't worry; you will by the time we're finished.

In between these covers, I'm going to share my own harrowing money stories, providing you with a feminine canon of cautionary tales, or at least as many of them as I can muster up the courage to reveal. (My cheeks are already burning as I recall buying the duet with Sting of "Every Breath You Take" with money that could have paid off my mortgage, so we'll see how it goes.) The point is, every woman has a vast collection of blushing, tawdry money secrets churning inside her, waiting to be acknowledged, lest they scream their way out of hiding in order to be exorcized.

Money—how we love it. Fear it. Earn it. Spend it.

Save it. Stash it. Lose it. Lend it. Lust for it. Hide it. Pray for it. Marry it. Divorce it. Sleep with it. Tell and eat whoppers for it. Cry rivers and drown out sorrows over it. Throw it away or send it packing with an eBay click. Worry about it. Worship it. Work like a slave for it, then squander it. Make deals with devils. Go on fateful dates with con men and undertake vows before God so that we'll never be hungry again. Most of all, how women like us convince ourselves that money will change or fix everything in our lives that's ever been broken or has gone south once upon a time.

One of the things we probably don't realize is how hypocritical we are about money. We crave it but we don't want to appear as if we do. We're much more comfortable if money just magically appears in our checking account. That's how I got a sudden windfall in my life, by writing a best seller, although my overnight success was, in fact, based on twenty years of hard work living and writing my book.

Don't get me wrong (because that's what we do all the time about money): There is never a day that isn't made brighter when a check with your name on it actually arrives in the mail. But the great troubling of most of our lives right now isn't too much of this good thing, but a pandemic of dread over not enough, the *lack* of money. Remember, abundance and lack cannot exist in the same space, so if your imagination is blocked by images of yourself pushing a shopping cart in your slippers, then you can't be sighing with pleasure over repurposing your never-used dining room into a cozy library, happily imagining what that dark bookcase would look like if you painted it a sunny yellow and backed the shelves with vintage wallpaper. (I've done it and it looks amazing, but that's another chapter in another book.)

In *Peace and Plenty*, I want to remind and reassure you and myself that fear is always a future-based phantom and a conscious choice. *Will there be enough? What will I do? How*

will we manage? Where will it come from? How long will it last?
There are so many "wills" in our financial calculations;
surely there must be a way to fix our financial problems.
But while we figure that out, we have to live today. That's
why I'm here to share with you essential morsels of domestic bliss, some new takes on old ways, the rediscovery
of the true meaning of thrift (hint: It comes from the verb
to thrive), fabulous footnotes to famous women's private
money woes, and hints from Yankee and English housekeepers to mull over in your heart while you bless each
day's portion of your daily grace. Like the golden threads
you've spun out of a bale of straw, there's a promise of
peace and plenty in between the lines of this book, a private message that's waiting just for you to find, cherish,
and use to turn your life around. This message of hope, encouragement, and comfort will sustain you, awaken your
courage, heal your wounds, and rouse your passion to begin again. This message has been handed down from the
past, passed through me as I write today for your tomorrow, so that you may take that leap of faith and grasp your
fresh start with both hands and all your heart.

In this, our private respite from the stresses of the
world, I want to help you think, meditate, and ruminate
on the wondrous. I want you to ponder all the possibility
hidden now in your difficult financial circumstances. I believe with all my soul that there's a private code, a deeply
personal, magical, mysterious, and mystical prompt embedded in what passes for ordinary. It's my great joy to be
able to help you dig these rough diamonds out from the
mountains of coal that life throws at us. We'll find a secret
cipher ready to be revealed in Margaret Mitchell's *Gone
with the Wind*, and Emma Bovary's spendthrift ways. We'll
discover why Daphne du Maurier's haunting *Rebecca* is a
fable for how women handle power and money, and how
Amelia Earhart never went anywhere without her "little
housewife." As far as I'm concerned, Miss Piggy is a financial prophetess, Pollyanna is profound, and Mae West's

investment strategy is all any woman needs to be rich. We need to find inspiration whenever we can, because when we're spiritually tuned in, everything is a clue pointing us in the right direction. Think of me as your personal guide.

Looking up to the Light and much farther than the landscape of your life might seem way beyond your abilities at this moment. Maybe, but not for long. My prayer for this book is that it will be the best kind of page-turner: a collaborative art between the two of us. For as the poet Robert Frost so brilliantly observed, "No tears in the writer, no tears in the reader. No surprise in the writer, no surprise in the reader."

Which personal surprise should I start with? Which private snapshot can I share to illustrate my deep understanding of the enormous range of unruly emotions—guilt, shame, foreboding, anger, remorse—that the lack of money and sense of financial insecurity can instantly trigger? Although our circumstances may differ, our emotional truths and often contradictory feelings over money are very similar and, I believe, uniquely feminine. So while I pray you haven't experienced all the lows I have, read on and see if portions don't strike a chord with you. I've a whole photo album full of sense memory snapshots, so I've got a pretty good idea what you've been going through lately, dear Reader, and I know it's been rough.

On to the sharing. I'll go first. Will it be the memory of leaving a famous Los Angeles hospital after seeing the best cardiologist in the country on an emergency basis through the intervention of friends? After a day of diagnostic tests, he's just told me not to worry, that my heart is strong and that, basically, I'm a healthy woman. The problem seems to be that I'm so stressed, my body has begun mimicking heart attacks due to the onslaught of repetitive panic episodes. As the picture comes into focus in my memory, I can see my shoulders rising by inches and feel my chest constricting, even as the doctor is reassuring me. It's nothing to worry about this time, but I'm told I need to get my anxiety under control. Oh yes, I will. Yes. You bet. My sister is with me and now she's driving the car out of the hospital parking lot, and our mutual sighs of relief and gratitude are buoyant.

Suddenly my cell phone voice mail beeps. I think it's from my husband. No, it's a nasty debt threat from a celebrity limousine company I owe money to. I should have paid the bill by now and God knows I want to, but at the time it was a choice between them and health insurance. Now they are threatening to call Oprah and somehow make my private debt a public matter. Of course, this tactic is illegal; by law they can't shame, intimidate, or bully me. Still, they do—and my body reacts with the pounding heart, sweats and shivers, dizziness, shallow breaths, nausea, and the same sharp pain in my chest that drove me to the doctor in the first place. As the maelstrom of emotion grips me like a vise, a cosmic finger snaps before my eyes, jarring me out of some hypnotic terror. A wise woman, her voice very strong and soothing, speaks to my heart: "Choose, Sarah. Which thought will it be? To be grateful that you're healthy or frightened over money? He's a bill collector bully. Of course you're going to pay your bills. But right now, health is the first wealth. Choose health. Choose wealth. Choose now."

Or how about a gorgeous Indian summer afternoon two years ago. I've just arrived at a lovely Long Beach hotel where I'll be staying for the next two days. I've been invited to speak at the California Women's Conference, and I'm thrilled to be here. After I check in, I telephone my husband back in England, who tells me that I've got to—right this instant—send a fax to the clerk of the court, proving that the reason I can't attend the debt hearing scheduled in a few days is because I'm out of the country. Although I had written a letter explaining the situation in good time, suddenly the court wants proof. Now I'm trembling and teary behind big sunglasses as I stand in line waiting for the hotel to send my fax and its attachment—the conference program page featuring my photograph and biography in between Bono and Cherie Blair. The court concludes that I must be where I say I am, and the hearing is set for another date. But I'm shaken to the core, ashamed and humiliated. And the timing couldn't have been worse. What right do I have to be giving other women advice on how to live their lives when I've messed up mine so completely? I feel myself shrinking inside, becoming very shy and small. The incredible withering woman. How did I get here? How will I ever get back to financial sanity and serenity?

The same way you will. One day at a time, through difficult decisions and tough choices, sharp shards of blinding insight and dazzling moments of truth, but most of all with spoon-fed optimism to accompany those hard-digested life lessons. By preserving our pennies, exulting in our elegant economies, saving our senses, and keeping our wits about us when all the world is losing their minds. We're going to learn life's most valuable lesson together: how to keep calm and carry on.

Oh, my darling Reader, the only way we can move on is to start over from scratch. Who could have imagined it? But blessed are we among women with the opportunity, desire, and sublime common sense to finally strip away the pretense; now real, wise, and savvy enough to count all the good remaining. Women have always known how to tame the fears of our loved ones. Now we need to do it for ourselves. Join me on an enlightening as well as enchanting, reassuring journey to emotional solvency and financial serenity, as you become secure in the knowledge and spiritual truth that peace and plenty shall always be your portion.

Blessings on your
courage.

Sarah Ban Breathnach

Part One

The Measure of Our Days

And what does January hold? Clean account books. Bare diaries. Three hundred and sixty-five new days, neatly parceled into weeks, months, seasons. A chunk of time, of life, waiting to be filled. One thing is certain. There will be more newness than ever before. All the world over men and women are facing changed values, an altered lay-out of life.

—PHYLLIS NICHOLSON (1947)

First You Cry

Even when the gates of Heaven are closed to prayers,
they are open to tears.

—THE TALMUD

I used to be a woman who cried at Hallmark commercials. Maybe you are as well. But for the last couple of years, as the economic ground beneath all I've accomplished and cherished has shifted so profoundly in a life-shattering reversal of fortune, I've trained myself to stay alert when the roar and the rumbling of what could be catastrophic change begins. As anyone who lives on a geographic fault line where earthquakes are frequent will tell you, it's the aftershocks you need to worry about. Just when you think you're safe again, you can get buried alive. Tears are too much of a distraction at times like this, so I've learned to adapt to a behavior that is completely contrary to my natural inclinations: no crying. I simply cannot allow myself the luxury of falling apart if the world does.

Not just yet.

Other times, the shock of whatever heartbreak has just befallen you is so great, and so unexpected, your visceral reaction is a hand to cover a stifled scream as your knees buckle. This is what happens to other people, but not you. You pay your bills on time, have a deeply personal relationship with God, do good works, are the best mother in the world, the most devoted wife, loyal friend. A moment ago you had dreams, vacation plans, routines, the car pool run, vet appointments, budget meetings, retirement pension, conference calls, soccer games, health insurance, dinner reservations, a home. Then the doctor calls. The Dow plunges. A drunk runs a red light. The bank forecloses. There's a menacing knock on the door. The court summons arrives, or a police car slows down then turns into *your* driveway. Photographs slipped through the mail slot reveal that your husband has *not* been working late at the office. In an instant you lose your job, your home, your health, your marriage, or the unthinkable, your child. We vanish in plain sight along with our good name, our identity, our honor, our sense of right and wrong. Our security. Our future. The day after tomorrow.

All the money's gone? How *can* that be? No, you don't understand. *I* didn't do anything wrong. There must be some mistake.

But no, there is no mistake. Only beautiful lives gone awry, promises that can no longer be kept, and hearts rent asunder. In this "ordinary instant," as Joan Didion so exquisitely calls the moment when each of our lives changes utterly and forever, we are catapulted into the realm of the unspeakable.

There are simply no words to express or console. No explanation, no reasoning, no self-help mantra, no belief big enough to surmount this anguish at this moment. No secret on earth to help you come to grips with the unfathomable. All we know is that we are stunned, shocked, hurt, grieving, and groping with too many unknowns to consider and too many contingencies to handle as we attempt, in wrenching pain and agonizing vain, the harrowing undoing of what cannot be undone.

And now, sweetheart, *now* you cry.

Misery Has Her Moments

Sorrow fully accepted brings its own gifts. For there is an alchemy in sorrow. It can be transmuted into wisdom, which, if it does not bring joy, can yet bring happiness.

—PEARL S. BUCK

Misery is, by her own nature, a passing phase of sorrow, one that does not linger uninvited. Her sojourns seem to be part of life's required curriculum, perhaps because Misery endows us with compassion and empathy. A time will come when—because we know how much it hurts—we will be able to help another.

Artists will confess, after a few drinks, that the pain of Misery can sometimes be bittersweet. Down through the ages she's been the most inspiring of muses. Poets write tributes to her, musicians sing her song, playwrights dramatize, and filmmakers embody her cinema verité with every take. What they all are trying to do is work with Misery's mystical power to transform, because after she's come to call, we are never quite the same. There is a composite echo, a deeper vibration to the adagio of our days and our response to life. I remember having a conversation with Rabbi Harold Kushner about life's tragedies; he told me something that I've never forgotten and so pass on to you. Be very sorry and pray for the "lucky" people, the people you might envy, those who have not known the vestige of sorrow, or grief, or misery before they are forty, because their ledgers of loss will be incalculable. Life is the ultimate forensic accountant.

So how do you deal with Misery? Some of us dance around her, playing out her many moods and wearing the mask of ennui as if nothing matters, when the truth is that *everything* matters. Others of us ignore her in a pointless pretense of dissociation and denial. Yet there is really only one way to deal with Misery. Accept her presence. Like most experiences in life, we must acknowledge the passage gracefully and let her move through our lives because she brings with her a hidden gift. But we must be patient enough for her to reveal it. And so we find ourselves reciting the narrative of our grief again to family, then friends who will listen, and then, when they won't, strangers on a train, our pets, or the peeling wallpaper in the kitchen, as Misery's morning cups of tea become tumblers of wine or whiskey mixed with our tears at twilight. Finally, miraculously, one night we stumble into bed and for the first time in a while don't toss and turn but sleep deep and morning comes. Oh yes, my darling Reader, Miss Misery does have her moments of healing.

"It is in the middle of misery that so much becomes clear," the poet and Jungian analyst Clarissa Pinkola Estés reassures us. "The one who says nothing good comes of this is not yet listening."

More Than Words Can Say

Let your tears come, let them water your soul.

—EILEEN MAYHEW

Perhaps your situation is the exact opposite—you wish you *could* cry, but the tears won't come. When we find ourselves in the realm of the unspeakable, we are in shock. Think of shock as Divine, impenetrable (for now) bubble wrap between you and the world. The angels have wrapped your frail body, fraught heart, and fragile soul in a protective, mystical membrane so that you won't break from the pressure and pain you find yourself in at this moment.

When we can't cry, we've shut down in order to shut ourselves off from whatever we can't face just yet. But the Compassionate One has already intervened on our behalf. The Bible tells us that when we can't pray, the Holy Spirit prays for us, and entreats God for what we cannot ask for ourselves. We have been taught to think of tears as signs of weakness instead of liquid triggers for a body's reserve of strength and endurance to kick in. Our first instinct as a mother is to hold our little ones close to us when they cry and coo, "Hush now, darling, *don't* you cry," when what we should be whispering as we comfort them is, "There, pet, there's the sweet babe. Have a *blessed cry* now; it's so good for you and soon you'll feel a lot better and grow up to be brave and strong."

"Rich tears! What power lies in those falling drops," the seventeenth-century English playwright, romantic novelist, and political satirist Delia Riviere Manley reassures us. Far from being self-indulgent, crying is an ancient form of articulated prayer. In Catholic and Eastern Orthodox religions, tears have always been considered one of the special gifts of the Holy Spirit; in the Hebrew Old Testament, an entire book of the Bible is devoted to crying—the Book of Lamentations.

Being Irish, I learned at Nana's knee about the Banshee, a Celtic mythological female spirit whose ghostly mournful summons heard in the night foretold a death, especially if it occurred at a distance. For centuries in the west of Gaelic-speaking Ireland, particularly in Connemara, certain women, wise in the ways of the supernatural or "other realms," were taught the proper way to grieve with sound, or *keen*, which is a long, high-pitched wail of abandonment and grief strong enough to shatter glass. The language of keening is the passionate calling forth of exactly what it is that you dread and fear, to rise up and meet you face-to-face on the scorched battlefield of your devastated heart. The sob is the soul's sacred battle cry for the Beloved.

To keen is to embrace those emotions too deep and too dark for words, struggling now for some, *any* form of expression. To let the sound of sorrow and waves of grief pass through you, picking up tempo and timbre as you go, is like breath on the reed of a woodwind or strings of a violin. To truly cry takes tremendous courage. The fiery anger wrestles in the pit of your gut; the despair catches in your throat; the fierce loneliness of the iron band of sorrow tightens across your chest.

Many of us resist the sacred relief of crying because the truth is, the act of crying physically hurts. Heartache is real. But we must trust that it hurts for a reason. For the love of all that is holy, do you really believe that God would leave us alone at such a moment? I don't. I won't and you can't, either, because how could we go on? And go on we must.

I'll never hush you, sweetheart. I'd rather you howl at the moon.

Heaven knows that I have.

You're My Thrill

The Peace and Plenty
Path of Thrift

*There is satisfaction in
seeing one's household prosper, in
being both
bountiful and provident.*

— PHYLLIS MCGINLEY

I don't know a woman alive who doesn't get a thrill out of thrifting—the finding of the perfect item at the perfect low price and not at the mall. But thrifting is so much more than a bargain bagged at a resale shop. For centuries, thrifting has been the heart of the homemaker's honorable estate and a sacred trust that included the right apportionment of her personal and domestic resources: time, creative energy, emotion, industry, strength, skill, craft, and labor; the management of property of all kinds, including money; the exercise of prudence and temperance; and the distribution of charity to those less fortunate. In other words, all those homespun virtues necessary to keep a family healthy, wealthy, wise, and secure were contained in the boon of this one expansive word. In the marvelous book *Thrift: A Cyclopedia*, edited by David Blankenhorn and written "for those who are not ashamed to think anew about happiness, extravagance, and thriving," we trace the origins of thrift as the path for achieving peace and plenty.

What thrift isn't: parsimonious, frugal, mean, scrimping, paltry, shoddy, stingy, sharp, or cheap.

What thrift is: bountiful, generous, compassionate, vigorous, growing, abundant, blooming, copious, healthful, efficient; filled with elegant economies, gratitude, simplicity, order, harmony, beauty, and joy (interestingly, all the six principles of *Simple Abundance*!); thriving, increasing, expanding, and plentiful.

We can trace the role thrift has played in the English household back to the thirteenth-century bard Geoffrey Chaucer's *Canterbury Tales*, as well as William Shakespeare's *The Merchant of Venice*. Probably the earliest meaning of the word *thrift* was "the condition of one who thrives," or being endowed with good luck, good fortune, wealth, and health. But what made thrift such an honorable aspiration was that its bounty was not conveyed by celestial benediction or favor of the Crown—but rather through the everyday choices made by prudent housewives who were neat, clean, industrious, imaginative, honest, clever, enterprising, and generous.

The invocation of thrift was considered as crucial to a bride's happy marriage as tossing rice, releasing doves, or wearing something old, something new, something borrowed, and something blue. Beginning in the sixteenth century, English nuptials introduced the custom of the bride's father or guardian slipping a silver sixpence coin into her left shoe as a harbinger of wealth and protection against want. The symbol of the sixpence represented the "reward" due to those drawn to the honorable estate of matrimony.

Intriguingly, thrift is also the name of a charming English flower, a sea pink perennial that blooms through April and September and flourishes in rocky crevices, requiring little soil for its sustenance. Usually the thrift flower acts as a barrier protecting the marshes from the

ebb-and-flow erosion of the sea. As a metaphor for our
own reconsidered economic lives, the metaphysical
boundary of thrift protects us from the ebb and flow of the
cost of living. It enables us to create our own protective
barrier to cushion us from want and distress through our
savings, the provision we've stockpiled through our persis-
tent thrift.

Without thrift "there can be little solid domestic happiness," the Pulitzer Prize–winning poet and essayist Phyllis
McGinley tells us in her *Sixpence in Her Shoe* (1964), written as an answer to Betty Friedan's groundbreaking *The
Feminine Mystique* published the year before. "For thrift is
neither selfishness nor cheese-paring, but a large, compassionate attribute, a just regard for God's material gifts. It
has nothing in common with meanness and is different
even from economy, which may assist thrift."

Phyllis McGinley is a woman after my own heart. She
loved being a wife, a mother, a homemaker, an author, and
a poet. She reveled in combining all the facets of her daily
round in her writing, working on her poems, essays, or
books while the stew or soup pot simmered. And she saw
no contradictions in combining all aspects of her life into
a tapestry of contentment—from meeting her husband's
train to celebrating being a suburban artist of the everyday at the White House. In her inspirational essay "The
Pleasure of Thrift," she describes how passionate thrift is
the guardian of domestic bliss: "Meanness inherits a set of
silverware and keeps it in the bank. Economy uses it only
on important occasions for fear of loss. Thrift sets the table
with it every night for pure pleasure, but counts the butter
spreaders before they are put away."

For many women, pulled up short by our own economic crises, becoming a novice in Mother Plenty's Order
of the Hearth enables us to create a framework for luxuri-
ating in a sustainable lifestyle protected from life's storms.
"Thrift saves for the future because the children must be
educated and because one must not be a burden in old

age," McGinley tells us. "Thrift keeps the house painted and the roof in repair, puts shoe trees in shoes, but bakes a jar of cookies for neighborhood children. It is never stingy..."

What I adore about McGinley's view of thrift is that "it has to be a personal joy which every housewife must work out for herself" by first examining what are her authentic extravagances. Do you love to cook? Then quality knives, organic chickens, and virgin olive oil will be your affordable luxuries—but through your prudent meal planning, the chicken will stretch to three delicious suppers, and the homemade sourdough bread accompanying your fresh chicken noodle soup will elevate leftovers to a family feast. For the woman who tallies contentment with thread counts and yearns to be tucked in under a silk duvet, then taking public transportation to work instead of parking a car can prove a fair trade-off. For the last year, my budget has included a category for shipping my cherished collection of still-life paintings from an English country manse where they once adorned a posh dining room's walls to a modest California apartment that doesn't even have a true dining room. But gazing at these beloved paintings will nourish my soul more than supping at a polished mahogany table, so my trade-off is incomparable.

"Every woman has to learn to be thrifty in her own idiom. Her economies must be like her luxuries—cut to the shape of the family budget or the family dream and they must never descend to indignities. Thrift implies dignity, the importance of human worth as well as of inanimate things," Phyllis McGinley reminds us. "It might lie for one person in a thing so small as properly balancing her check book or for another in something so large as learning to make all the draperies for her windows...And, like laughter or sachets in bureau drawers, it is a pleasant thing to have around the house."

In our journey to peace and plenty, we're going to be looking at thrift with fresh eyes—not as an exercise in

curbing shopping but as a home-grown remedy for contentment and creativity that begins with being grateful for
what we have and learning to embrace the honorable art of
"making do" to stretch for what we might not have at the
moment, whether it's money or gratitude or enthusiasm.
As you pull back from spending and learn to distinguish
between your needs and your wants, you'll find regular
"Thrill of Thrift" features throughout this book intended
to boost your morale and stoke your creative fires.

The Thrill of Thrift

Sweet Mercy Medicinal

Frequent tears have run
The colors from my life.

—ELIZABETH BARRETT BROWNING

Women had a lot to cry about during the Depression and the Home Front years. Keeping bodies and souls together with a continuous feed of courageous optimism and cheerful vivacity was considered vital. Women's magazines of this era acknowledged and provided regular remedies to soothe red faces and swollen eyes after having "a good cry."

Here's my favorite homemade après-crisis restorative. It calls for items you probably have in your refrigerator and cupboard—a cucumber-and-chamomile-tea rinse for the face that I call:

Sweet Mercy Medicinal

½ cucumber, peeled and seeded
¼ cup hot, prepared green tea
¼ cup hot, prepared chamomile tea

Puree the cucumber in a blender and strain the juice. Mix the teas together and add the cucumber juice. Stir well and refrigerate for at least half an hour. This mixture will keep for a day or two in the fridge. If you've been crying on and off, dab your face with some, rinse with cool water, and then pat your face dry with your softest towel.

Also have on hand a pitcher of water with cucumber slices and drink from it frequently. Often when we're emotionally distressed, we forget to do things as simple as sipping water while we slosh back the wine and whiskey. Reach for the water first, because dehydration can make you swoon.

Crying jags also leave us headachy. You can ease the throbbing with a little aromatherapy by inhaling the scent of an essential oil combination of violet, peppermint, and orange peel. I've made a Sweet Mercy kit that contains the homeopathic Bach Flower Essence Rescue Remedy, a lavender-scented eye mask, my headache oil, and some beautiful vintage handkerchiefs, luxuriously lace-trimmed or monogrammed, which I'm always on the lookout for at flea markets and estate sales (they make thoughtful, affordable birthday and holiday gifts, too), tucked into a pretty fabric jewelry roll or pouch. What you are doing by preparing this reviving self-nurturing kit for yourself or a friend going through a hard stage is granting permission to grieve gracefully and gratefully.

"Heaven knows we need never be ashamed of our tears," Charles Dickens wrote in *Great Expectations* in 1860, "for they are rain upon the blinding dust of earth, overlying our hard hearts."

Paradise Lost

That day I oft remember, when from sleep
I first awaked and found myself reposed
Under a shade on flowers, much wondering where
And what I was, whence thither brought, and how?

—JOHN MILTON, *PARADISE LOST*,
"EVE," BOOK IV, LINE 20

So how did we get here? Like most women, I've had the jarring experience of waking up the morning after the night before wondering where in the world I was and how I got there. Sometimes I imagine what it might have been like for Eve—the Mother of Us All—to awaken for the first time, finding herself naked, lying next to a strange creature—a man—and in Paradise.

I've not been alone in my Eden reveries. Down through the ages, the story of Adam and Eve has served as inspiration for artists, theologians, philosophers, statesmen, saints, sinners, and sages. Probably the greatest fleshing-out of the Book of Genesis is the seventeenth-century English poet John Milton's (1608–1674) epic saga *Paradise Lost*. Published in 1669 and never out of print since, this international best seller is arguably the most influential poem ever written in the English language, a feat made all the more astonishing by the fact that Milton wrote it after becoming blind. He would conceive (or channel) the verse in the night, memorize it, and then dictate it the following morning to his daughters or scribes. It took him twenty-nine years to write what eventually became a colossal twelve-book canon. Scholars spend their entire lives reading *Paradise Lost*, many devoting their careers to understanding and interpreting Milton's enormous biblical vision, the first ever written in blank verse (unrhymed poetry). When you think of the great poets in history, the headliners all owe a huge debt to John Milton.

And once you start reading it for yourself, it's actually a page-turner. So many of the Western world's concepts originated in Milton's imagination, including our ideas on the war between the sexes, original sin, good and evil, love, lust, loss, disobedience, betrayal, revenge, retribution, and redemption, not to mention archetypes, metaphors, literary allusions, even vocabulary; it's virtually impossible to completely unravel his impact on contemporary everyday life. *The Oxford English Dictionary* attributes 630 words to Milton (as compared with 229 from Shakespeare), including *earthshaking*, *self-delusion*, and *pandemonium*. Milton's Pandemonium is Satan's palace in hell, where noise, confusion, and pain reign.

Sound familiar?

Lately many of us feel as if we've been thrown out of Paradise without so much as a fig leaf…and we never even got a chance to take a bite of the apple. Maybe you've lost your way, your bearings, your home, your job, or your pension through debt, divorce, disaster, or death. Maybe your security and serenity have been wiped out because of someone else's misdeeds or malfeasance. Maybe your life is hell on earth at this moment. What you had before is gone and what's taken its place is sheer pandemonium.

But you are not alone. It was never part of my grand life plan to end up lost, alone, and out of necessity living with my sister and her family in her small apartment in California until the dust settled, sharing the bathroom with my aged cat, Mikey, especially when I have a gorgeous home and writing sanctuary in England (once the private chapel of Sir Isaac Newton), bought with the sweat equity of my life's work—but now part of a distressing divorce after a short and disastrous marriage. Just a few months ago, Mikey and I roamed the gardens of our Eden to sit and lie under the shade of an ancient apple tree. Echoing Eve, I wonder, *Whence thither brought, and how?*

When cataclysmic change arrives, why does there always seem to be such rapid and ruthless reckoning required, especially before we can even process what has happened? I can't be alone in thinking that events always move more quickly than we can deal with them; life's "preliminary hearings" are often scheduled before we can even blink.

The litany of loss seems enormous, the chasm between past and future made all the more fathomless by the detailed accounting to strangers of assets, now ashes, to be bartered, sold, or divided. What is even more wounding is the intersection of randomness and exactitude as we are called to account for someone else's debts, deceit, or reckless behavior. This is not right. This is not fair.

The shattered soul sits outside the Gates of Paradise in dust and disbelief. So many of us must start over from scratch. So few of us can afford to replace our past. *How long have we been here? Are you all right? I don't know yet. Give me time to figure it out.*

But there is no time.

You can't go back. You can't go forward. You can't stay here or stay put. When fire and brimstone are falling down upon your head, you can't take the time to figure out anything, especially where it all went wrong.

As Milton foretold, what happened is "all hell broke loose." But Reader, trust me: This experience is essential. It will make our new life all the more sweet when we find our way back. And we will find our way back.

Reversal of Fortune

Disaster is private, in its way, as love is.

— NADINE GORDIMER

Although the cartography of personal disaster and its passages are familiar—shock, denial, anger, bargaining, depression, acceptance—our emotional response to financial calamity is private and particular. A fashionista is going to have a different reaction to a money setback than a frugalista—which set of coping skills would you prefer at the moment?

It has been said that in a crisis, people fall back on what they know best: thieves to scams, gamblers to the turf and table, bigamists to one more golden ring. When my life derailed, what I knew best was self-help and gratitude. Or to be more precise, self-help through gratitude.

I remember after *Simple Abundance* had been on all the best-seller lists for more than a year, a hedge fund ran a full-page color ad in a glossy luxury magazine aimed at the very rich. After announcing "Abundance Is Not Simple," it wrote in rather dismissive copy that perhaps the author of this book was learning that handling windfalls was a difficult discipline, and there comes a time in one's life when we all need wealth management advisers.

Well, they had a point. One minute I was a freelance writer without a comma in my checking account and the next I was a millionaire entrepreneur with a staff of ten on both sides of the Atlantic. But no matter what personal situation I've encountered in my life, I've come to rely on shelf help. Actually, the only reason I ever ended up an inspirational writer was because nobody else had written what I desperately needed to read. Believe me, I tried to find it. The editor of a motivational book club once told me that I was their *best* customer; I had bought just about every self-help book published in the past decade. Yet few self-help books have offered me more than strident exhortations to pull myself together, when what I needed was gentle encouragement and coaxed truth, a tiny mustard-seed-size insight that slowly takes hold in the barren soil of the soul and grows strong roots, so that by the time the truth blossoms out of nowhere, it can't be pulled away.

When I realized to my horror that *all the money's gone*, I began to search out vintage memoirs, biographies, letters, and diaries, especially those by famous women writers and artists who seemed to play out charmed lives in the pages and canvases of their art and under the public gaze. Women who experienced enormous reversals of fortune in between the lines of real life; the perfectly poised, coutured, and coiffed who had money, fairy-tale marriages, beautiful homes, gorgeous children, successful careers, and enviable fashion spreads in magazines but knew private pain in the public fall from grace (usually because of their wretched husbands), yet handled themselves with dignity, aplomb, and courage. Writers like Rumer Godden, whose stockbroker husband ran off with all the money she'd given him to invest for the family, leaving her destitute with two children, at the height of her brilliant success with the novel and film *Black Narcissus*. Or the Anglo-Irish writer Elizabeth Bowen, who lectured and taught literature in America during the 1950s to save her family's beautiful home, Bowen's Court, only to be forced to sell it and then learn of its being demolished. Or Vivien Leigh's "fatefully irresistible" decision to follow Larry Olivier to Hollywood to make more money to pay for both their (costly) divorces back in England. The more real women's stories I could collect, the more sense I could make out of my own situation, especially the husbands who managed their wives' careers and spent all the money until there was nothing left on the gray ledger sheets but humiliation.

"There was a time when my life seemed so painful to me that reading about the lives of other women writers was one of the few things that could help. I was unhappy, and ashamed of it; I was baffled by my life," the writer Kennedy Fraser poignantly confesses in her luminous collection of women's lives, *Ornament and Silence*.

> I would sit in my armchair reading books about these other lives. Sometimes when I came to the end, I would sit down and read the book through from the beginning again. I remember an incredible intensity about all this, and also a kind of furtiveness—as if I were afraid that someone might look through the window and find me out. Even now, I feel that I should pretend that I was reading only these women's fiction or their poetry—their lives as they chose to present them, alchemized as art. But that would be a lie. It was the private messages I really liked—the journals and letters, and autobiographies, whenever they seemed to be telling the truth. I felt very lonely then, self-absorbed, shut off. I needed all this murmured chorus, this continuum of true-life stories, to pull me through. They were like mothers and sisters to me, these literary women, many of them already dead; more than my own family, they seemed to stretch out a hand.

Kennedy Fraser believes that "honest personal writing is a great service rendered the living from the dead." And I agree. But the lifesaving nuggets I cherish most are those heartfelt revelations from the living. Emotional sustenance that is enriching enough to give you the inner strength you need to throw the covers off at three in the afternoon, turn on the shower, wash your hair. Next, shuffle toward the kitchen and put on the teakettle and while the tea is brewing make yourself some scrambled eggs and hot buttered toast. Now sit, sip, and savor. Let out a big sigh—the first signal, as far as I'm concerned, alerting the Cosmos that a significant life-altering awakening is about to begin. Because it is. In fact, you're about to trigger a seismic shift in your thinking and awareness, coming face-to-face with your own money memoir.

After the Fall

When life changes abruptly with a financial reversal of fortune, we immediately become so caught up in stalling our own house of cards from collapsing that we don't realize that, by this point, we've already crashed and burned; at the very least, we're the walking wounded. Because of this, I experienced long stretches of emotional amnesia and economic dementia when it came to recalling my first few heady years of wealth in the late 1990s. For a long time while I was attempting to deconstruct my own personal financial disaster, I just blanked on details, episodes, events, and even the identity of the mystery woman I was trying to become through spending as if there were no tomorrow.

Everything happened so fast. The last time I looked, I'd been driving the car pool, changing the kitty litter, and waiting for the chopped meat to defrost in the microwave so I could make meat loaf. Within a short time, *Simple Abundance* had sold millions of copies, been translated into dozens of languages, and I had all the world's golden gifts lying at my Manolo Blahnik–clad feet. I was sought after and fussed over, made to feel important and grand, which, admittedly, is quite fabulous. I had enough money to establish the Simple Abundance Charitable Fund (which supports nonprofit causes through my royalties and has to date given out more than $1 million in grants), pay for my daughter's college education, fly the Concorde, and purchase the former chapel of Sir Isaac Newton in England to use as my writing sanctuary.

However, as I went back to unravel the truth about my financial situation, clarity became impossible; there were so many layers for me to sift through from the ashes of the mess I'd gotten myself into through a combination of good intentions and naïveté.

For instance, once I appeared on *The Oprah Winfrey Show* in March 1996 and *Simple Abundance* hit the bestseller lists, we could barely keep track of all the "business opportunities" presented to me—but it was clear that everyone was working their own angle. I became very protective of the trust readers had endowed me with and wanted to guard the integrity of the *Simple Abundance* philosophy. The best way to do that, I reasoned, was to use my new wealth to support my burgeoning business (instead of the business supporting me). So I hired a brilliant creative team to give me advice on designing a website and print magazine. No one on the team suggested that I protect myself. The lack of that lesson became very apparent when we scheduled our presentation to potential Silicon Valley investors the very week the dot-com bubble burst and I was left to honor my obligations with nothing to show except a huge loss.

Inevitably, the larger my public persona grew, the smaller my circle of intimates became. Isolation is one of celebrity's more uncomfortable footnotes. And while acclaim, awards, and applause are often very agreeable fellows to have a drink with, their conversation rarely moves past small talk. As Coco Chanel so succinctly warned: "That's what fame is: *solitude*."

Initially I was flattered by all the attention. After a few frenzied years, however, I grew overwhelmed and, frankly, exhausted by the sheer volume of requests: to speak, give money, franchise my name, extend the *Simple Abundance* brand, sit on boards of directors, and most of all write more books—as fast as possible. Now there were so many people depending on the success of my next project. I remember taking offense during a newsmagazine interview when I was asked what was so simple about having nine assistants. Fair enough, but I was sensitive to the criticism. There's a Life 101 red flag for you: If you don't like the question or scrutiny, ask yourself why. The reporter was right. My life had spun out of control; I had so many personal assistants because I didn't have time to grocery shop, cook, clean, answer the mail, or even pack for a trip. On weekends when I was alone, damned if I could find *anything*. When I wasn't with my teenage daughter, I'd catch up on badly needed sleep.

My staff were amazing, talented women with zest and flair; I loved each one dearly, and I wanted them to be happy in their work. But I didn't keep my staff on a budget because I couldn't keep myself on one, whether it was decorating, revamping my wardrobe, funding nonprofits, restoring a historic English home, or creating a stunning prototype for a *Simple Abundance* magazine. I discovered that women just love to spend money, and if it's not for themselves, for someone else they know is just fine. If I found a perfect pair of black trousers, one of my assistants would suggest I order three so there would be one in each closet at my three different homes. It seemed at the time that I was being practical, not extravagant. Isn't this what rich women do? The French designer Hubert de Givenchy once said that all a woman needed to be well dressed was the perfect black trousers, a black cashmere sweater, good shoes, and a well-cut trench coat. That's all I was going for, but in multiples.

For the truth was, I didn't have time to think: I was always working, always writing, always on to the next project, always on call. As my work began to spread and touch women around the world, I was invited everywhere, usually in conjunction with fund-raising for charities. I felt so blessed by my success, I was sure it was a fluke and that I had to "earn" it every day with more and more responsibilities. I felt obliged to share it in every way possible; I didn't want to disappoint anyone. Does any of this sound familiar? This is how women self-sabotage and self-destruct. Unless we have constant witnesses to our hard work, we are convinced we pull off every day of our lives through smoke and mirrors.

Yet I was so painfully shy and self-conscious at personal appearances that the only way I could do any of them was to travel with someone. I chose to be accompanied by a man who did my hair and makeup. This went on for a couple of years, and while it managed to keep me feeling confident enough to keep on showing up, you can imagine the expense. Equally, I was so uncomfortable with being photographed that I hired one of the world's most famous celebrity photographers "to get it right" and paid a fortune for a few head shots, which are gorgeous, but really not appropriate for most of my work, unless I'm going to be in a Busby Berkeley Broadway extravaganza. (However, I shall leave instructions that only these Brigitte Lacombe photographs are to be used for my obituary. I wouldn't want them to go to waste—and besides, this is how *I* want to remember me.)

Although my confessions are extreme, they are variations on the theme of a woman's secret wounds of the soul: low self-esteem or, as I called it more accurately in my book *Something More*: "self-loathing." What we lack in self-esteem we more than make up for at our favorite boutique or department store. Women spend to plug the leak, until life's levees break; before you know there's a flood tide and you're drowning in debt and haven't a clue what you bought for $25,000.

I believe the mustard-seed insight for us both might be the phrase *I didn't want to think*, which is how we all become oblivious to our own demise. I swear to Heaven if I were in charge, I would have every Saturday purchase over $250 called in upstairs so that a Divine Credit Mistress could have a brief word: "Madam, are you sure you want to spend this money in this way, or are we just feeling fat today? In that case, might I suggest our hot water and lemon 'time-out' at no extra charge."

"Spiritual empowerment is evidenced in our lives by our willingness to tell ourselves the truth, to listen to the truth when it's told to us, and to dispense truth as lovingly as possible, when we feel compelled to talk from the heart," Christina Baldwin reassures us in her stunning book *Life's Companion.* I certainly hope she's right. It has occurred to me as I've been detailing this litany of personal financial loss that in my first few years of overnight wealth, I made just about every money mistake possible, and yet I've just gotten started. There are some doozies down the road.

Maybe this is making you feel better, because your money mistakes must pale in comparison. And that's so important. Good. I'm grateful you can see that right now. I'm looking hard for the silver lining, and if you can learn a lesson on my dime, then it won't have all been for nothing. But this much is certain: It's taken me time to face my financial fears; time to muster the courage to begin to correct them; time to recover from the shock of all the collateral emotional damage that comes with how we handle our money. It will take you some time as well.

Time: the real currency for the past decade. But who has time to do anything but react? Especially when financial calamity arrives?

When there is a death in the family, we understand that there is an entire grief cycle that can't be avoided (although certainly many of us try our hardest to do just that), and family, friends, and professionals are there to help. After a devastating death, the world expects us to stay in bed, to cry, fail to eat, get drunk, not show up for work, and not wash our hair for a week. We are given psychological permission to drop out for a prescribed period of mourning. It is the necessary response to the precious loss of life.

Death is inarguably the biggest calamity humans must cope with. However, I think we also need compassion to understand that when people abruptly lose financial resources such as savings or pension, or the ability to earn a living, or the security of their home, there is also going to be a grief process. This, too, needs time to unfold as we come to grips with new and confusing circumstances.

Having to abandon places, houses, jobs, or our cherished possessions can be soul shattering. The enormity of the human drama and sorrow being replayed on the nightly news as homes are demolished and lives torn apart by earthquakes, tornadoes, hurricanes, wildfires, and floods grabs our collective heart because it's something that could happen to any of us. Acts of God may not be insurable by humans any longer, but there's no shame attached to losing your house by a freak mudslide, only best wishes, help, and community support.

But losing your house to foreclosure? Hmmm. The arched eyebrow wants to know: What were you up to? Do you gamble? Take drugs? Drink? Are you a spendthrift? Bank foreclosures don't happen to good people.

Well, they do now.

Even with the daily dropping of the Dow a public reality, few of us can bring ourselves to admit financial difficulty to even our closest friends until it's too late. This shame is so deep, we bury ourselves alive with imagined condemnation as well as our own self-punishment. It's sad but true: No one can shun you as deeply as you shun yourself.

When you lose money, shock ripples through every moment of every day. Suddenly finding yourself drinking your morning tea in a chunky ceramic mug after you moved back in with your mother, daughter, or sister instead of greeting the day in your own beautiful kitchen with your special rose-patterned porcelain tea set can clobber you senseless. The reassuring rituals and comforting routines now missing only seem to compound the ache when you must acclimate to a life you have not chosen and toward which you only feel fear and loathing.

You want your teapot, damn it, and I wish I could give it back to you, sweetie. But what's more important is that you're hurting and need some comfort. You need something to keep you calm, so that you can carry on. Something to nudge your attention away for a moment from all that's lost and toward the good waiting to be found and appreciated from this day forward.

Stay with me. I've got a few lovely diversions that work wonders.

The Grace of Gratitude

*Grace fills empty spaces, but it can only enter where there is a void
to receive it, and it is grace itself which makes this void.*

— SIMONE WEIL

I've been writing about Gratitude for nearly twenty
years, professionally and publicly (in my books) and pri-
vately (in my own Gratitude Journals). But back in 1991
when I first started experimenting with Gratitude as a
spiritual catalyst for changing my life (in case you're wondering, skeptics make the best seekers), I recall being
disappointed at how little I could find written on the subject, with the exception of a slender meditation by the
Benedictine brother David Steindl-Rast titled *Gratefulness,
the Heart of Prayer*. Certainly there was no such thing as my
Gratitude Journal, which was born because gratitude was
such a new and wondrous step toward changing how I
perceived my life.

And why did my life need to change? Like fifty million
other working mothers, my daily round had become a tug-
of-war between other people's demands and expectations
and my own genuinely conflicted desires and unrequited
needs. I multitasked from one obligation to the next so
fast that my spirit felt as if it were constantly sprinting to
catch up with me, which it finally did when I collapsed into
bed. Mornings were a major source of dread: My first conscious breath was a sigh; my awakening thought was how
to make it through the day.

Of course, like most women I rarely complained to anyone else, but I whined to myself and God, until, literally, the sound of my own complaining nearly drove me mad.

One morning I woke up physically exhausted and spiritually bankrupt; money was tight, too. The freelance market was shrinking fast because the only story in town was downsizing. I was so sick and tired of concentrating on what was missing in my life, Heaven knows I didn't want to write about it. I felt drained, depleted, discouraged. Worrying about money had squandered my most precious natural resources—time, creative energy, and emotional resilience.

That morning, I'd had it with the sound of my own inner complaining and I think God had as well because I heard the marching order to sit down at the kitchen table and start writing an inventory of what was *good* in my life, right at that moment.

Think Pollyanna on Prozac. When I stopped some six hours and several pots of tea later, to my great astonishment I'd created a master list of my life's many overlooked blessings. I had more than 150 and none of them had anything to do with money! And then I had an everyday epiphany: I realized I didn't need a single thing, except the awareness of how blessed I was. That was the very first time Gratitude beckoned and invited me to use its transformative power not to revamp my life, but to rejoice in it.

When I type the word *gratitude* into search engines today—years later—the books, websites, articles, newsletters, and research projects the computer directs me to number more than two hundred thousand, and are increasing daily. My favorite is the weighty tome *The Psychology of Gratitude*, edited by Robert A. Emmons and Michael E. McCullough, which is the first compilation of the empirical, scientific research on gratitude conducted by prominent scientists. When explaining how they chose their topic, they stated in the article "Counting Blessings Versus Burdens: An Experimental Investigation of Gratitude and Subjective Well-Being in Daily Life":

> The construct of gratitude has inspired considerable interest in the general public... Although intuitively compelling, many of the general claims in popular books concerning the power of a grateful lifestyle are speculative and as yet scientifically untested. In one popular book on gratitude, for instance, the author asserts that "Whatever we are waiting for — peace of mind, contentment, grace... it will surely come to us, but only when we are ready to receive it with an open and grateful heart" (Breathnach, 1996).

Isn't this amazing? Although scientists are usually latecomers to the party, once they're with you, they're true believers. Through conducting highly focused and controlled studies on the nature of gratitude, its causes and consequences, Emmons and McCullough have concluded that people who keep Gratitude Journals are more optimistic than people who don't, take better care of themselves, exercisé more regularly, report fewer physical ailments, and experience more alertness, enthusiasm, determination, and confidence to meet life's challenges; they also reported more moments of contentment than distress.

We know all this. But have we remembered it? Not unless we're actively keeping a Gratitude Journal. For new readers, keeping a Gratitude Journal is the soul of the *Simple Abundance* philosophy, not an optional insight tool. The Gratitude Journal is a polite daily thank-you note to the Universe. You know how insulted you are after you've knocked yourself out for one of your kids and all you get in return is surly silence. How many women have asked, "Did you like it?" frustrated out of their minds as they recall the long hours cooking or sewing or shopping that brought their offspring such bounty. Well, an ancient spiritual axiom teaches, "As below, so above."

Because you are not spoiled rotten, at the end of every day you write down the five things that got you through it and brought moments of peace or a feeling of plenty. The *Peace and Plenty Journal of Well-Spent Moments* is specific to these two themes, which will begin to shift your focus from worrying about "financial security" (which is unattainable) to an appreciation of today's "financial serenity." To activate that switch, look for little ways to thank the Great Giver for your ever-increasing sense of *well-being*, which is what wealth feels like: A friend treats you to lunch; the repair bill is less than you imagined; you find $20 in the pocket of a coat you haven't worn in a while; you're thrilled with a DKNY skirt for $5 at the new thrift shop; there's a rebate check you'd forgotten about in the mail; you bring your coins to the coin machine and it's double your guesstimate; your coupons at the supermarket end up saving more than you spent; you get the family an H1N1 flu shot at the free clinic and, while waiting in line, accept a stranger's offer of the new novel she's just finished: It's Dan Brown's *The Lost Symbol*, which you'd been dying to read but were waiting until it came out in paperback.

Some days filling your *Peace and Plenty Journal of Well-Spent Moments* will be easy, but other days—and we all have them—the only thing that we feel grateful for is that the day is over. On those nights, I've started writing one of the many biblical promises for prosperity at the top of my page and dating it. My favorite one for dispelling gloom is "'For I know the plans I have for you,' declares the LORD, 'plans to prosper you and not to harm you, plans to give you hope and a future'" (Jeremiah 29:11). Like asking for only one day's Grace, I have never experienced the feeling of Heaven not hearing my prayers when I accept the wonder of the Prosperity Promise as my own. And who, upon receiving this promise from God, wouldn't settle down for sleep peacefully and be tucked in by Mother Plenty?

Living Beyond
Your Means

Follow me — and you will have fun. Follow me — and I will lead you off the beaten track where two and two make five or even ten or twelve — who cares? At any rate, we'll burst the bonds of reason and the fetters of care — double-cross the statisticians and the bookkeepers while we get what we want out of life…I want more, don't you?

— MARGERY WILSON,
HOW TO LIVE BEYOND YOUR MEANS (1945)

When you're worried about money, the contented hours seem few and far between. You *are* living beyond your means, and it's anything but fun or comfortable. *If only*, we say to ourselves over and over again, gnawing a deep ravine of regret from morning until night into the cavity of our soul: "*If only* I had $50, $100, $500, $1,000, $5,000, $50,000, I could pay all these bills, solve all my problems, or get this new business started." "*If only* I hadn't spent it on…" "*If only I'd been more vigilant instead of trusting…*" *If only.* But like everything else, it seems, the number of people offering practical, compassionate advice dwindles as personal emotional worries become global economic woes, sweeping the world in a pandemic of fear. Being in the red, we're told, "is the new black" as heaping portions of parsimony and panic are served up around the world.

Making it even more difficult to rein in our terror, the personal magic number that will "fix" all our financial problems seems to rapidly increase. Have you ever noticed this? If it's $5,000 you need, by the time you scrape it together, suddenly there's another $3,000 needed to cover an equally pressing need. No matter whether you're rich or skint, the secret of financial serenity seems to be balancing your personal perceptions to life's daily portion. It's never the amount of money that will save the day; it's the amount of fear that needs to be calmed to get through the day, especially as you learn to put your financial house in order.

It's no wonder that we're as confused and conflicted over money as we are. As someone who has literally gone from being overdrawn in my checking account one day to depositing a royalty check for $250,000 the next, this I know for sure: Money changes everything. Or seems to. But one thing it doesn't really change is *your* authentic emotions or openness about money. That's because from sudden windfalls to staggering debts, we can't talk to anyone about money unless they have as much as we do, or as little. I'm sure I'm not the first to tell you this, but money is a taboo subject with family or friends. If it's a windfall—whether from royalties, stock options, an inheritance, or the lottery—and you suddenly have more than anyone else in your circle of intimates, you will be expected to pick up every check for the rest of your life, not to mention pay for everything from emergencies to indulgences. If it's the reverse, such as foreclosure or bankruptcy, no one will want to talk to you; like a disease, people are afraid poverty is catching. It seems that the only people who want to talk to you about money are those who want to take it off you. Which, of course, is why the very word makes us nervous.

So why don't we start here, with the word *money*. We barely even know what the word means anymore. Still, it provokes an emotional reaction triggering the fight-or-flight mechanism or a fifth of scotch. How does saying or even thinking about the word *money* make you feel?

Serene? Probably only if you have a comma in your checking account and no bills past due. Uneasy, nauseous, headachy, unable to breathe, panicky? That sounds more like it, especially if your checking account is anything like mine right now. I've got some big payouts due soon. Payouts long ago spoken for even before the next check is earned and deposited as I pay down a mountain of debt, including two mortgages on houses I can neither live in right now nor sell, because of a complicated divorce. It used to be that a friendly bank manager contacted you if you missed a mortgage payment; now they send you a frosty e-mail informing you that next week a mortgage payment is due—you'd better get ready for it and not spend it on anything else. So today, as I write, when I think about the word *money* I feel antsy, edgy, and needy.

But what do I need? My first response before writing this book would have been "more money," but after a year's pondering on the page about money and its meaning in our lives, and without my own home to live in while I write, I know that my soul is thrilled with just the thought of a space of my own. I believe that each new year comes with a gift—but we need to ask for it. I'm praying for wisdom to achieve financial serenity.

However, I also know that the beginning of wisdom is practicality. Women need something soothing, practical, and palpable to focus on, especially when the panic attacks start, which is why I created a few new home-grown feminine remedies intended to break the relentless cycle of remorse or the frantic waves of money fears. Learning to consciously shift our own destructive energies to emotionally positive ones is how we learn self-preservation in the best sense.

I won't pretend that when your financial affairs crash down upon you and you're buried in emotional, psychic, and fiscal rubble, just being a good woman is enough to pull you through. But it is a comfort to know that another woman has weathered a similar crisis and come through

safely. Since times are tough, I created for myself a treasure trove of encouraging distractions to ease my anxiety
as I untangled my financial affairs and longed for serene
composure. We all need extra doses of confidence to start
our lives over from scratch. What worked for me will
work for you because it has worked for generations of
women before us: morale-boosting reassurance and hidden truths revealed in women's lives, stories, films, fables,
recipes, and red-checked-gingham-wrapped tips gleaned
from women's books and magazines spanning the first half
of the twentieth century, particularly during the Great Depression and the Home Front years of both the Great War
(1914–1918) and World War II.

On the *Peace and Plenty* path, there's one philosophy
that I've carefully cultivated and three different insight
tools that I've used every day as I've divined and designed
personal contentment prompts. All of these treasure tools
can help you live beyond your means spiritually and cre-
atively through the rediscovery and appreciation of well-
spent moments that cost little or nothing but, like sweat
equity and compound interest, bring big dividends. They
are the *Peace and Plenty Journal of Well-Spent Moments*, the
Contentment Chest, and the *Peace and Plenty* Comfort
Companion. Using just one of these tools will induce a
brief pause in your day for a spiritual recalibration that
recovers a sense of optimism and brings a smile to your
face. Playing with all three as you process and ponder
ways to restore balance and prosperity to your daily round
can have you feeling so contented that in a few months,
you'll marvel that it took a global economic meltdown to
reawaken your awareness of life's truest blessings—what
matters most to you.

The Thrill of Thrift is the heart of the *Peace and Plenty*
philosophy, but *thrift* in this case harks back to the original
medieval meaning of the word, which was "to thrive" and
had nothing to do with frugality. Let's be honest here:
Cheap is not cheerful, but homespun thrift wraps us in a

warm tapestry of fulfillment so that we are able to experience the fullness of life, no matter how much water is in our glass. Throughout this book, I'll be sharing my collection of what I call the Thrill of Thrift treats, all of which have at one time piqued my feminine curiosity (*Can this work?*) or made me swoon with purrs of pleasure upon discovering remedies or activities that unexpectedly soothed my soul and quieted the wants.

That's why gradually we'll consciously make room in our busy days for restorative indulgences, elegant economies, and other bijou morsels of ecstasy: the charm of home comforts—pocketbook suppers, pin money stashes, or the morale of new curtains. The earthly delights of planting a Gratitude Garden, the relief of a pre-caution cupboard. We'll prime our creative well with vintage bliss musings and learn how keeping proper account books bestows a sense of pride as well as getting the bills paid on time. We'll calm those nagging worries of what tomorrow might bring by reintroducing rhythm and rituals into today's daily round and by choosing, whenever possible, the hush of life's holy humdrum over all the daily drama on the twenty-four-hour news channels. We'll turn the page on our past mistakes (and keep each other company) as we courageously take steps to restore our creditworthiness (first in our own eyes, and then in the world's) and redeem dreams by creating ceremonies that make our common days sparkle.

One of the most important lessons I divined from writing and living *Simple Abundance* through so many dramatic changes in my circumstances is that a woman's personal contentment is not a frivolous luxury but a spiritual directive and that true wealth and well-being are one and the same. In *Peace and Plenty*, I'll prove to you—one cozy home comfort, earthly delight, or vintage bliss at a time—that making the most of what you have and learning to appreciate the precious but fleeting well-spent moments of every day's sacred ordinary is the path to true financial serenity.

Let's begin again, my cherished friend...

The Peace and Plenty Journal of Well-Spent Moments

In the coming years we shall need all the charm, aplomb and philosophy we can get. It will be the task of women to keep the world from despond, to keep the prettier gestures of good living going with meager materials... We will not fail in any crisis to come. To the extent of our ability we will keep the torch of civilized home-life burning. We will create beauty with whatever materials are at hand. We will fan the embers of kindness in a brute-stricken world... We will heal and hold to our hearts the wounded, the young, the needy. It is a great privilege to be a woman today.

— MARGERY WILSON (1928)

Worrying about money never paid a bill. If it did, at least there'd be a legitimate reason for indulging in worry. Actually, worrying about money repels, rather than attracts prosperity. Worrying about money shuts down our creativity and sends toxic signals — fear, lack, deprivation, despair, anger, frustration — which is exactly what we attract. And when we're in this mood, it's very difficult to feel grateful.

However, it has occurred to me that when I muse

about Gratitude, what I'm really doing is meditating about happiness. So are you. The pursuit of happiness, the stumbling upon it, the recognition of it, the acknowledgment and appreciation of the precious, fleeting moments of fulfillment in our daily round that truly make a difference in how we feel, day in and day out, triggers sublime spiritual serendipity. When we are worried about money we instinctively contract, becoming smaller, withdrawing into ourselves, pulling away from the goodness of life in a defensive manner because we are afraid on a deeper level that whatever we have left will be snatched away.

It's going to take a powerful elixir to break through financial fear. It takes spiritual moxie — high-caliber enthusiasm, also known as courage. It will also take the alchemy of an ordinary day and a gifted woman — that's you, wherever you may be reading this.

"But how to live beautifully today — on less than usual? Faced with the shortages, priorities and allotments of consumer goods, we must make life and happiness for ourselves. No longer is it to be delivered on our doorstep wrapped in cellophane," Margery Wilson, one of the leading American literary domestics during the Great Depression and World War II, wrote in 1942. "We have more to do — and less on which to do it. Yet down in our hearts we know that we have the skill, the courage, the ingenuity, the imagination *and* the all-important good-taste to make a very fair success of living with the materials at hand."

I don't know about you, but that's just the perfect dose of inspiration I can use today, which is why I captured that quote in my *Peace and Plenty Journal of Well-Spent Moments*, so that on the days I didn't feel I had much to be grateful for, I could go back to that thought, personalize it, write it out, say it aloud, and let the wisdom wash over me and seep inside. I wrote it out like this:

In my heart, I know that I have the skill, the courage, the ingenuity, the imagination, and the all-important good-taste to make a fair success of my life with the materials at hand: my creativity, my emotions, my time. Thank you for these priceless gifts. Please bless me with the grace and wisdom to use them well starting tomorrow.

I recorded nothing else that day, but I slept deeply that night for the first time in ages and awakened the next morning with a new resolve.

Using this creative insight tool, you will never come up short in your own personal storehouse of cheerful and determined optimism, no matter what happened to the Dow. Not having money to spend doesn't mean we can't have well-spent moments every day.

Margery Wilson arrived in Hollywood in 1914 from Kentucky seeking fame and fortune with little more than a suitcase, a smile, and luscious brown curls. She quickly became a favorite of the pioneering film director D. W. Griffith, who is considered the father of cinema. It may be hard to imagine now, but Hollywood then was little more than scattered tiny bungalows, dusty, unpaved roads, citrus groves, one trolley, and a sign in the hills advertising a new housing development. Oh yes, and dreams. But nothing is more real than a dream and it seemed that life could turn on a dime, especially at the intersection of Hollywood and Vine. It certainly did for Margery when Griffith cast her as "Brown Eyes," the doomed Huguenot girl, in his iconic film *Intolerance* (1916), a million-dollar epic interweaving four story lines throughout twenty-five hundred years of history and three thousand extras. For a decade Margery enjoyed an enviable career as one of the top female silent-film stars, appearing with Douglas Fairbanks Sr. and Hollywood's celebrated cowboy star, William S. Hart.

However, life is a cycle of both personal and professional change, especially if your financial success is based on entertainment and technology. After Al Jolson appeared in the 1928 film *The Jazz Singer*, the "talkies" took over Hollywood. Being adaptable and entrepreneurial, Margery Wilson never missed a beat. When cultural and economic change arrives, resilient people are versatile and find ways to reinvent themselves or repackage their experience into new careers. Already known for her beautiful voice, Margery made the wise decision to step behind the camera and created a successful new career teaching diction to actors.

Margery also thought she'd try her hand at women's advice and became one of the first successful female self-help authors with her publication of *Charm* in 1928, followed by *The New Etiquette*, *The Woman You Want to Be*, and my personal favorite: *How to Live Beyond Your Means*, published in 1945, the last year of World War II. By the time this book was published, people had been stretched so thin by the Great Depression and World War II that hope had flatlined and their precious natural resources of time, creative energy, and emotion were depleted.

Wilson would have none of this. She was going to fill her readers to the brim with optimism, the most valuable commodity in the world. It cannot be bought and sold, but can be caught and given away.

"Here is a golden opportunity to learn how to get the most you can out of living—to squeeze significance and happiness out of every moment, every hour, out of everything which happens in the daily round of existence," Margery told her readers as she shared "her own hard-won knowledge that it is useless to kick against the bricks of a universe which refuses to yield before your insistent demands." After all, "the universe has been in business a long time, but there is more to be had out of this old world for a very little amount of effort—if only you are willing to search for it." Margery's advice: "Be more elegant. Be serene. Be more gracious. Graciousness is the most profitable personal attribute in the world. What dividend it pays! Second to cheerfulness, it pays off in actual cash.

And we're interested in—the extra values we can get. It is the tangible reward, the money in hand, the worldly advancement, promotion and profit, and the extra joy as well, that concern us in this book. For our time, money and effort, we want more!"

Welcome to your new insight tool, the *Peace and Plenty Journal of Well-Spent Moments*, inspired by the thought that if we're already living beyond our means, let's make the most of the life we have.

What is a "well-spent" moment? Well, the expression is a play on words—we really spend very little on the things that make us truly content. The things that matter most are priceless. Those moments of connection, kindness, laughter, encouragement, and inspiration, those flashes of intuition and coincidences occurring all the time.

In June 1942, *Vogue* took up the idea of "Well-Spent Moments" by encouraging readers to say their "good-byes (and no regrets to other summers and other summaries of what to do with them). For this is our first summer at war. And our tastes have changed as radically as our lives. Whatever the change, whether we have a little or a lot of money; whether we have a little or at lot of time, we will want that money and that time to bring in the biggest returns."

I discovered as I was trying to work with my Gratitude Journal during this time of financial upheaval that I was so exhausted from all the resolve, determination, work, and effort expended during the day, by the time I was ready to turn in, my before-bed ritual of writing down five things for which I was grateful just petered out. I was simply too tired and, yes, worried about money. Maybe you've noticed this as well. So I just recited what I was thankful for as I dropped like a stone. The following morning, it was as if my entire memory had been erased. I knew there were things to be grateful for, but I couldn't recall a single one.

Still, I *know* the magic and power of Gratitude to

change our lives. I needed to find some creative way to engage my mind.

The miracle of searching for peace and plenty isn't merely in the acknowledgment of what's working in our lives; it's in the *remembering* of it, too.

"Is there something you wish were different? Is there something missing in your life?" Margery Wilson asks us in *How to Live Beyond Your Means*. "If you will just look around a bit you will, more than likely, find that the way out of the difficulty lies right under your nose. You already possess the means of your deliverance. There is some thought, a small beginning, a letter to write, a call to make, an action to begin that will result in solving any problem you have."

Each day while on the *Peace and Plenty* path, we'll record just *one* thought or appreciation that endows us with a sense of comfort or encouragement for ourselves or our loved ones. Perhaps it's the next step, a eureka moment you didn't have this morning that gives you something to follow through with tomorrow. "When Elijah helped the poor widow, he did not bring in something NEW. He said to her, 'What have you in the house?' It was, as you know, a cruse of oil, and from that small beginning she was delivered from poverty," Mrs. Wilson assures us. "A miracle, you say? Well, almost everything we do is a kind of miracle. Much comes from little. Light has power over darkness. Love has power over discord. Life yields great returns, pressed down and running over."

The Thrill of Thrift

The Contentment Chest

*Gradually, as you become curator of your own
contentment you will learn to embrace the gentle
yearnings of your heart.*

—*SIMPLE ABUNDANCE*, JANUARY 1

Here is what I do when I want to jump out of my own skin
because I'm so worried about money. Once you begin
practicing this ceremony, you'll wonder how you ever lived
a contented grown-up life without it. Oh, you say, contentment's not your strong suit? It soon will be.

First, I call a time-out for twenty minutes. I walk away
from the computer, television, or telephone. I take a pretty
Tiffany-blue eleven-by-fourteen-inch box from my shelf
and open it. I allow myself to savor its contents. Inside
are all kinds of things that make me smile—clippings from
different magazines or newspapers, cards and letters I've
saved, matches from wonderful bars and restaurants, paint
and fabric swatches, photographs, brochures, a rapturous
curl of salmon-colored silk ribbon.

Here's a travel promotion on cardboard about great
train journeys I hope to go on someday: the elegantly restored Victorian and glamorous South African Rovos Rail
between Cape Town and Pretoria; the art deco Orient
Express from London to Venice with stops in Paris, Inns-
bruck, and Verona. The seven-night journey on the shock-

ing pink Golden Chariot from Bangalore to Mysore and the Nagarhole National Park, where I shall disembark for a jeep safari; or the Trans-Siberian Express from Moscow westward to Vladivostok on the breathtaking Golden Eagle knocking back blinis and ice-cold vodka shots.

Next, there's a clipping to remind me how much I love the idea right now of slipcovers for dining room chairs, with buttons down the back, like the spine of a Grace Kelly sheath; that exuberantly colored, vintage-1920s hankies make fetching bracelets; and how a toddler's blue-and-white smocked gingham dress circa 1950 from Best & Co. pulled together with a swath of white silk ribbon makes the most adorable lampshade I've ever seen. I feel better already. Yes, I feel . . . dare I say it? contented. And you can, too.

That's the purpose of a Contentment Chest, and you can begin to create one today. I know that somewhere you have clippings, because most women are inveterate clippers from catalogs and magazines and savers of every piece of paper that's ever crossed our palms. We clip because we want to remember something beautiful or pleasant or intriguing or dream about another way of living, especially if it isn't practical. Who knows — maybe it will be in the future. But who cares? Just looking at it makes us happy right now. And that's *all* that counts right at this moment.

Women also tear and clip because we long to be organized, to have our unruly dreams in some sort of tidy, trim, decorous form. This would be fine if we already had neatly marked filing folders waiting to receive these insights — but that would require prescience, and when we worry about money it is hard enough to view the present clearly, let alone the future. Unfortunately, worries about money have a scurrying, furtive effect. We hide the shopping bags, we hide the bills, we hide the buyer's remorse, we hide the yearning. We hide the guilt. We hide our once beautiful dreams in a tattered, soiled trench coat of denial. Our sacred passions and our genuine wants — for stability and serenity — become secretive and shameful because we believe that if we can't afford our dreams now, we must snuff them out or hide them.

In reality, all we have to do is find a holding place for our new dreams and desires, while our edited circumstances eliminate what's no longer working in our lives. But unless we have a place — a bulletin board or a scrapbook or a collage frame in or on which to collect these happy impetuous ramblings — our clippings become clutter and then forgotten, half-folded impulses in the back of books on the nightstand or the bottom of the basket in the bathroom.

Today I want you to take twenty minutes to go around the house and create your own stash. If the clippings you find don't register a zing from your heart, start fresh. Be on the search for a pleasing lidded box — or make your own. A penny pleasure is finding the perfect one-yard fabric remnant to cover an ordinary gift box and transform your yearnings into something tangible to soothe your ravished heart. As you collect what makes you happy, one clipping at a time, your capacity to dream begins anew. As you become thankful for each moment of contentment and write it down to remember it, your capacity for comfort grows. "It may be that true happiness lies in the conviction that one has irretrievably lost happiness," the Chilean novelist María Luisa Bombal wrote. "Then we begin to move through life without hope or fear, capable of finally enjoying all the small pleasures, which are the most lasting."

PS: If you work in an office every day, keep the Contentment Chest waiting for you at home. Create a pleasing ritual around it with a glass of wine or juice, or a cup of tea, as you unwind from the day's clamor. Once a week, bring one new picture to prop up on your desk and ponder for five days in a row. You will be *amazed* at the power of gazing consistently at something you want to bring into your life. By the end of the week, you just might visit that website, make that call, send for information, join that class — completing the one deliberate action necessary to begin transforming your life from desire to fulfillment.

The Thrill of Thrift

The Comfort Companion

*What fun it is to generalize in the privacy of a notebook.
It is as I imagine waltzing on ice might be. A great
delicious sweep in one direction, taking you your full
strength, and then with no trouble at all, an equally
delicious sweep in the opposite direction. My note book
does not help me think, but it eases my crabbed heart.*

— FLORIDA SCOTT-MAXWELL

Remember how much fun and joy life provides on a
"good" day—the delicious sweep in full strength
across the ice pond of time and space? Hmm, has it been
that long for you, too? Well, on a good day you wake up
refreshed, your hair behaves beautifully, your clothes are
comfortably loose, all the lights are green, you're early for
every appointment, there are no lines, there's always a
parking space, deadlines are met with ease. Dinner, from
leftovers, is delicious, inexpensive, and served with gusto;
the discount wine sips like a *grand cru*, there's a new, riveting English mystery on TV, and you arrive at the computer
at the perfect moment to steal that genuine Michael Kors
signature satchel for $28.99 on eBay just in time for sweet
dreams.

A bad day needs no poetic recall because we can't seem
to wake up and snap out of it. Bad days begin, in the biblical sense of Job or Jonah, after we've been tossing and

turning all night not sleeping but fretting about paying Peter's expected boiler repair by borrowing from Paul's next semester's tuition. But lying awake and fretting about money produces nothing but frustration and exhaustion. It's rather like waking up to find at the foot of your bed a cute, mysterious pet called a "Mogwai," brought home from Chinatown with a tag around his neck in Mandarin warning you not to expose him to bright light, give him water, or feed him after midnight. But of course that's exactly what you do, because you don't understand Chinese characters and aw, he's so cute. Give us a cuddle, then.

That's the thing about nighttime money worries. They don't seem so bad when you first start mulling over possible solutions. But by the time your money Mogwai has fed off your emotional and creative energy, been splashed by your tears, and been blinded by the bathroom light for the fifth time as you frantically look for the NyQuil, he's morphed. Stumble down to the kitchen at dawn's early light and you've got a pack of gremlins whizzing around the kitchen on blenders and beaters. Careful to wear your slippers on the way to the cupboard.

So this is what I do to snap out of misery while I'm waiting for the tea to brew. I go to the kitchen counter, where I keep my scrapbooking basket with scissors, glue sticks, and tape. I open the Contentment Chest and select one magazine clipping. Today it's a picture of a serene-looking woman dressed in white, lounging on a faded shabby chic floral couch, relaxed and dreamy as if in a reverie, looking at pages in a scrapbook. I read what she is reading about the need for women to create "A Place for Quietude," torn from *Victoria* magazine long ago.

"A room where one sleeps and dreams and grieves and rejoices becomes inseparably connected with those processes and acquires a personality of its own. This room is not a pretty or a dainty one, but it has always been a retreat for me, the one spot in Belmont where I might be alone and possess my soul in quietness..." So Lucy Maud

Montgomery, the creator of *Anne of Green Gables*, confessed to the pages of her commonplace book, the personal journals she called her "life-books." Far more than a diary, these blank scrapbook pages (thousands of which chronicled her life from 1889, when she was fifteen, until her death in 1942) were filled with drawings, photographs, clippings, pressed flowers, souvenirs, short-story ideas, accounts, receipts, remedies, ribbons and recipes, fashion plates, knitting patterns, and novel plots and became — for a woman who gifted the world with such contentment and grace — her paper companions of Comfort and Joy. These albums also contained her "grumbles," which she might document in a sketch or a rant, but by admitting them to her album she acknowledged what was happening in her life on a daily basis. With acknowledgment came acceptance, the soul's alchemist. By the time an incident appeared in any of her twenty novels or five hundred short stories, it had been transformed from worry's dross to life's nuggets of gold, enchanting the author herself and millions of readers around the world for the last century.

We can begin to chart our daily journey to peace and plenty with the blank pages of what I call the *Peace and Plenty* Comfort Companion. Our designated place for quietude — for we can no longer count on the luxury of a private room in which to beat our retreat — is in between scrapbook covers capturing the golden fragments as well as the grainy grumbles of our daily round.

"How was one to begin anew when the heart has gone out of life?" Lucy Maud Montgomery asked her paper soul one day, surely a question every woman must ask herself at one time or another, and maybe even this morning.

With one clipping that makes us smile, a glue stick, and a large blank page on which to paste it.

The Thrill of Thrift

Creating a Comfort Companion

It's been a rare year, o paper soul...Maybe I should fold you away to pull you out again in a decade, see whether the flowering that now seems promised, came; see whether it was untimely frostbit, or died without fruit, because you chart the real deeps of me.

— KERI HULME

Oh, where will I find the deeps of me this chilly winter's morning? Here, still burrowed in the bundle of blankets and books on my sister's four-poster bed in California, hidden in a jumble of pillows, duvet, books, magazines, legal briefs, and financial forms?

Or there, scattered helter-skelter, the pickup sticks of what to take and what to leave behind, now silently hushed beneath layers of dust on my writing desk at Newton's Chapel in England? Both places, really. The SBB of today, sleepy thoughts still unformed, groping a word at a time with every sip of English Breakfast tea, gazing at the pea-soup fog that obscures the California coast, wet, gray, and cold this morning. December rains have begun and I'm shivering with bewilderment as much as chilblains. Are these dots and dashes of consciousness making a connection to my June 2009 SBB? Traces of a woman being wrenched away from her gorgeous home, garden, beloved possessions, including her scrapbooks. Rain that day as well, warm, round, dense droplets of midsummer showers mingling with my salt tears.

How could these two very different days—one scurrying, one surrendering—conjure an instant recall without the intervention of my paper soul—my commonplace book, my artist's album, my scrapbook? Details of dreams, detours, derailments captured in a combination sketchbook, journal, and portfolio. My life-book. I remember the eureka I felt with the creation of my Illustrated Discovery Journal, a visual autobiography of one's Authentic Self through collage, during the *Simple Abundance* process, from private page to public book. Readers have often told me that they are with me, diving in tandem between the lines of their copies of *Simple Abundance* and in the collages of their Illustrated Discovery Journals. Perhaps it's because honest intimacy *is* authenticity.

What holds my interest this morning and perhaps yours: Can the creative process of collage—the blending together of disparate images and materials—work its wonders in helping to untangle the complex financial skeins of emotion always present just beneath the surface of our daily round? I believe so. Would you like to experiment with me? I always feel better when I have my own personal, empirical evidence to corroborate my wealth-increasing rituals. I did it with the *Simple Abundance Journal of Gratitude*; I did it with tithing. Women are their own best research-and-development practitioners. Listen, if someone who's paying her bills on time confides that tying a green ribbon around a faucet increases the flow of money in her life, I'll waste no breath telling her she's foolish. I'm already rummaging in the ribbon jar for the perfect bow. *Any* self-prompt that reminds you to focus on flow, not ebb, contributes to your greater sense of abundance.

If you are familiar with *Simple Abundance*, you know

that after the Gratitude Journal, I believe every dream I ever brought into the world was accomplished through the intercession of my Illustrated Discovery Journal. This creation is a visual autobiography of your Authentic Self, or the emergence of the different parts of your life into a beautiful wholeness. The difference between the IDJ and creating a Comfort Companion is that the collages we arranged in the IDJ were targeted to a *specific quest*: a redecorating project, unraveling a relationship's snags, trying a new personal fashion style, finding the perfect haircut, uncovering an authentic passion that could be the foundation for a new career. With the Comfort Companion, we'll be keeping a visual diary of our daily round in real time — a fusion of sketchbook, diary, and personal memorabilia that tracks the triumphs and turmoil of our lives, especially our personal tug-of-war becoming comfortable with all aspects of money. You're going to learn along with me how to transform our constant craving for financial security, which is impossible, into the wisdom, well-being, and wealth of financial serenity. Glimpses, flashes of insight in images, reminders of wealth and success are dramatically drawn into our life when we are clear in our intention — to create a life of peace and plenty for ourselves and those we love. When we collect these seemingly random images together in one cache, the impulse becomes an imperative — a new soul's directive.

It couldn't be any simpler or more abundant than that. What is it you want when you want more money? Peace of mind. A respite from crises. Breathing spaces and light-filled rooms. A silent phone. All the bills paid with a "thank you" and a smiley face notation. A good night's sleep. Vitality and Optimism. Cheerfulness and Hope. That's why the most productive thing you can do today is to begin to keep this scrapbook; it will explode your creative thinking and blast through the boundaries of money deprivation that you've unconsciously erected by listening first to your family financial lore, then to your husband's or best friend's money opinion, and on to the nightly news and the rest of the world.

Whenever you can step into your imagination, you are creating, especially when you are focusing your creative energies on acknowledging and savoring moments of Gratitude, Simplicity, Order, Harmony, Beauty, and Joy—the six graces of *Simple Abundance*. From scrapbooking to the poetic, purposeful Thrill of Thrift rituals, you will learn how to gradually change a lifetime of spending habits and emotional responses toward money by nurturing and increasing your sense of peace and plenty every day.

What is it you want from Life at this moment? Peace and plenty. Say it aloud softly to yourself. *Peace. And. Plenty.* Now, is there any circumstance in your life that cannot be transformed by injecting a little peace and plenty into the situation? I don't think so. After "Thank you, God," these three little words are the cosmic equivalent of Einstein's Theory of Relativity (why time seems to increase or slow down based on our circumstances, when the speed of light is constant) or—as the great mystic physicist put it—"the refinement of everyday thinking."

What you need to begin, at least for the first time, is a blank scrapbook or artist's sketchbook. Please get the plainest version you can find; I still recommend the size be approximately eleven by fourteen inches, and—at least until you've got the knack of this pastime—the most inexpensive blank notebook available.

Of course, I realize that in the years since I wrote *Simple Abundance* and created the original Illustrated Discovery Journal, the hobby of scrapbooking has exploded around the world. There is now such a splendid array of supplies available, you'll be dazzled standing in a craft aisle. But being dazzled to the point of vertigo won't get you very far, and if you go the scrapbook extravaganza route right now the only thing you'll feel tomorrow is buyer's remorse. "We are always afraid to start something that we want to make very good, true, and serious," the famous writing coach Brenda Ueland wrote in 1938. How right she is. I've taught Illustrated Discovery Journal workshops for nearly twenty years now, and I can tell you, the hardest part of teaching this Divine Insight process is getting someone to believe that there is no way to make a bad beginning or get it wrong. But this truth is easier to understand if you can rip out a less-than-perfect blank page rather than throwing away a bead-encrusted, cleverly stenciled photomontage that cost $25 in raw materials because of an ink spot or because you misspelled a word.

So if you're reading this at night, what paper ephemera do you have with today's date on it? A café or bookstore receipt? An appointment card. A traffic ticket. A horrible bill. A page from a Page-A-Day calendar? A lovely card from a good friend. A lottery ticket? Do you know how much you spent today? While you're tabulating data, what's the weather today? Just make a connection for a moment between the weather and your mood as well as how much cash you had on you to spend indiscriminately. Did you have an argument with anyone in your family about money today? Did you need to call a client and ask where your check is? Or were you on the receiving end of a dunning phone call, or a heart-stopping invoice with PLEASE!!!!! scribbled on it? Gather these seemingly boring and insignificant clues together. You'll soon start to create your treasure map to wealth, well-being, and wholeness.

And what's more, you'll have fun doing it. Now, when was the last time you associated fun with money and *not spending*?

Part Two

Money—An Education in Ourselves

Education is a wonderful thing. If you couldn't sign your name you'd have to pay cash.

—RITA MAE BROWN

Discovering Your Family's Financial Tree

Money is better than poverty, if only for financial reasons.

—WOODY ALLEN

One of the first stops on our journey to understanding our own personal relationship with money is the discovery of our family's financial tree. Just as we inherit blue eyes or brown, right-handedness or left, we inherit as a legacy our family's conversations about money, both spoken and unspoken.

I grew up in a family of big spenders. My parents didn't have a family fortune to squander, only Dad's weekly paycheck. But on some unconscious level, I knew that even if I wasn't to the manor born then at least I'd be living in one someday. Those were the days, however, when middle-class young ladies believed the only route to the Big House was by "marrying well." So it was with mixed feelings that I became Lady Bountiful all by myself. Like most little girls of my generation, I was waiting for the prince to come and sweep me off my feet and take me to his castle, ironically only to have my upper-class British ex attempt to take mine away from me because he got used to the idea of being Lord of My Manor.

Although my parents didn't have any money, they did possess a wealth consciousness that I now recognize as priceless: Our family lived in abundance, not lack. The problem was that our reality of true abundance was only on the surface. A favorite phrase in our house was "Money doesn't grow on trees." It was, however, spent freely until the branches went bare—not really an ideal model for impressionable children. But then spring returned every year to start the whole process over again. We were a feast-or-famine family, and that became a pattern in my life. I don't mean to suggest all my parents' lessons on this subject were worthless; they were generous people, taught four little children good manners at great restaurants every Sunday, entertained lavishly, and shared their good fortune when we had some with everyone who crossed their paths. My father was the biggest tipper since Diamond Jim Brady; I thought all the waiters and porters fussed over him and us because Dad was such a big shot (and in their/our eyes, he sure was). My mother doubled every recipe she ever made because someone down the street or in the parish "might need it" (and they always did). I don't think I even realized we didn't have any "real" money until I was a freshman in a private Catholic high school and started to hear the word *debutante*. When I asked my parents when I was going to have my coming-out party, they laughed and told me I'd already made my debut—on the day I was born. And if I didn't remember the occasion, that was only the proof of what a great party it had been!

The downside of all this largesse was that my parents were so carefree with money, they never saved a dime. When the time came for my hardworking father to retire, there wasn't a nest egg; he continued working in a series of ever-diminishing menial jobs until the bitter end. After he died, my mother lived the next five years of her life riddled with fear, burdened with debt and guilt because she relied on the slender checks her children (who were all struggling on their own) sent every month to supplement her Social Security. After her funeral, when I was going through her papers, I discovered a slim red ledger in which she kept track of her accounts. The pain evident in the penciled figures and erasures still haunts me. And I wonder: Have I ended up having to start all over again from scratch at this stage in my life because of these early unconscious but crucial influences? Did I expect to be entering my sums into a little book? Am I more comfortable doing that, restricted by financial constraints, than being a millionaire when my books were kept by certified public accountants and my bills were paid by a personal assistant? Next time around, I'm certainly going to be present and accounted for.

I'm sure that everything in our past influences our present relationship to and with money. Fortunately, we can be conscious now, because we've identified the pitfalls in our predisposition to handling money. It is an important step in our appreciation of what *plenty* means for us individually and an awareness that cannot be rushed if we want to associate money with peace and not anxiety. Having had the experience of prosperity, I can tell you this for sure: I know in hindsight that a closet crammed full of designer shoes and handbags, and the surge of glee that slapping that plastic card down to pay for them brings, as giddy and extravagant as it might have seemed then, cannot match the quiet relief, reassurance, serenity, and, yes, sense of the luxurious that having the money in the bank to handle any crisis provides. No Prada purse ever felt as good as being able to pay an emergency vet bill, put down a security deposit on an apartment, or pay for prescription drugs. As the Victorian novelist Mary Adams wrote in 1902, "The great crises of life are not, I think, necessarily those which are in themselves the hardest to bear, but those for which we are least prepared."

Your Personal Money Myth

Myths which are believed in tend to become true.

— GEORGE ORWELL

When I was a little girl, there were two days in the year that were cause for celebration in my family: January 1 and July 1. On these two days, my parents would celebrate with a toast, usually a big tumbler of Johnnie Walker Red on ice, and proclaim, "We made it to January, we'll make it to July"—or vice versa. I wonder if that's why I chose a profession that calculates royalties from January to June and July to January. Hmmm.

Whether we like it or not, our personal behavior patterns with money and feelings about money have come from the financial environment in which we were raised. And until we understand the emotional triggers and the motivation behind our money practices (your weakness might be designer shoes on eBay, or completely handing over your money to a broker to spend). Whatever it is, your personal money-myth dragon must be discovered before it can be slain.

Here's a perfect example for a lot of women, including me. *Yank* magazine reported in the March 23, 1945, issue that "the greatest shortage right now is in cotton goods. Not long ago the Office of Civilian Requirements asked

4,499 housewives [nobody seems to know why the agency didn't query just one more housewife to get a nice, easy round number] what clothing was hardest to buy. The most consistent shortages were reported in house dresses, sheets, underwear — particularly children's — and diapers. A recent Government order for 90 million yards of herringbone twill can be cited as the cause for the shortage."

After discovering that the reason your grandmother and mother always used towels until they began to resemble cleaning rags was that they never knew when they would be rationed new ones, you'll understand why you use your towels until they're threadbare, too. They may not be hanging up, but I'd bet they're in whatever passes for your linen closet. Unless you are like Oprah, who dreamed of having luxurious towels the moment she hit it big, most of us are stingy when it comes to buying towels because reverence for the threadbare was a learned practice. But you now have both the freedom and the clarity to throw out every ratty rag in your house and begin treating yourself to some new towels at the next white sale, usually held in January and July. Special sales are also featured in August and known as "getting ready for college."

New towels are a way to give your house a face-lift every season. Having special hand towels in the bathrooms and special tea towels in the kitchen fills you with feelings of contentment. But we don't think about adding a new towel to our carts when we are picking up household essentials, because we have been trained to think of this as excess and extravagance. It just wouldn't be right to have hand towels that match our bath towels. What would the women on Wisteria Lane think! Let's put to rest once and for all these myths that have kept us financial and emotional paupers. Take an inventory of what you need and what you want. Make sure that everyone in the family has the basics and then jazz up your wants. You'll be surprised how much whimsy, style, and elegance you can create with two hand towels.

Since our parents can only teach us what they know—and consequently, we can only teach our own children what we know—bad money habits are passed down from generation to generation. If you had good money role models in your life, congratulations. You have a good start toward repaving a prosperous yellow brick road to your future even in these dark forest times. But as many people who have done all the right things with their money have discovered to their horror in this uncertain economy, trusting the old ways of creating wealth might not be in our best interest. We all have to reinvent our money strategies. Discovering your personal money myth is a very empowering activity to help you begin.

"To me, money is alive. It is almost human. If you treat it with real sympathy and kindness and consideration, it will be a good servant and work hard for you, and stay with you and take care of you," Katharine Butler Hathaway wrote in 1932. "If you treat it arrogantly and contemptuously, as if it were not human, as if it were only a slave and could work without limit, it will turn on you with a great revenge and leave you to look after yourself alone."

Do You Know Why You Spend?

Family Legacies or Heresies

I can't take it with me I know
But will it last until I go?

— MARTHA F. NEWMEYER

Tracing our genealogy from our ancestors can be both fun and a passionate pursuit. The stories you've been told about your family can also shed some light on your own financial tendencies, and the stories that you find are bound to add some delicious insights into family quirks, legacies, and legends. I love the marvelous genealogy series called *Who Do You Think You Are?* in which celebrities trace their family trees and always come up with startling surprises—both good and bad. It's a fascinating watch, and I realized that the idea could be adapted to excavating our family money legacy. I started my search with my grandparents on both sides of my family, using family lore and whatever public records could be accessed.

The lessons we glean from their lives are most likely based on the stories that resonated with us as young children. My father Patrick's family emigrated from Belfast, Ireland, during "the Troubles," which was the Irish Civil War of 1918–1922. My grandfather Joseph Crean arrived at Ellis Island on May 11, 1921, with $125 in his pocket. He was twenty-nine years old and stayed with his brother Dominic, who lived on East 79th Street in New York City. My grandmother Rose Crossan Crean was six months pregnant with my father at the time and still living in Ireland with her family.

My family's oral history tells us that Grandpa Joe went to work as an electrician for Macy's in New York City. My grandfather was present at the first Thanksgiving Day Parade in November 1924, so every year we watch the Macy's Thanksgiving Day Parade to stay connected to the memories of what was, once upon a time.

When my father was two years old, my grandmother Rose brought him to the United States with less than $50 in her possession. Rose and her baby were "released" to her husband, who by then lived on 49th Street, in the middle of Hell's Kitchen. But our family lore was not focused on struggle; it was filled with the wonder of coming to America. The messages, sacrifices, and dreams of my grandparents were passed on to my parents. Anything, yes, anything is possible—but success was achieved by hard work, especially during hard times. Achievement was in our DNA, in our destiny, nature, and aspirations. We knew how to win our chosen race. What was unclear was how to manage the winning spoils of the race.

My parents were both children of the Great Depression. The pain of not having, and not having enough, ingrained contradictory beliefs in both possibility and scarcity in two generations of our family's psyche; a deep crevasse of uncertainty, worry, and pessimism that battles for control with the optimistic dreamers in all of us. We had many great legends in our Irish family: from inventors and artists to an Olympic champion and a banished hero fighting for Irish independence from the British. To compensate for our darkly pessimistic side, we became overachievers, always hoping that one more accolade could insulate us from failure and poverty.

We also shared a shameful whispered secret known as the "Crean Curse." According to family legend, the Creans could make fortunes...but couldn't hold on to their wealth. How deeply ingrained in my psyche was this drama? The family motto was: "Enjoy it while you have it." And they did. Our family saga started in Ireland in the town of Sligo in 1640 when the O'Creans were the wealthiest merchants in the area. Our family built Sligo Abbey, which still stands today and holds a tomb of Crean ancestors. But that all quickly changed when Oliver Cromwell decided to quell the Irish upstarts and took the land and our birthright. In response the family dropped the *O* from our name, which means "descendants of." No one wanted to be identified as Irish Catholic in the land of the Protestants.

Not to be held down, my ancestors moved to Belfast and my great-grandfather Patrick Crean filed a patent for curing fire bricks around 1890. These bricks had holes in them, and heat from a fire warmed the air. The process revolutionized brick manufacturing at the time, for it cut brick-curing time from seven days to twenty-four hours. Fame and fortune quickly followed, and Patrick and his brother Michael parlayed their assets into coal and shipping. Soon they dominated the landscape. Then it happened. Fate stepped in with a plan of her own. Michael, an asthmatic, died in his fifties. His death alone would have been a tragedy to the family, but Michael was also the linchpin in the family's wealth; Patrick was the dreamer and Michael was the businessman. In less than fifteen years the fortune was lost on various bad business schemes and Patrick died, leaving a family of six children to pick up the pieces. They did, in the form of the Irish Republican Army.

Now, we're not really sure how many of the siblings were involved in the Irish independence movement, but my great-uncle Desmond was the one who was jailed for treason against the Crown. He and other prisoners were confined to a prison ship and went on a hunger strike; he wrote a book of poetry, *Songs of an Old IRA Man*, during his imprisonment. The English, of course, seized all of the family's remaining property and possessions and Desmond was exiled instead of hanged. Our family moved to the United States, to the land of possibility, freedom, and new beginnings, where the streets were paved with gold. Starting over is a theme our family is accustomed to and does well. But it does make me wonder how many "back to the beginnings" we're supposed to have in life. I suppose as many as we need, but I'm telling you right now, this starting over from scratch is beginning to wear thin on my nerves.

And me? Do I have the guts to tell you that while I absolutely adored spending, especially not having to look at a price tag—suddenly having a lot of money to look after was difficult for me? Why? Because I didn't understand money, I couldn't say no to requests for it; I thought I couldn't possibly have deserved so much, so fast, so it was imperative to share the wealth. Because I felt I'd never truly been loved before, sudden wealth also triggered my fears that now I'd be loved *only* because of it.

Money. As I've said, it's both the most complicated and the most passionate relationship in our lives. That's because our lives *do* depend on money: how we make it, save it, spend it, share it, manage it, respect it. We'll explore our complex relationship with money gently and slowly so that we both—writer and reader—have a safe place to excavate our deepest fears about money and its meaning in our lives. I'm grateful for this sanctuary of peace and plenty, but my heart is racing at the moment. "Talent is helpful in writing, but guts are absolutely necessary," the Quaker writer Jessamyn West reassures me.

I hope she's right. Because this conversation is really pushing me past my comfort zone.

Southern–Fried Cash

Wealth consists not in having great possessions but in having few wants.

—ESTHER DE WAAL

Money does push us past the boundaries of our comfort zone. That's why we do everything possible to numb ourselves so that we're not thinking about it.

On the Southern heritage side of my family, it was a life of different circumstances—but struggle all the same—that created our financial tree beginning after World War I. My Kentucky grandmother Lucy Lyttle Donnelly White was widowed with three young children, and she was forced by financial circumstances to change the parameters of her life. Her young family's brief adventure began in 1920, when my grandfather Cecil B. Donnelly became one of the Treasury Department's first G-men and moved them to Washington, DC. Shortly thereafter, he became ill with the Spanish influenza; he died when my mother, Drusilla, was only two years old. Making ends meet became my grandmother's plight for the rest of her life. She began a career as a stenographer for a traveling court circuit around Clay County, and left her children during the week with "relations."

This excerpt from Granny's daily journal in 1964 sheds much light on my own mother's indoctrinations toward money:

October 6, 1964
Dru called Sunday

Jane called Monday

Cecil called Monday night [note: these are her three adult children]

Today I remembered my fire insurance/Homeowner's policy, $8,000. The payment was $45.87. I gave a check on my special account, I think I had $615.00.

I deposited $137.00 to my checking account and must have had $60.00 or should have. I'll call it $200 so as to be in round numbers.

I deposited my Social Security check $72.00

Bill Rawlings [note: Jane's husband] $25.00

John Lyttle [note: a cousin] $25.00

Dru Donnelly [note: my mother] <u>$15.00</u>

$137.00

God is good and keeps my head just above water. I had my trees trimmed, cost me $45 altogether with the wreckage of all my utility lines.

Had my roof tarred about $30 and the rat hole stuffed for $1.50.

Thank God I was able to do it.

Round numbers and rat holes! In 1964, my grandmother's monthly income of $137 was the equivalent of $941.23 today, well below any era's poverty level, but she never, ever stopped thanking her God for his gifts to her.

Gratitude in all circumstances is her bright legacy to our family; one that makes the checkbook balance and gloom fade, at least for a little while. "The wise lay-out of money, and the resultant feel of complete financial security must give a sort of quiet happiness which is the essential basis of successful homemaking," the English essayist Phyllis Nicholson wrote in 1941. "There are no text-books on the subject. For some unexplained psychological reason we all talk about money in the abstract, never in the concrete. No one says how many pounds they possess. They merely say they 'are dreadfully hard up.' I never met a woman who confessed to being rich!"

Pilgrim Mother Mentors

*It isn't for the moment you are stuck that you need
courage, but for the long uphill climb back to sanity and
faith and security.*

—ANNE MORROW LINDBERGH (1932)

By the third Thanksgiving of the Great Depression in November 1932, American housewives and the women's magazines they read had passed through the same desperate psychological stages a person confronting death (or one who must learn to live with and through a life-altering trauma) endures—shock, denial, anger, bargaining, and great grief—before settling in for what is often the longest stage of an emotional or economic transformation, depression. A new Democratic president-elect, Franklin Delano Roosevelt, was getting ready to take over the White House, but it would be another four months before FDR's rousing Inaugural Address reminded Americans that all they had "to fear is fear itself." There would be seven more lean years of economic uncertainty followed by five world war years. How did our grandmothers and great-grandmothers drag themselves out of bed to make the biscuits for breakfast? An image of my Kentucky grandmother rolling out dough in her salmon-pink chenille bathrobe has come to represent grace under pressure in the archives of my heart.

It was the women's magazines that shored up feminine courage, fortitude, and perseverance in between thrifty recipes and fashionable dress patterns, and they did it spectacularly. The *Ladies' Home Journal* in October 1932 declared "It Was Up to the Women" to bring about an economic recovery, calling for women readers to start an apron-string revolution to bring about "freedom from want."

> It is not enough to be willing to make the best of things as they are. Resignation will get us nowhere. We must build what amounts to a new country. We must revive the ideals of the founders. We must learn the new values of money. It is a time for pioneering—to create a new security for the home and the family...As a nation, we have been desperately ill. Now, like any other convalescent, we are in that querulous stage when one regretfully looks back upon the past, without feeling quite strong enough to face the future. But it is a time when we must look forward instead of back, and stop the weeping and moaning and hand-wringing...the wailing wall is still overcrowded but a new and happier philosophy is beginning to appear. There is less and less complaining. New satisfactions are being found in simpler living and simpler pleasures. Almost everyone is poor—by comparison with three years ago—but no one is ashamed of it. Keeping up with the Joneses is out of fashion...Where we were specialists in spending, we are becoming specialists in living. There is a new American thrift for new pioneers—a thrift of endeavor and of accomplishment...It's up to the Women!

The Thanksgiving editorial written by Marjorie Shuler in *The Pictorial Review* (November 1932) urged readers to reconsider gratitude as a prism with which to view their lot in life and as a catalyst to jump-start positive life changes, no matter what they had lost in the previous three years.

> To give thanks is to be rich. For the very state of being grateful is acknowledgement that something has been received.
>
> That something may appear trifling, a salary sadly reduced, wool stockings instead of silk, pot roast and noodles when your taste is for turkey and caviar.
>
> But just to say "thank you" implies having a possession, and possessions when handled with serenity and confidence and courage have a way of multiplying. On the other hand ingratitude is poverty. It is the denial of possession. It is the robber which takes away even what there is...But for each generation there is a new frontier. For each generation there is a trail to be broken. Not always is the way to be found by physical effort or fighting; sometimes it is sturdy, strong, courageous, intelligent thinking.

When discouragement comes, I comfort myself by thinking of the long line of heroic women behind me—not only those in my family, but every woman settler, explorer, adventurer, and homemaker who tamed wild land and wild times around the world. I particularly love to meditate on the first band of Pilgrim women. There were eighteen women on the *Mayflower*, and although none of them died during the crossing from England to Massachusetts, by the time of the first "Thanks Giving" meal, a year later in 1621, only four women had survived the brutal winter, spring sowing, and autumn harvest. Four very tired women who needed to take care of fifty men and children daily. With the men almost entirely focused on building houses and the village, the women had so many chores, they performed them in shifts. For aside from cleaning and cooking, there was plowing and planting, preserving and putting away, caring for the livestock, making soap and candles from tallow (animal fat), tending the stock and creating herb medicinals. There was so much work that they lived on one portion of daily grace and very meager food—and if they didn't drop dead with their hand to the plow or wither away in a nighttime sweat from a succession of diseases contracted on the voyage, they took it as a sign that God meant for them to go on.

And you know, they were right. I love the bare-bones simplicity of this truth. Sometimes in life, and today might be one of those days for you, all we can do is put one foot out of bed in the morning, and then in front of the other, literally. I figure if you wake up in the morning, you're meant to go on—continue at what you're doing, ask Heaven to show you what you're doing wrong if you are, or what you should be doing differently. Since God knows we are not meant to manage alone, Providence will be there to help and answer if we ask for help. I think this is called "blind" faith, but it is the substance I'm living on right now, the evidence not yet seen, and it is nourishing.

All women are endowed with the same spiritual DNA as our Pilgrim mothers—a genetic code of resilience and strength, ingenuity and creativity, perseverance and determination. Our Destiny, Nature, and Aspirations are Heaven-sent, so why wouldn't we be given the wherewithal to fulfill them?

The lean days when the budget won't budge are our Pilgrim mother moments. Whenever anything happens (and every day there's a lot) that triggers the feelings of angst or distress, just ask yourself a few questions, as I do when I'm experiencing a panic attack:

Is my family safe?

Is there a roof over our heads today?

Do I have to chop wood to keep warm?

Do I have to carry water in a bucket from a creek three miles away to drink, cook, bathe in, clean with, and garden?

Do I have to melt snow or collect rain for my water?

Do I have to warm my water over the fire before I can take a bath or have a cup of tea?

Do I have to eat only what I grow or slaughter?

Will I have to make candles today before I burn them for my only source of light?

If you can answer no to any (and hopefully all) of those questions today, it's an immediate reconnection to the Divine, or hopefully a smile at least and a genuine thank-you, the only prayer Heaven ever asks of us to experience peace and plenty. God bless our Pilgrim, pioneer, settler, and Native American mothers.

Money In, Money Out

*I enjoy my success for I've worked and thought hard for it.
I have never had any assistance and very little
encouragement from anyone. My ambitions were laughed
or sneered at. The sneers are very quiet now. The dollars
have silenced them.*

— LUCY MAUD MONTGOMERY

Maud Montgomery had been keeping track of her "money in, money out" accounts since she was paid $15 a month for her first teaching position on Prince Edward Island. According to *The Lucy Maud Montgomery Album*, a compendium of her "life-books," journals, ledgers, and albums, in 1896 she received a check for $5 for her first published story, "Our Charivari," which appeared in the American children's periodical called *Golden Days*. In 1909, Maud received her first book royalties of $1,730 from the sales of *Anne of Green Gables*, which had been published the year before. By 1910, flush with pride, success, and money, she was able to privately boast to her journal: "Whatever worries life may still hold for me...it does not seem likely that lack of money will hereafter be among them."

It's been said that God created the world round so that we couldn't see very far ahead.

I know how Maud felt, because receiving my royalty check after *Simple Abundance* hit number one on the *New York Times* best-seller list on April 14, 1996, was a euphoric occasion—flowers, champagne, compliments, accolades, invitations, and great rejoicing. Even if overnight success does take an average of twenty-five years, it brings a wild, giddy, glorious ride. What's more, the sneers, snickers, and sarcasm of others stop immediately. It's very pleasant. And when checks for more than a million dollars have your name on them every six months, it's very easy to believe your money problems are a thing of the past. At the time, there was a marvelous ritual in publishing circles every Wednesday evening when the *Times* best-seller list for the next week was faxed to publicists and publishers around 6 PM. I'd get a call. Yes! Crack open the bubbly. Then one Wednesday evening the following year, 6 PM came and went without a call. The silence hung in the house like a shroud. "It's a little depressing to become number one because the only place you can go from there is down," Doris Day consoled me. And while it stung to be number two, there's really nobody around to offer you sympathy. I left the champagne in the refrigerator and poured an Irish whiskey, usually reserved for medicinal purposes such as wakes and root canals.

Maud's success continued. By 1917, the New York publishers Frederick Stokes and Company agreed to pay her 20 percent royalties and offered her an "advance" of $5,000 against these royalties—a spectacular sum. Maud felt that she had "attained a good foothold" in her profession, and she notes in her journal in 1919 that when she adds up her books, she now has $76,000. "How the thought of possessing such a sum would have made my eyes stick out twenty-four years ago! It is not a bad showing, considering my initial capital—my pen and the scanty education I managed to get."

But Maud was familiar with the financial difficulties of family and friends, and she explored these familiar financial dilemmas in the plights of her fictional characters. In *Anne of Green Gables*, Anne's beloved guardian Matthew Cuthbert dies from shock after reading in the newspaper of the failure of the Abbey Bank, which held the mortgage to his farm.

As is the case in most families when one person suddenly wins or earns a great deal of money, the poorer relations felt entitled to ask for loans. From the time Maud started receiving a regular amount from her royalties, she also started lending. In November 1931, she grumbles (with good reason), "I have lent over ten thousand dollars to various friends and they won't even pay the interest. As for the principal, they evidently look upon it as a gift! If I had never lent a cent I would not be counting my pennies as I have to do this fall."

Of course, two years into the Great Depression (1929–1941) everyone in the world was counting their pennies. Throughout her career Maud had trained herself to write a book every two years, but with ill health, emotional depression, and the pressure of having to financially take care of an ever-increasing extended "family," her very real worries about money began to affect her writing. In a rare occurrence that reveals her vulnerabilities, these worries spilled over into her public life when she began to ask fans writing her to recommend her books to others. The low point seems to have come around Christmas 1932, when Maud was forced to type her next book in order to save money. This seems to have devastated her. "In twelve days I have typed 100,000 words. I have not typed the MS of a book since *Anne of Avonlea* (1909). But it would cost fifty dollars to have it done and this year every cent counts, so I [typed] it."

It always seems to me that it is the smallest shift in circumstances that reveals the most about a person. For Maud, the serious nature of her financial situation was revealed in her typing her manuscript herself; when I left my marriage in England, I left behind two houses and a lifetime's possessions and designer clothing in order to take the cat. No woman needs an explanation of what that gesture meant.

As a record of triumphs or adversity, Lucy Maud Montgomery's "Money In, Money Out" is as valuable a memoir as I've come across in documenting Life's ebbs and cash flows as well as a spiritual practice for financial serenity. "We should regret our mistakes and learn from them," Maud notes, "but never carry them forward into the future with us."

Yet how many women, including myself, have carried our money regrets in sacks full of sorrow, murky memories, and recriminations when they could easily be left behind as lines in an illuminating ledger, lightening our load and straightening the path up ahead toward peace and plenty.

The Art of Forensic Accounting

Friendship, like credit, is highest when it is not used.

—ELBERT HUBBARD

There comes a time in every woman's life when she has to come face-to-face with some inevitable facts: Your children have lives of their own, you'll never be twenty-five or size 8 again, and your FICO or credit score counts as you rebuild a life of financial serenity.

I've spent many a night over the past few years dreading even finding out my score, let alone trying to improve it, and I'm sure I'm not alone. However, before we can begin to climb out of the credit hole we find ourselves in today, we have to get real with ourselves. That means following the advice of Jack Webb from the 1950s television police drama *Dragnet*: "The facts, ma'am, just the facts." Ironically, just like our credit scores, compiled from different credit reporting agencies, Jack Webb's detective Joe Friday never actually said this. According to the book *My Name's Friday* by Michael J. Hayde, Sergeant Friday really said, "All we want are the facts, ma'am." If a famous quote from a recorded TV show can be so misrepresented, imagine what you're going to find when you go looking for your own facts. You may very well be hounded by debt collectors (who buy and sell our debts) for a bill you paid years ago. Hence the advice: Never believe a bill collector.

This is not the time to indulge in the emotional story of why we're where we are. That will only fill us with despair and actually hinder our progress. Tackling our FICO score (named after the first credit scoring company, Fair Isaac Corporation, which began keeping track of creditworthiness in 1956) is easier if we act as if we're forensic accountants, following the money and looking for errors in the books.

At the base of our FICO score is our actual credit report. In the United States, there are three agencies that track our credit history: Experian, Equifax, and TransUnion. (If you live outside the United States, you will want to find the credit reporting agencies appropriate to you.)

Now, there are many companies out there that want to sell you your "free" credit report, but don't be fooled by their catchy jingles and celebrity spokespersons. These companies just want your money. There really are only two places to request your report without a fee. By law in the United States, you are *entitled* to see your credit report from each credit reporting agency at no cost every twelve months.

The only legitimate source for this really *free* information is the FTC, the Federal Trade Commission. You can request your report through www.annualcredit report.com, calling toll-free 877-322-8228 and following the automated system, or by mail. You can download the Annual Credit Report Request Form at www.ftc.gov/ credit or write to: Annual Credit Report Request Service, PO Box 10521, Atlanta, GA 30348-6281.

When you call the toll-free number, you can only request one report at a time (Experian, Equifax, and Trans-Union). Still, it's worth the effort and it is free.

It will take a few weeks to receive your report. Once you have made your request, take a moment to acknowledge the important step you've just taken; give yourself "credit" in the true sense of the word and celebrate in a small way. You have made an important decision, acted with courage, followed through, and I'm so proud of you, as you should be, too. Coming to terms with our financial situation, whether we want to improve our credit score or protect ourselves from identity theft, is what grown-up women do, and it's crucial to find out where we stand in the eyes of others. Taking charge of our financial life is liberating, and you can relax, you don't have to face the music until the report arrives. All the better to brace yourself, my dear.

Keep Calm and Carry On

In this world without quiet corners, there can be no easy escapes...from hullabaloo, from terrible, unquiet fuss.

—SALMAN RUSHDIE

I'm sure these last few years of cataclysmic financial shocks and shudders have affected you. They've affected everyone—that's why it's called a global economic crisis. But recessions become depressions when the numbers being crunched are your own. If you are a woman who has prudently planned and carefully saved for your retirement and your children's education, to suddenly lose what you thought was safe is devastating, because you lost more than money, you lost your dreams. Trust. Hope. Maybe even faith. To wake up every morning worried about losing your house, or job, is to meet despair at dawn. It's one thing to downsize your life out of choice, but it's a completely different one to have your dreams derailed by the bad choices of other people who didn't even consult you, never mind get your consent. And so we've all been gripped by some feral emotions—anger, betrayal, fear, grief. But you're going to be okay. And I will be, too. Maybe this is the opportunity for all of us to overhaul our lives in positive ways. Maybe this is the time for us to discover for the first time what trust, hope, and faith really mean. To us. To rediscover what matters most. To you. To me. That's what I pray for all of us.

Writing of watching her father, hedge fund manager Victor Niederhoffer, live through a Wall Street financial downfall that lost the family millions of dollars, not just once but twice, the filmmaker and writer Galt Niederhoffer reflected on what's left behind after personal economic ruin:

> Now the world is facing a bankruptcy of sorts and the emotions that go with it—fear, shame, embarrassment, hopelessness, self-doubt. What can we do when money is lost other than toil to make it back? We can look for the opportunities *created* by loss—and pursue them with passion. In loss, my father, and later I, saw an opportunity for reinvention. I watched my father break down and rebuild. I followed in his footsteps. As a daughter I found it a hard lesson to learn. As a mother, I realize, it may be the most important thing I can teach my children.

I must admit that since I've been back in America, I've noticed that the doom and gloom bombarding us from the electronic media is particularly difficult to process; it feels like I've got vibrating swirls of static electricity buzzing my brain. It's difficult enough to deal with the demands of sorting out your own financial matters (like that pile of unopened bills growing across the kitchen counter), but against the background noise of 24/7 news that batters you during your early-morning coffee, through the computer all day long, and continuing until you turn the television off late at night, the task is magnified a hundredfold. When there are seven hours and six minutes before the U.S. market opens and you know this, though you are not a trader by profession, you're meant to be occupying your time in a more fulfilling way. And no, it's not cruising all the adorable Mary Engelbreit collectible teapots on eBay. Trust me on this one.

Our new fascination with being connected to live re-ports — whether it's the Dow during the course of the day, or an eBay auction, counting down the minutes until yet another unnecessary purchase fights for room in your closet — reminds me of a hospital ECG hookup, which monitors heartbeats. Even when the beat is steady, those wires and green electrical impulse lights make us edgy be-cause we're always expecting the next sound to be the high-pitched whine of the flatline.

"The world is too much with us," the English poet William Wordsworth wrote more than two hundred years ago. "Getting and spending, we lay waste our powers." Today I'm going to ask you to deliberately turn away from the world. Don't read the newspapers or watch the evening news for a week — longer if you can stand it. Believe me, if there's something you need to know, you'll hear about it. And when you talk to other people, always make sure that you leave them with a smile or a story that makes them feel good. I've started conversations with "Tell me something good." Try it. It works!

Here's a great one to share. In 1939, when the English government feared a massive Nazi invasion, the Ministry of Information commissioned a series of simple but strik-ing red posters to reassure and rally the British people — YOUR COURAGE, YOUR CHEERFULNESS, YOUR RESOLUTION WILL BRING US VICTORY and FREEDOM IS IN PERIL — which appeared all over the country on bill-boards and at train stations. Another poster was prepared and more than two million copies printed, which was to be distributed only should the *worst* happen. It read simply:

Keep Calm
And
Carry On

Despite living through air raids, the bombing of Britain, the evacuation of London children to escape the Blitz, the drastic rationing of food and other essentials from eggs to thread to stockings—women resorted to "dyeing" their legs in cold tea and then drawing long black lines up the backs to simulate hosiery (female ingenuity at its most fashionable)—the worst actually *never* happened. The poster was pulped. Then a decade ago, an English bookseller found one of these posters in the bottom of a box of old books he'd bought at auction. He framed it and put it beside his cash register. There were so many requests to buy the poster that he had it reproduced. Now, seventy years after the invasion that never happened, the slogan has taken on a cult status. The reassuring message speaks volumes to those undergoing economic anxiety in five easy-to-remember words.

Keep calm and carry on.

I have this profound personal prompt framed on my desk. Its quiet confidence never fails to bolster my spirit. No matter what may happen in the course of today, if you keep calm, and carry on, there is nothing that you and Spirit can't handle together.

The Gathering

We are a fact-gathering organization only. We don't clear anybody. We don't condemn anybody.

— J. EDGAR HOOVER

When it comes to facing the music of our lives, it is far more productive to get on the dance floor than to sit this one out. It is time for the gathering, dear Reader, while we await the arrival of our credit reports.

Doesn't a "gathering" sound like a lovely time for all? Hold that thought as you address this task. For this "gathering" is literal—you are going to collect every bill sent your way and bring them all to the party. Depending on your financial attitude (FA), this task may present different levels of difficulty. I have identified five attitudes as embodied by some of my favorite characters in fiction, so let's map your FA archetype to get a glimpse of how this will go for you:

- **Scarlett O'Hara:** The mail comes in and is tossed onto the table, the desk, the dresser, and the counters while she gets ready for the party. It isn't that Scarlett is lazy; oh no, the opposite is true. Scarlett works hard for her money and takes care of her family and provides for them as best she can. It's just that some things are so stressful, she puts them off as long as possible. Scarlett will probably have her mail scattered, so if you see yourself in her, grab a basket and start collecting the bills.

- **Auntie Mame:** "Let's go" was probably one of Auntie Mame Dennis's favorite phrases as she got on with feasting at the banquet of life until her couture ensembles burst at the seams. If you have an Auntie Mame attitude toward life, you are busy, very busy. There are so many things that need to be done in a day, and you are wildly enthusiastic about the endless adventures that life has to offer. Alas, you're also easily sidetracked. It's far more pleasant to make a call to your credit card company to increase your credit line than to actually balance your checkbook. You may not be sure where you put the bills as you were getting ready for your weekend with the girls, but pick up your prettiest hatbox and start looking.

- **Madame Bovary:** Marriage seemed like a good idea on paper, but it delivered boredom for Gustave Flaubert's 1857 French heroine Emma Bovary, leaving her little choice but to turn to adultery and sophisticated spendthrift amusements. "A woman who had laid on herself such sacrifices could well allow herself certain whims. She bought a Gothic prie-dieu, and in a month spent 14 francs on lemons for polishing her nails; she wrote to Rouen for a blue cashmere gown; she chose one of L'heureux's finest scarves and wore it knotted around her waist over her dressing-gown." You are now sitting with the aftermath of endless unconscious decisions. You've tried to have fun, but now you face the weariness of impossible debt and no way out. Have no fear, there is a way out and you will take one step at a time. You know where all your bills are, in boxes in the closet or desk drawer. Now is the time to take them out and put them in a designer tote to make carrying them easier.

- **Rebecca Bloomwood:** In the film *Confessions of a Shopaholic* (based on the novel by Sophie Kinsella), Rebecca, a financial journalist for the magazine *Successful Savings*, sprints through life and department stores as fast as her credit card allows, trying to escape from the frugal and unfashionable life led by her serviceable-brown-shoe-wearing, parsimonious mother. Becky loves how shopping makes her feel—and don't we all know that intoxicating swoon when a velvet scarf "makes my eyes look bigger, it makes my haircut look more expensive, it makes me look like a different person." Swoons are expensive, though, and Becky finds herself relentlessly pursued by her debt collector, who follows wherever she goes. Are you being stalked by bill collectors as well? No worries; by the end of this process your phone will be ringing again, but with calls from friends you want to see. Your bills are probably already in shopping bags, so you're ready for what's next.

- **Della Street:** In Erle Stanley Gardner's first Perry Mason novel, *The Case of the Velvet Claws*, we are introduced to loyal, hardworking secretary Della Street. We learn that Della comes from a well-to-do family who lost all their money in the stock market crash, forcing her to reinvent her life. You might be Della if you are trying to work yourself out of a life of bills from a time when finances were better: before divorce, before the economic collapse of the recent past, before a Casanova con man spent or stole all your money, or before you were laid off from your job. Just like Della, you will land on your high heels without a sprained ankle. So gather your bills up in an accordion legal file as you help Perry gather the facts of the case.

You may have another heroine in mind as you approach the daunting task of gathering your paper debt together. The important thing is to eliminate the browbeating we often give ourselves when we make mistakes. That's why dipping into literature and films to vicariously enjoy other women's shopping sprees or their remorse is good for the soul and the pocketbook. Jane Austen hated to shop, but knew she had to trim the bonnets for her readers. In Virginia Woolf's 1923 short story "Mrs. Dalloway in Bond

Street," Clarissa Dalloway believes the search for the perfect pair of gloves — French kid, white, tight, and but-
toned — can change her life. And if I could find such a pair
at a flea market for $10, I might think so myself.

The only thing that counts right now is who we choose
to be in the face of our own financial situation. Choose
someone brave! As Emily Brontë reassures us, "No cow-
ard soul is mine."

Or yours.

How Bad Is It Really?

Solvency is a feeling of being comfortable with money—not anxious about it, and not careless with it, either. Solvency is a confident feeling of being prepared for any circumstance, of living within our means at all times.

—JULIA CAMERON AND MARK BRYAN

Now that you're calm enough to try to separate your fears from the state of your fortunes, how bad is it really, your money situation? Do you even know? If not, I completely understand. I've rarely wanted to know precisely how much money I've had or owed, preferring to adopt early on my granny's round-number method of moving through life. I was an ostrich long before I could wear the feather boa because the head-in-the-sand tactic worked equally well whether I was broke (well, if there's nothing I can do about it, then why torture myself with worry?) or I was a millionairess (well, if I have so much money that I don't even have to look at the price tag, then why bother to think about it?).

Listen, women are scared of anything that even resembles money (and if it were pearls that we were exchanging instead of coins, we'd be afraid of oyster shells). We're scared it won't be there, scared there won't be enough, scared it won't last. We're scared of the husband screaming about the spending. Scared the ex won't send child-support payments regularly. Scared we'll only be loved for our money. Scared that without money we won't be loved. Scared that if we know the truth about our own situation, we'll have to take responsibility for that knowledge. Let's say you earn more than your husband, or your husband has been laid off from work. Let's say that even though you now have to bring the bacon home and fry it up in the pan and he seems to have plenty of time on his hands to help at home, maybe to throw a load of laundry into the washer or start a meal before you get home, he doesn't. Instead he plays golf, heads to the pub for a noon pint, goes to the gym, plays solitaire on the computer, watches sports on the couch, and builds increasingly large piles of papers on the kitchen table, calling it "work."

Let's just say for the sake of conversation this is what he does and now you're ticking off a list in your head every time you pass him in the hall. Your fuse is getting shorter and shorter. The word *bum* seems to hover in the back of your throat and you don't really think that of him generally, but maybe you do today. Still, that would mean you have to speak up and start a conversation you've been avoiding for the last two years when he was supposed to have started looking for a job.

A couple of years into my English matrimonial fiasco, I read an article about "freeloading" husbands. That article so scared me that I obsessively folded it into increasingly smaller origami shapes and kept it in my handbag. Every few days I'd take it out and furtively read it, my discomfort mounting each time. The idea of even acknowledging to myself that I'd married a "freeloader" made me want to scream with rage, resentment, and, yes, fear. Because if this suspicion ever floated to the surface of our lives, I wouldn't be able to stay in the marriage. Of course, I had no business staying in it for many other reasons, also willfully ignored. Several years later, by the time the article shredded in my hands from being opened and folded so many times, I'd had enough. But I was still afraid and continued to feel fear as I started divorce proceedings and then a new life from scratch. Fear was associated with money, just as once love had been.

You see, our hopes and fears, desires and despairs,

aren't really about the money we either have at the moment or don't have; they're about what's standing between us and the truth. It could be that uncomfortable, agonizing conversation you can't bring yourself to start. It could be your origami secret. But it could also be a lifelong avoidance of anything that doesn't feel good. Whether we spend or hoard, our personal pattern of handling money is based on emotion—how money makes us feel. Just as with dependency on drugs, food, alcohol, gambling, sex, or any other addictive behavior, our trigger is an emotion. We have an addiction to money and money addiction can take many shapes, but the one constant is that we're all afraid. All of the time.

Solvency is the word that Julia Cameron and Mark Bryan use for what I refer to as "financial serenity." In their illuminating and compassionate book (despite its tough-love title) *Money Drunk, Money Sober: 90 Days to Financial Freedom*, they reassure readers, "Our goal is solvency: the return of choice, sanity and personal dignity in the use of money. More than a positive bank balance, solvency is a balance in our lives as a whole."

Now, I don't know about you, but I think even imagining a fiscal balance in my life is nothing short of miraculous. Yet I have the faith that it is also achievable, because whatever we can imagine, we can pray for the grace to accomplish, and I've never known a prayer for one day's portion of grace to be denied. This is what makes the pursuit of financial serenity over financial security so powerful. For when we seek peace and plenty, Providence bestows upon us the restoration of our sacred imagination. Soon we'll begin to do something extraordinary. Something heroic. Something that, once again, we've never even been able to imagine. We're going to call a financial ceasefire between our hearts and our heads and begin a diplomatic relationship with money.

The Reckoning

Truth is truth to the end of reckoning.

—WILLIAM SHAKESPEARE, *MEASURE FOR MEASURE*

No matter how long we push it off, one thing is certain. If we are ever to get our financial house in order, we must reconcile our books. By now, you should have received your credit reports and have gotten your bills together. Whether you do it today, tomorrow, or a week from next Tuesday, pull out your calendar and schedule an afternoon to create your new financial future. This isn't about bemoaning what you spent on redoing the kitchen before the bottom fell out of the real estate market. It's not about having a fight with your spouse over the size of the bills for that new truck or SUV now that gas prices have gone crazy. The only point of this exercise is to get straight with yourself, understand where you stand financially today, and then make a plan for a better tomorrow. It is an exercise in conscious money management.

Online banking is one of the greatest gifts offered by the age of technology. If you are able to download your credits and debits, you can save a lot of time. If not, it's no problem; you will just write down your expenditures by category, so you can get the whole picture of your financial life.

For the time being, set your credit reports to the side and make the following labels on an index card: CURRENT BILLS; PAST DUE 30 TO 60 DAYS; OLD DEBTS. Sort your bills according to their freshness dates. You're going to look first at the status of your current bills. There are many wonderful books that will tell you how to handle the repayment of your debts from a logical standpoint. The advice is factual and well taken, except when the choice is between a credit card company charging high interest and dear Aunt Em, who lent you money to go back to school. There are two considerations for every bill you owe: the financial and the emotional. Long after the debts are repaid, the emotional hangover lingers if things have not gone well in the relationship.

Now go through your bills and draw a star on any bill that has an emotional charge. Did your pediatrician make room for you on a Saturday when your child wasn't feeling well? Does your church fill your soul spiritually every week? These decisions don't have to be logical; you want them to be authentic to the quality of your life. With these bills, make a fourth pile labeled HONORING. It's probably not going to be possible to clear these obligations quickly, but the honor method of payment will help you relieve the guilt.

To honor something, it must be in your consciousness in a positive way. Once you have budgeted for the essentials—food, clothing, shelter, child care, savings, transportation, and insurance—you will have a good idea of how much money you can put toward debt reduction. This becomes the pot of money you dip into to pay the rest of your bills. If there is a particular debt that bothers you, then take 1 to 10 percent of the pot and make an honor payment toward the balance owed. Over time you will fully repay those emotionally charged obligations, but this small step in the right direction will signal to these emotionally important creditors that you have the best intentions toward repaying their kindness.

At the end of this exercise, you will know the truth about what you can pay and what you have left over. Now is the time to revisit your budget with a more informed eye. What is really essential to your life and the well-being of your family? What options do you have for creating a more positive cash flow in the family? Can you cut back on the food budget without endangering your family's health? In most cases, the answer will be yes, if you are willing to put in the work of planning and cooking. By eliminating two nights of takeout for a family of four, you can put $40 to $60 back into the pot of money each week. All it takes is some time and creativity to rethink lifestyle choices. By taking the first step and facing your financial fears, you become your own best defense against making financial mistakes in the future.

To complete today's activity, you are going to reduce the four stacks of bills to two: those you can pay this month and those you can't. For those bills that have to wait until you have more income, you'll need to make some phone calls to creditors and make a plan you can stick to, but that's a task for another day. You will be amazed by the enormous amount of energy you have expended just creating and moving these piles. Tonight you may be exhausted, but tomorrow you will feel renewed. This is definitely an accomplishment to record in your *Peace and Plenty Journal of Well-Spent Moments*. You need to focus on this accomplishment to keep up your energy and continue moving forward.

So let's "pack up our troubles in our old kit-bag and smile, smile, smile." If you don't have an old kit-bag handy, any basket, container, or hatbox will do. The prettier the better. Show your bills and yourself that you have honor, integrity, and respect. Don't worry, you'll figure it out, and for tonight put it away in the closet.

"Money is only money, beans tonight and steak tomorrow," Meridel Le Sueur wrote in 1955. "So long as you can look yourself in the eye."

Job well done, Babe. I'm proud of you, and so is your money!

Here There Be Monsters

When it comes to money, fear is constantly constricting and debilitating, like a companion or a voice in your head, reminding you of all the bills you have to pay, intruding on times that should be pleasurable, keeping you up at night.

—SUZE ORMAN

When we feel so scared, so utterly panic-stricken over the lack of money, we lose the ability to hear ourselves think clearly over the din of our pounding hearts. Of course, most of what people worry about never really comes to pass, but try telling this to the woman pacing your bedroom floor at night, inviting the inevitability of impoverishment to stay a little while longer. Fear becomes first its own phantom, then a self-fulfilling prophecy.

The fear of the unknown has always repelled or galvanized the human spirit—it is the source of the primordial fight-or-flight instinct. I love to pore over old maps. In my Contentment Chest, I keep a copy of a seventeenth-century map of Lincolnshire, England, that exquisitely details the area near my home, Newton's Chapel, circa 1698. The map surveys approximately thirty-five miles of the then "known" world nearby. There's Woolsthorpe, Colsterworth, North Witham, South Witham, Sproxton, Grantham, and Stamford, which was the main coaching stop on the road from London to Scotland. There's London to the south, but to the northeast, off to the upper right-hand side of the map at land's end and the beginning of the North Sea, there's a severe drop in elevation marked with beautiful calligraphy warning: BEYOND HERE THERE BE MONSTERS. And if that was not enough to deter intrepid explorers, next to the careful lettering is a picture of a bright green sea dragon spewing fire.

You may not be lost in merry olde England, but your spiritual lack of direction is an equally daunting wilderness to tame. With so much churning in your heart and soul, you can't take accurate readings of the longitude or latitude of lack. You're steering by dead reckoning. You've begun to have some revelations, to accept what may be some unpleasant realities, and to face the facts, but right now you may feel farther away from your dreams than you ever thought possible.

You're no longer in the old state of denial, but you're far from the promised landfall of peace and plenty. And if you're like me, financial worries encroach on every waking and nonwaking hour, leaving you exhausted with no place to go for comfort or even a respite from your financial crisis.

It is a physical reality: When you can't sleep, you can't think. You wake up practically paralyzed by dread and in a cold sweat. You can't answer the phone, read your newspapers, open your e-mail. All you can do with the bills is pick them up off the floor and stack them unopened on the kitchen table. You're so dazed and confused, you shouldn't be allowed to cross the street by yourself, or get behind a steering wheel.

"I have found that when negative emotions control the purse strings, money will not flow purely and evenly. When it comes to money, emotions can speak louder than reason or necessity. Your emotions, expressed through your financial actions, have gotten you to where you are now and will continue to shape your financial future if you let them," financial analyst Suze Orman cautions us in *The Courage to Be Rich: Creating a Life of Material and Spiritual Abundance*.

Time for a leap of faith to the kitchen table. I'm calling a time-out for both of us. Put the kettle on. Now take a blank piece of white paper. Write the word SCARED in the middle of the page. That's your known world.

SCARED

What would you say to a child who came to you asking if everything was going to be all right? Women have always known how to banish monsters under beds or hiding in closets. We know how to comfort the fears of others; we just don't remember to use the same tender, loving tactics on ourselves.

Now transpose the *a* and the *c* in *scared* and you'll find not only another word, but a world of difference.

SACRED

Doesn't that make you feel better already? It works for me, every day. I have come to believe that if something scares me, it's probably a Divine prompt for me to go ahead, not run away, for this "teaching opportunity" is sent to help me heal.

Let the fear pass through you—and keep moving toward peace and plenty. You've actually come a long way from where you were at the beginning of our journey together. You're thinking new thoughts about money, you're asking new questions, finding life-altering answers, and you're moving with every step toward a more honest, more authentic, more serene way of life. You're changing what scares you into what will bless you through the spiritual gift of choice.

Today when your mind veers toward monsters that scare you, use your powers to fix your attention on finding the sacred of this situation.

"Your emotional state ultimately determines your financial state," Suze Orman encourages us. "By having the courage to face and overcome your inner obstacles, however, you will change the outer trappings of your financial life forever."

Making the Calls

You Are More Than the Bills You Owe

You gain strength, courage and confidence by every experience in which you really stop to look fear in the face. You are able to say to yourself, "I have lived through this horror. I can take the next thing that comes along." You must do the thing you think you cannot do.

—ELEANOR ROOSEVELT

Apart from the obvious benefit of becoming debt-free (oh, the glorious thought!), one of the positive benefits of facing our own financial demons is that the bills and their collectors lose their power to have us quaking in the corner. You are not alone in looking at a mountain of expense and wondering how you are going to take it on and ever resolve these issues. It's like the old joke: How do you eat an elephant? One bite at a time. Once you make your first call, you will be amazed at the energy you feel to take on the project with full force.

No matter how much money you have left after paying the essentials, you must make a payment on an outstanding bill. This simple act is a sign to the Universe that things are changing for the better in your world. Here's a secret: Your creditors want to hear from you. In fact, they'll be more astounded that you called than you'll be to have picked up the phone.

As for your mountain of debt, think of this as a cosmic estimate of your earning capacity. One of the great joys of having money was that I was able to pay everything off every thirty days; I will again. But I'm holding on to the memory that I could always pay my debts. Providence doesn't view the situation as $100,000 in debt; the Mother of Plenty sees that you are worth more than $100,000, otherwise you would have never received that credit to begin with. Today is the day that you start to believe in yourself again, as you restore your creditworthiness.

To start, pick a bill you care about. Maybe it is for a doctor who cared for you when you were ill, or the car company that loaned you the money when you desperately needed new wheels. It isn't important to the exercise which bill you pick. The only thing that really counts is that you value the debt.

Before you make the call, make a decision on the amount of money that you can pay on it. Even if it seems like a low amount in proportion to the debt you owe on the bill, you know that you are making a good-faith payment until you can pay more. A friend of mine was faced with $3,000 in one unexpected medical bill for her son. He had a problem with his eye that required an MRI one November that cost $1,500, the amount of his insurance deductible. Then, because the surgeon was very careful and gifted, he wanted another MRI repeated in January prior to the operation. Yes, you guessed it, a new calendar year and a new deductible of $1,500. In less than three months, she'd amassed a $3,000 bill without the funds to pay. She called the creditor and set up an automatic payment of $25 a month. Satisfied, they stopped calling her to collect. It may take her years to pay the whole bill off, but faced with all the other debts for the surgeon, anesthesiologist, hospital, and insurance, the best she could do was good enough. The operation saved her son's vision, and the payment plan saved her sanity. The best you can do will be good enough for you, too.

Once you have your bill, it's time to decide who to call.
It is always best to call the original creditor, even if a bill
has been turned over to collection. The doctor or vendor
has a vested interest in receiving your money. It's best to
call before an account goes to collection, but if it has, it's
not too late to clean it up. Before you call, have a quiet
meditation. I pray for Amazing Grace to supply my needs.
Once you are ready, practice this sample conversation to
help you get a feel for it:

> YOU: Hi, my name is _____, and your name
> is _____? Thank you, [repeat her
> name]. Your doctor/company was kind enough
> to provide a service for me/my child/my family
> on _____. I wasn't able to pay the bill then,
> but I would like to make arrangements to pay it
> off with you. [Then be silent; let them solve the
> problem for you.]
>
> VENDOR: How much can you pay?
>
> YOU: I would like to set up an automatic payment
> of $_____ a month until it is paid off. My bank
> can send you a payment every month on the
> _____ of the month.
>
> YOU: Thank you so much, [repeat her name], I re-
> ally appreciate your help.

When you take the first step to honor your debts, you will
be honored back. The only way to start the flow of receiving in your life is to give first to those who have honored
you. Record this moment in your *Peace and Plenty Journal
of Well-Spent Moments* as evidence of your accomplishment
and of the agreement itself. Regardless of what it feels like
right now, when we can thank our creditors for believing
in us, we can start to believe in ourselves again.

The Glad Game Revisited

Be Glad. Be Good. Be Brave.

—ELEANOR HODGMAN PORTER

Do you remember Pollyanna? "The Glad Girl"? Now, don't snicker at the thought of her name, even though it's come to refer to a cloying determination to find the good in any situation.

Women usually have two kinds of people in their lives, and they're emotionally and energetically polar opposites. First are those friends who are the essence of positive energy and optimism; being in their company invariably lifts us up, encourages and inspires us. Then there are our other friends, the toxic ones who might commiserate with us, but manage to bring us way down, leaving us limping, exhausted, and drained. It's an invitation for tea and sympathy with the devil. These people are spiritual energy vampires, and on some level we know it.

When we are rebuilding our financial lives, we need to guard our energy—physical, emotional, psychic, creative, spiritual, and monetary—as if it were the most precious natural resource on the earth. Because, Babe, it is. And we only have so much of it. We need to protect it, guard it, cherish it, be kind to it, supportive of it, nourish it, bless it, give thanks for it, and defend it.

"Pollyanna did not pretend that everything was good," her creator, Eleanor Hodgman Porter, insisted. "Instead she represented a cheery, courageous acceptance of the facts. She understood that unpleasant things are always with us, but she believed in mitigating them by looking for whatever good there is in what is."

When *Pollyanna* was originally published in 1913, no one was more shocked than Mrs. Porter at the sudden and widespread appeal of her eleven-year-old orphan's ability to find the silver lining in any black cloud. Although the book was published without any publicity, word-of-mouth recommendations made it a best seller. Eventually it sold more than a million copies in a year, and spontaneous "Glad Clubs" sprang up all over the country. Coming as it did just before World War I, during an era of great uncertainty and change, *Pollyanna* spoke to people who were uneasy about their future. Suffragette demonstrations were getting more heated, and women were being jailed in both London and America; Woodrow Wilson became president and the Federal Reserve System was founded to make sure that there could never be another run on the banks and collapse of the stock market such as the Panic of 1907. People were nervous, especially as governments, the media, and financiers were telling everyone that things were just fine.

"I have never believed that we ought to deny discomfort and pain and evil," Mrs. Porter explained. "I have merely thought that it is far better to greet the unknown with a cheer." Very shortly, *Pollyanna* was translated into a dozen languages and was so popular that the character's name entered the English vernacular to describe irrepressible optimism. Pollyanna was such a golden girl that Helen Hayes brought her to life on Broadway in 1916 and America's silent-movie sweetheart, Mary Pickford, played her in 1920 in a film.

Pollyanna may be hopelessly sentimental, old-fashioned, and outdated as a novel (though I find it charming reading for a winter's day), but this business about Heaven giving us eight hundred reasons to "cheer up, it's not so bad!" deserves reconsideration. Perhaps this is exactly the nugget of good news we should meditate upon as we face uncertain times ahead full of the unexpected. As the little ray of sunshine tells us, "Just breathing isn't living."

It's easy to look back on the past and beat ourselves up for all the wrong turns, incorrect assumptions, and false hopes that have led us to our current financial disappointments. We label them "mistakes" and write them down in our book of life as failures, then wonder why we feel overwhelmed, oppressed, and too scared to try again.

We can't change the past, and in hindsight we usually realize we wouldn't want to completely erase every choice, every risk, every decision, but one of the most important steps to achieving the serenity we so deeply hunger for is to change the label from "mistakes" to "attempts." There is always something in our situation and our past lives to be glad about, to rejoice in, to be thankful for, even if it's just that our past is over. That's what Pollyanna has taught me, and I share her wisdom with you with all my heart.

Be Glad. Be Good. Be Brave.

The Thrill of Thrift

Putting on a Brave Face

Happiness hangs by a hair.

—MARY O'HARA (1943)

Into each woman's life "duvet days" and "lost weekends" occur, and what a blessed relief comfy pants and reading in bed in the middle of the day can be—a rejuvenating tonic for the soul. Just to make the scene more appealing, imagine the sound of icy-cold sleet on the roof as you sip a cup of Earl Grey in your warm, cozy nest. It really doesn't take much to make us happy. But two days off for good behavior can, on occasion, especially in the last grips of winter, imperceptibly slide into a funk that masquerades as a malaise or *la grippe*. We don't feel well, and since almost everyone else feels the same, we all watch days slip off the calendar, like in bad black-and-white films, with barely a whimper.

Although we've done nothing, we're exhausted and can't make the effort for anything. If we're lucky, we have kids at home who have to get up and go to school. If we don't have some kind of external obligation—like a job—we find ourselves mired in mysterious malcontent. Mail begins to pile up on the kitchen counter, along with overdue library books, DVD rentals, and cereal boxes—which seem to weigh a ton or why else haven't we put them back? We stop answering the phone, replying to e-mails, or emptying the sink. It's on days like these that we can barely get ourselves dressed and out the door. We feel sad, but we don't know why. We feel stuck and we are. We feel scared, and the safest place we know is the four-poster. Hey, I'm the woman who's always giving you permission to take a nap, so dashing for cover can't be all that bad, can it?

No, certainly not for a day or so, even three. But three days is my limit, and it should also be yours. After three days, fish and feminine daintiness aren't fresh.

When the last thing to cross the mind of the deliberately prone is the thought of madame's *maquillage*, not to mention recalling the last shower, shampoo, flossing, and plucking stray hairs out of strange places, a grown woman is probably on the road to perdition, by which I mean a serious depletion of her precious natural resources—time, creative energy, and emotion—which is why she feels like hell. Did you know that psychologists as well as hairstylists can date a woman's depression back according to the bands of growth of her roots? Much like the rings in the trunk of a tree, a woman reveals her psychological health through her personal appearance.

For this reason, it is exactly when we want to turn our face to the wall that the mirror beckons. Believe it or not, keeping up appearances can make all the difference in how well we end up weathering life's storms. And lately we've had a lot of them.

But did you know that during the Great Depression and the Home Front years of World War II, women's magazines regularly encouraged readers to treat themselves to a new lipstick, permanent waves, and cuticle cream and use their "pin money" or ration coupons to do it? Women were taking over men's jobs in the factory and the field, but they were never to forget the magic, mystery, and miracle of being feminine. A bowl of warm gruel would taste delicious if it was served by a smiling, well-groomed woman in a pretty apron. The time it took to create self-nurturing and beauty rituals was a priceless morale booster, and everybody from family to country benefited. Putting on a brave face was considered not just patriotic, but heroic. When times are tough, real women see red on lips, hands, and feet, and the difference between courage and lack of confidence can be as crucial as a pin curl.

When I need a personal prompt, which happens seasonally, I begin by sorting out my makeup, which gives me the happy benefit of rediscovering what I have that I've forgotten. There's something very calming about sorting your makeup, discarding the old, cleaning your brushes, and then arranging everything on your vanity or bathroom shelf. Now, it's impossible to sort your makeup without trying a few and sundry pencils and pots...and the next thing you know, you're winking into the mirror. Figure out your basics; for me that's tinted moisturizer, blush, eyebrow pencil, nude eye shadow, eyelash curler, mascara, and lipstick. Raid your china cabinet for some pretty dishes and cups to use for your makeup. Put your basics in a pretty, small dish so you know exactly where to find them every morning after you brush your teeth—and make the connection that if something looks pretty, you're bound to keep it that way. And that includes yourself.

"We are after beauty—you and I. Beauty in everything connected with us. Our faces, our bodies, our homes, our loves, our friendships, our lives, our goals," an editorial in the *Delineator* magazine in 1934 encouraged readers. "Don't let any of it fade! Don't let your face fade! It must grow into greater beauty every day."

And if that doesn't bring a smile to your face, it's time for a new lipstick!

Part Three

You Might as Well Live

A lot of people will also urge you to put some money in a bank, and in fact—within reason—this is very good advice. But don't go overboard. Remember, what you are doing is giving your money to somebody else to hold on to, and I think that it is worth keeping in mind that the businessmen who run banks are so worried about holding on to things that they put little chains on all their pens.

—MISS PIGGY

Money Changes Everything

What I know about money, I learned the hard way—by having had it.

—MARGARET HALSEY

You're tired of trying, fed up with being broke, and horrified at how long it will take you to get back on your feet, assuming you ever do. Forget every other problem in your life; if only you had more money, everything would be great! "Wow, the Mega Million jackpot is $266 million tonight. You can't win if you don't have a ticket, so put me down for twenty tickets." But c'mon, if you're destined to be so lucky as to win the lottery, you don't need twenty tickets, you need only one. Somehow I'm sure I'm not the only woman in the world to have these thoughts about probability and luck.

Last night I watched a television documentary about lottery winners, and it was like watching a slow-motion train wreck to see, time and time again, how winning the lottery sure did change their lives. The specific stories are morbidly fascinating, about how they rushed through their money, facing the envy of friends, feelings of entitlement from greedy relatives, guilt over giving or not, lawsuits from former spouses, and the pleas, scams, or threats over money from complete strangers. Some winners became recluses because they were always being hounded for handouts; one winner's brother was arrested for hiring a hit man so that he'd inherit the money sooner rather than later; other winners, in England, Europe, and the States, died miserable, mysterious deaths. "Foul play," we call it in America; "death by misadventure" is how Scotland Yard puts it.

As riveting as these sudden windfall snapshots are, the overall common denominator among most of the winners is even more telling—within a short while they were back where they started financially, if not worse, reduced to debt, food stamps, welfare benefits, and life in a trailer, their car, or on the streets.

The lesson that's out there for us all to see, although we don't want a private viewing, is that money does change the outside packaging of your life, it does change the circumstances you find yourself living in, but it doesn't change your core. If you haven't worked through your emotional feelings about money before it arrives, you won't know how to do it afterward.

"For many people, sudden money can cause disaster," admits certified financial planner Susan Bradley, founder of the Sudden Money Institute in Palm Beach, Florida. "In our culture, there is a widely held belief that money solves problems. People think if they had more money, their troubles would be over." In fact, when someone receives sudden money, "they frequently learn that money can cause as many problems as it solves."

I know you don't believe her; no one ever does. You're sure it would be different in your case. Well, you may not be wrong. But here's the only way I think it would be different: if you started treating the money you do have with as much respect as you think you would with millions. I found a diary entry from a few years ago, when I began to meditate about this book. And in my musings, I tell Money that I love her. I love the sense of order she provides, the luxuries, the distractions. I loved being able to give family and friends super gifts. I told Money how she made so many things easier, faster, more stylish, and, initially, more fun. Money opens doors to more choices, more decisions, more temptations, and the real possibility of more (and more expensive) mistakes. Fun vacations and designer clothes. Homes worthy of magazine spreads; parties they're still talking about. Education for your children or yourself with no student loans for your loved ones. New business opportunities. Charitable work that makes you feel blessed and humbled when you see what good has passed through your hands to help others. Money does all that.

"Well, if you love me so much, why do you keep giving me away?" Money said defensively. "Why don't you hold on to me and love me, cherish me, look after me, and protect me in the same way that I wanted to love, cherish, and protect you? Stop letting me go! I don't want to see you at risk, frightened, fragile, and vulnerable. My job is to take care of you, Sarah. But you are making my job impossible. We have to cooperate."

It's hard holding up your end of a conversation like this unless the answer is "Okay—my buck stops here."

Then Money said to me: "Why don't we discuss it every day? A real conversation—a heart-to-heart. Let's work on bringing solvency back into our life, one choice, one decision, one dollar at a time—together."

And I said, "Yes, my love, yes."

Anyone Who Says Money Doesn't Matter Never Had to Live Without It

Money brings some happiness. But after a certain point,
it just brings more money.

— NEIL SIMON

Lives of the rich and famous, before they were rich and famous, have always held me in their thrall. When I was young, I adored the television show *The Millionaire* (1955–1960) about the mysterious millionaire John Beresford Tipton, who sends his majordomo, Michael Anthony, to knock on doors and give complete strangers a million dollars. I used to daydream with such vivid imagination about Mr. Anthony, with his black bowler hat, umbrella, and briefcase, knocking on the door of our little suburban house on Long Island that when there came a real knock, I rushed to open it. "It's Mr. Anthony for me. It's Mr. Anthony for me." My family looked at me like I was crazy, but in my parallel universe he was due any day now.

I also love the story of Jim Carrey writing a $10 million check to himself in 1987 to be deposited in 1995 "for acting services rendered." And it was. Notice that the cycle was a full seven years, a very mystical number signifying completion.

The Universe has written me many similar two-comma checks, and cashing all of them eventually was wonderful. My brother and sister tell me that from a very early age I always believed that I was going to be rich, and so even without realizing it, I was thinking and growing rich. When I was writing *Simple Abundance*, I used the Napoleon Hill method described in his groundbreaking book *Think and Grow Rich*, published in 1937. This technique grew out of a suggestion that the Scottish American billionaire Andrew Carnegie gave Hill—a "Master Key" that would inspire millions of the Great Depression's forgotten, struggling against fear, to pull themselves up not by their bootstraps but by the power of their minds. "You can write your own price tag," Hill told them, "and if you are ready to receive this miracle of natural law, then you will understand what I mean when I say that whatever the mind can conceive and believe, your mind can achieve."

One of the best examples I've found of Hill's method working is the success of the legendary Broadway playwright Neil Simon; anointed by *Time* magazine as "the patron saint of laughter," Simon was a child of the Great Depression, born in 1927. After World War II, he got a menial job like we all do, working in the Warner Bros. mailroom, and then started writing comedy sketches with his brother Danny Simon, Woody Allen, and Mel Brooks, becoming the funny man for Sid Caesar, Jackie Gleason, and Phil Silvers in radio and early television. He even won Emmy nominations for his work. But the theater was his first love, and he was determined to succeed there, later explaining, "The theater and I discovered each other and she would one day be mine no matter how many rewrites it took." He finally got his foot in the stage door with his first hit, *Come Blow Your Horn*, which opened on Broadway in 1961. It took Simon three years and twenty complete new drafts to get *Come Blow Your Horn* to laughter pitch-perfection. This determination and perseverance were what Napoleon Hill referred to as "Definiteness of Purpose," which would enable one to work with "a Power greater than poverty."

Once Simon had his first hit, the plays started opening and the money started rolling in, and it has never stopped. ("An avalanche of abundance" is how Hill describes it, meaning that once you change your thoughts and commit to your dream, nothing succeeds like success.) Simon, the beloved creator of over thirty plays including *Barefoot in the Park*, *The Odd Couple*, *Sweet Charity*, *The Sunshine Boys*, and *Brighton Beach Memoirs*, describes the joy of feeling truly rich this way: "Sudden money is going from zero to two hundred dollars a week. The rest doesn't count." Two hundred dollars could pay Simon's rent, cover his bills, allow him to go out to dinner when he wanted, and not worry about surviving from one day to the next. That money meant peace. That money meant plenty.

The moment when his situation changed from not having enough to having enough—a sacred realm—was all that mattered.

"Having enough" is the destination for all of us on the *Peace and Plenty* path. But we have to know how much that is right now for us; chances are the $200 that did it for Neil Simon in 1950 won't do it for us this week.

Knowing that all your financial needs and the needs of your family are taken care of; knowing that you are comfortably sheltered in a home that you love waking up in and coming home to each night; knowing that there is money in the bank for emergencies, for rainy days and leaky roofs, sunny days and barbecues, for a wonderful vacation, for pursuing your passion, whether it's writing, theater, painting, traveling, kayaking, cooking, or parenting; knowing that your foreseeable future is planned by you and funded by you; knowing that should you become ill, you have the health care you need; knowing that you can pay all your bills every month, that you don't have to depend on anyone other than yourself and the grace of Providence, knowing all this is "having enough."

"Don't listen to those who say, you're taking too big a chance. Michelangelo would have painted the Sistine floor, and it would surely be rubbed out by today. Most important, don't listen when the little voice of fear inside you rears its ugly head and says, 'They are all smarter than you out there. They're more talented, they're taller, blonder, prettier, luckier and they have connections,'" Neil Simon encourages us today. "I firmly believe that if you follow a path that interests you, not to the exclusion of love, sensitivity, and cooperation with others, but with the strength of conviction that you can move others by your own efforts, and do not make success or failure the criteria by which you live, the chances are you'll be a person worthy of your own respect."

And you will have satisfied your soul's yearning for peace and plenty. You will have enough because you are enough.

The Rich Are No Longer Different from You and Me

Let me tell you about the very rich. They are different from you and me...

—F. SCOTT FITZGERALD

Yes, they have more money than we do...

—ERNEST HEMINGWAY

Never let facts get in the way of a good story. There are many versions of this famous exchange. F. Scott was supposedly droning on about how different the very rich were from you and me in a short story, "The Rich Boy," and his rival Hemingway gave him a withering send-up (even naming Fitzgerald as the source of this wealthy fawning) in his story "The Snows of Kilimanjaro." As you can imagine, this profoundly affected their tenuous friendship, and the sore feelings always just festered below the surface afterward. However, Fitzgerald's obsession with wealth all his life played out in his ambitions, choices, risk taking, love affairs, marriage, and of course his writing. He gave the world some of America's literary crown jewels, including the Jazz Age novels *The Great Gatsby*, *Tender Is the Night*, *This Side of Paradise*, and *The Beautiful and the Damned* as well as a collection of 160 glittering short stories, mainly written for decidedly middle-class mores in such magazines as the *Saturday Evening Post* and *Collier's* during the 1920s and 1930s. Fitzgerald was so in demand that he was paid $4,000 per story during the Depression (the equivalent today of $40,000) for such delicious meringues as "Bernice Bobs Her Hair," "The Curious Case of Benjamin Button," and "A Diamond as Big as the Ritz." His writing style was much imitated but rarely matched.

The rich were universally hated during the Depression, much as bankers, hedge fund operators, and all those who take a bonus paid by the taxpayers are now. Critics tried to dismiss Fitzgerald because he was forever associated with the Lost Generation of the 1920s, all tousled hair, white flannel trousers, and a bottle of gin stumbling across a lawn of America's collective consciousness. When he died in 1940 from alcoholism at just forty-four, having spent many years ill, troubled, deeply depressed, and in exile in Hollywood, doing very little writing, his critics had a field day describing the curse of not fulfilling his early "promise" because he continued to try to explain the behaviors of the very rich to the rest of the world, at a time when the wealthy were just loathsome.

At first glance, the rich really do seem different. It's not just the beautiful homes, the jewels, the artwork, the fabulous fashions, the jet-set lifestyles. It's the sense that they are so sure, so safe, so "destined" to a life of luxury, gratification, and entitlement that the rest of us can only dream about. But then something like the Bernard Madoff scandal—the Ponzi scheme scam of the century—comes along, and the seemingly unbridgeable gulf shrinks, the differences disappear, and we all learn again that we're the same under the skin. Safety and certainty can vanish in the blink of an eye no matter how many zeros one thinks one has.

In the aftermath, the same people who were once buying jewels are now selling them at Palm Beach pawnshops and Beverly Hills privateers for a fraction of what they had paid. Even more appalling are the stories of auction houses calling the monied "clients" who used to buy from them to inquire if perhaps they would prefer to "quietly" dispose of their jewelry. The international art and antiques market has been flooded with treasures, but the "inventory" will take years to reach its true value on the open market. People are walking away from million-dollar homes, and the market for the mega-homes (over $50 million, just imagine) has fallen through the floor. Good Lord, people are walking away from everything.

When I was writing *Simple Abundance* in the early 1990s, the great demise of the esteemed English insurance broker Lloyd's of London caused the same tsunami of grief, wailing, gnashing of teeth, and bewilderment among the British aristocrats and upper middle classes who had invested in the centuries-old establishment. Lloyd's of London was created in 1688 as a shipping insurer for English merchants who were sending vessels around the world in search of precious cargo—spices, cotton, tobacco, and slaves. Wealthy individuals agreed to undertake part of the risk of sending out ships and signed their names underneath one another in true all-for-one style. This tradition is how individual shareholders became known as the Lloyd's "Names," and it's where the expression "when my ship comes in" originated. The gold-plated promise was this: If Lloyd's could not pay out on an insurance claim, the Names' pledges would be called in immediately. In return for leveraging this risk, the Names would receive an annual payment or annuity, which was very substantial.

Some of these pledges went back for generations, without these individuals ever doing anything but laugh all the way to the bank as Lloyd's of London became the world's most famous insurer (of, among other things, Betty Grable's legs, Bruce Springsteen's voice, and Abbott and Costello's working relationship). Then in 1992 Lloyd's found itself overextended and for the first time couldn't meet its obligations. So it called in the "Names." Overnight titled families and individuals found themselves with nothing more than the shirt on their backs—and if milord's shirt had gold cuff links, they were snatched as well. Nothing was sacred, everything became very personal as fortunes became bankrupted and lives shattered.

Great stories, like lives, are actually about the cycle of change. The rich become poor. The poor become rich. The downtrodden rise up. The powerful fall. The lonely discover love. The bored toss love away. Change is the essence of life; change is the great challenge, the great constant. Change is the ultimate teller of tales. Change brings conflict, crises, and circumstances that thank God we didn't know we'd have to face this morning. But those circumstances will change, and all we have to do is hold on until life writes another chapter. Look between the lines of your own life. Who would have believed your story? And guess what? It's bound to get better. It always does. We just have to get through this bad patch, and we will. Besides, look at how much you know about life now that you didn't before.

"Poverty and riches often change places. The Crash taught the world this truth, although the world will not long remember the lesson," Napoleon Hill wrote in 1937. "Poverty may, and generally does, voluntarily take the place of riches. When riches take the place of poverty, the change is usually brought about through well conceived and carefully executed PLANS. Poverty needs no plan. It needs no one to aid it, because it is bold and ruthless. Riches are shy and timid. They have to be attracted."

And with every small step we take, every tiny gesture we make as we use these powerful creative and emotional tools—from our *Peace and Plenty Journal of Well-Spent Moments*, to the Contentment Chest, to our Comfort Companion and the treats to come—we are wooing financial serenity, day in and day out.

Money and the Meaning of Life

We grow in time to trust the future for our answers.

—RUTH FULTON BENEDICT

Our faith in the present dies out long before our faith in the future," the anthropologist Ruth Fulton Benedict observed in 1915. Women are particularly susceptible to the fantasy of micromanaging "tomorrow," which is why I was fascinated to discover that during the Great Depression, the one industry that grew in leaps and bounds was fortune-telling.

In fact, the pervasive yet hidden habit of visiting fortune-tellers became so alarming that the August 1933 *Ladies' Home Journal* ran a lengthy exposé of a famous fortune-teller written by her ex-secretary in order to reveal the shenanigans and elaborate stings perpetrated on hapless victims, the majority of whom were middle-class women who, like you and me, wanted to know what their future held. Unfortunately for all the clients of Madame Zamos and her ilk, the future held little happiness and even more penury because they gave all their money away to morally bankrupt individuals.

One of my most financially successful friends recently told me about her encounter with a psychic years ago. At the time she was deeply immersed in her "starving artist" phase, struggling to cover expenses one month to the next.

Her main questions were all about money, and the psychic seemed to sidestep each of them. Finally my friend asked directly whether she would end up rich or not. The psychic seemed a bit bored. "Oh, I thought you understood. Yes, you will make all the money you could dream of and more, but by the time you do it won't mean much to you."

My friend was both relieved and puzzled. She was delighted by the idea that someday she would be rich, and she derived a lot of confidence and determination over the years as a result. But she was confused about the idea that money would eventually come to mean so little. How was that possible? The idea of money being so devalued made her feel uneasy, even though at the time she had no real idea what that prophecy could mean.

Now, years later, she reveals that both halves of the prediction came true. She has enjoyed a life of international luxury, outstanding professional success, and financial abundance that literally would have been beyond her imagination years ago.

Just as the psychic predicted, however, all that money and success has not buffered her from other difficulties in life. She and her family have faced serious health problems, emotional turmoil, and fractured relationships that are much more the focus of her daily life than the money could ever be. She told me that she was deeply grateful for the opportunities and beauty that having money brought into her life, and realizes that everything her family has been through would have been even more difficult without it. But she also wonders if having had the money to throw at solving the problems didn't postpone the reckoning we all find ourselves facing now. She said it seemed that the questions she asks herself now boil down to one thought beautifully, if abruptly, expressed by Nathaniel Branden, the author of some of the most compelling and respected works on self-esteem.

Time and again, in books and speeches, Branden

makes the point that "no one is coming." No one is coming to miraculously change the course of our lives, make us happy, or do all the things we don't want to do so we don't have to do them. People can love us, can support us, friends can cheer for us and comfort us, but no one else can be the engine of our own destiny.

When I was in my twenties, I lived in London and became incredibly curious about the world of spirits. Not God, mind you, but the lower spiritual realm—divination—which is seeking to know the future or hidden things through supernatural powers. Because I really didn't know too many people in England, I started hanging out with the wrong crowd because they asked me to *pay* them a visit, literally: spiritualists, psychics, mediums, tarot card readers, numerologists, astrologers. Not that all these people were bad; they were just bad for me. I did meet a few charlatans who weren't interested in my destiny or soul—just the money they could extract by manipulating my misery. But if a gypsy in a turban and gold hoop earrings who sees "clients" in a fringed silk tent in the middle of an antiques market on the Kings Road consults her crystal ball and tells you to put a raw egg underneath your bed, then to pay her the equivalent of a month's rent and give her the gold bangle bracelet you got for your twenty-first or forty-fifth birthday as a "seed offering" and you do it, as I did, you can bet that your future's going to include a stinky apartment, a pissed-off landlady, an empty wallet, and disillusionment.

Look, there are some very gifted psychics in the world, but gifted or not, what they're reading is your physical and emotional energy. If you're worried and distraught, you are broadcasting this information, Babe, loud and clear. The last thing you need is someone picking up on the beams of distress and then projecting that they are your future. Because once you get something like that in your head, it becomes a self-fulfilling prophecy. The other thing you must remember is that even if the prophecy is wonderfully mind-blowing—and I've had a few of those, too—earthly time and spiritual time are never the same. In my case, in fact, the spiritual time was *decades* later! Divine Timing is completely different from ours, but it's never late and always perfect. Probably, just not tomorrow.

These days I continue to wish on stars, open fortune cookies, swirl tea leaves, watch what planets are in transit, and occasionally delve into bibliomancy. One of the oldest forms of divination, bibliomancy is forecasting events by opening the Bible and seeing what message is waiting for you. For when you seek and follow the prompts of Divine Insight, your good fortune in Life is assured, here and now—and your monetary outlay is limited to the cost of a Bible, an investment that will pay you dividends for years to come.

The Thrill of Thrift

Pin Money Secrets for Haute Couture Contentment

One of the secrets of a happy life is continuous small treats.

—IRIS MURDOCH

It was the young "petite, pert and pretty" Catherine Howard, the fifth wife of English king Henry VIII, who first introduced long, slender, bejeweled, silver straight pins from France to keep her hat on before she lost her head as an adulteress in 1542. Nonetheless, hat pins caught on at court and remained popular for centuries or as long as fashionable women wore hats. In the late Victorian era, as hats "exploded into almost insupportable spectacles of stuffed birds, flowers, and veils," Jeanine Larmoth writes in *Victoria* magazine's *The Romance of Hats*, these millinery creations were so monumental that they "required safe anchorage. Hat pins ensured that even if the car went as fast as fifteen miles an hour, or if the wearer went wild applauding a matinee performance, the hat would remain immobile and glorious. In the twenties, hat pins found themselves on the crest of the costume jewelry wave, in materials as dissimilar as celluloid and coral. Today the hat pin, for too long an object prized by collectors only, is once again a practical treasure."

Practical treasures are what interest me today, as I think they might you, which is why I thought we'd meditate on pin money and the meaning of feminine contentment. You see, because hat pins were expensive, it became traditional for a woman's husband or father to give her a small personal supplement to her annual clothing allowance called her "pin money," which was intended to pay for these objects of desire as well as other small but necessary luxuries such as cosmetics, toilet water, dressing table accoutrements, and (don't tell) chocolate bonbons and trashy novels. This in turn created the hat pin purchase ritual at New Year's, when the shops would unveil the coming season's "look" in hats and hat pins and ladies opened those heavy white envelopes full of cash given them by the men in their lives at Christmas. Like hats, a woman could never really have too many hat pins. Personally, I think the whole fabric of women's mystery and power began to unravel when we stopped wearing hats after Jacqueline Kennedy's pillbox, but we'll save that plea for another day. It's the pin money revival that I'm encouraging because it's guaranteed to bring a smile to your face and a spring to your step. You must start it immediately.

Basically pin money is for whatever little sundries you might want to indulge in during these tightwad times. But the glory of starting a pin money stash is that you must accumulate or save your pin money before you spend it. And in the saving, the watching your pin money grow and increase, there is sublime serenity and absolutely no guilt. Even if you are a woman of independent means, your paycheck probably goes elsewhere: mortgages, health care, automobiles, gas, car insurance, groceries, school fees, dentists, children's clothing, computers, mobile telephones, not to mention credit card bills for the rest of your life. Where in your current budgeting is there a line item for personal pleasure? Was there ever?

Whatever your past allowance for yourself, with a pin money plan you can start exactly where you are at the

moment. Having just found $1.15 in loose coins under-
neath the couch cushions, don't put it in your change purse
or the petty cash soup crock where you normally collect
quarters; drop it instead in your pin money jar. Take pleasure in hearing the ping as the coins fall to the bottom.
Or if times are very tight, figure out a percentage of found
money you can skim off the top for the pin money collection, because if things are dire you can't ignore the need
to shore up other accounts first. Try to add to it every
day—make it a mystery game. Where will you find your
pin money tomorrow? This is a marvelous primer for ingenuity because you find yourself economizing with zeal.
What you don't spend at the shops, you can fully invest
in your pin money. Banks are all very well, but when the
chips are down, a smart woman keeps her money under
her hat.

Once you have saved $100 or its equivalent, then you
may dip in for your indulgences. But again, do it slowly.
In the meantime, make a list of your desired indulgences.
Label the prettiest file you can find PIN MONEY POSSIBILI-
TIES and fill it up with your inevitable clippings from mail-
order catalogs or glossy magazines. It's time to get back
to *Simple Abundance* basics. Keeping a pin money account
helps you acknowledge the little things, the affordable luxuries that you love—the ones that, if you bring them back
into your life, will contribute enormously to your sense
of well-being. Good coffee, French triple-milled soap, a
scented potted jasmine, a perfect tea set for one, a selection
of miniature bottles of after-dinner drinks, exotic teas, a
pretty new blank journal to keep track of your *Peace and
Plenty* Well-Spent Moments, a large, fresh artist's sketchbook for a new *Peace and Plenty* Comfort Companion, Cre-
tacolor watercolor pencils, good-quality writing paper, a
fountain pen with midnight-blue ink, vintage buttons and
ribbons, a proper sewing basket outfitted with divine hab-
erdashery items, foaming bath gel, small jars of your favorite jams, a delicious tin of shortbread biscuits, a box

of four French truffles, an antique-lace-trimmed handkerchief with your monogram scented with real rosewater kept in a crystal decanter...you get the idea. My pin money desires are vintage sewing items, I suppose because they connect me to a time when women created home art with needle and thread and what started as a necessity (darning socks) became elevated. I have several large Mason jars that are my secret pin money caches filled with silk flowers, buttons, antique lace trim. They line the mantel in my office and represent, in their individual trifles, my passions, solace, contentment, and, yes, serenity.

"There are no little things," the Victorian novelist and newspaper columnist Fanny Fern reminds us in a collection of her columns called *Ginger-Snaps*, published in 1870. "Little things, so called, are the hinges of the universe." By this time Fanny (born Sarah Willis Parton) was the highest-paid newspaper writer in the world, earning $100 a column. Like most women literary domestics, she began her writing career for pin money.

There's no telling what doors the pursuit of pin money might open up for women once again. And gingersnaps? Mmmm...let's add them to the list.

What Money Is and What It Isn't

*Talent on its own sat gracefully only on the very young.
After a certain age it was what you did with it that
counted.*

— LIZA CODY

I always wanted to be an actress, but my mother insisted that if I pursued this unstable line of work, I needed to have secretarial skills to pay the bills. So instead of college, I went to business school and took acting classes on the side. Since I ended up with more typing gigs than acting roles, especially living in Massachusetts, I made my escape as soon as I could. I thought my chances were better in London instead of New York where everybody was an actress, and because all twentysomethings want to see the world, off I went. I had a round-trip ticket good for a year, $1,000, and a whole airline fleet's worth of dreams.

Within a month, I ended up working as a secretary for Sam Wanamaker, the American film director, actor, and visionary behind the groundbreaking reconstruction of William Shakespeare's New Globe Theatre in 1997 — a fifty-year obsession of Sam's that began when he visited London as a GI after World War II and that, unfortunately, was completed after his death.

In 1972, the Globe project was only a summer tent

production. That fine June day, I showed up at what I thought was a "cattle call" audition for actresses; the line of young hopefuls curved around the block. By the time I got in the building, I realized that all these gals were secretaries and they were being interviewed by the woman who was leaving Sam's employment as soon as she found her replacement. She was eager to select a new hire as quickly as possible.

According to her, Sam was a feisty, dramatic, and passionate man, larger than life, and if he didn't get his way immediately, he responded the way an angry toddler might in a fit of pique, by holding his breath and throwing books across the room. This horrified the gentle English roses, and he was running through one a week. Instead of my typing and steno speed, I was asked how I felt about having a book thrown across the room at me. Thinking she was joking, I said, "I'd throw it back."

"I think we've found her, Sam!" With this pronouncement I was brought into the inner sanctum. Because I was an American, everyone but me thought it was a good match; however, my money wasn't going very far now that I'd found a flat to share, and I desperately needed a job.

Two weeks later, Sam's life was serene, beautifully organized, rehearsals were going well, and anytime a book got thrown across the room, I'd eventually retrieve it and place it back on his desk. He particularly liked the index card itinerary I created for him that he could carry in his pocket with "Need to Know" info: telephone numbers and addresses. This was during the Dark Ages before PDAs and electronic assistants made such a system obsolete. Sam told me I was the best secretary he'd ever had. Then, one happy day, Sam asked the dangerous question of what had brought me to London. I chose my moment to tell him I wasn't really a secretary, but an actress. Sam let out a long low groan similar to the bellyache of distress just before the lion roars—and I took a step backward toward the door. My timing was perfect, though, and Sam Wanamaker made me a deal I couldn't refuse: Stay with him until the end of the season, which was in September, and he'd personally call Joe Papp at the New York Shakespeare Theatre Company and get me an audition.

By the time September came, I'd fallen in love with England and didn't want to go home to the United States just yet. However, Sam's season was over and he wouldn't have another job for me until the following summer.

I tramped around for a few weeks looking for work with Kelly Girls as a temp and then saw an ad for a fashion copywriter, which I wasn't, but why not? I loved clothes and had developed my own "look." I called and was told to bring my "portfolio." I stalled with an explanation that some of my belongings had been delayed from the States and the receptionist told me then to mock up the current issue of British *Vogue*, using the photographs but writing my own copy beneath them. In a burst of creative energy and enthusiasm (from the Greek word *entheos*, "inspired from the god within"), I worked nonstop over the weekend and on Monday, glory be, I got the job. I began my career as a writer. Smashing. Brilliant. What fun.

Oh, and the salary?

"The position pays £25 per week" (then about $62.50).

Oh...Great. When can I start?

I share this story because it's part of my money autobiography, and because in calling back these early fiduciary occasions I can see with a clarity that is now stunning how differently I *thought* about money through the decades. But also because now, if I want to stay on the path of peace and plenty, I need to go back there—to return to that "Great. When can I start?" attitude—and so do you.

I also want to shift how you're feeling about money right now. Money may be a lot of things to you at this moment, most of them unpleasant: worry, loss, anger, anxiety, fear, shame, frustration, embarrassment, regret. What a maelstrom of misery money is for so many of us, so much of the time. It's no wonder money flees from us—how much fun to be around are we?

However, if you or I win the lottery tonight (hey, it could happen), tomorrow morning money would become: excitement, exuberance, relief, happiness, buoyancy, golden bubbles, champagne all around, and smiles as you pay off your bills and the extended family's chunk.

But can you see that all these contradictory feelings—whether we have money or don't—are temporary? They're phantoms standing between us and what money really is and has always been: *Divine Energy*.

Yes, the same cosmic breath that separated the Light and Darkness of creation and paid, through you, for bread on your table is Divine Energy. The Sacred Source. Spiritual Substance. What we're praying for if we pray the Lord's Prayer and ask for our daily bread. The *manna* the Israelites, lost in the wilderness, waited for Heaven to deliver every morning.

When we're just starting out to make our way in the world, we're willing to trade experience for money. We combine what little experience we've got with moxie—the ability to face difficulty and adversity with courage, pluck, and perseverance. Because we don't know yet that we can fail, it never occurs to us that we will, and as long as we keep thinking that way, we won't. At this stage in life, money is a pure exchange—energy for currency. We trade our raw talents, creativity, vitality, stamina, time, emotion, intelligence, ideas, execution, inspiration, and youth for currency (paper or coins) to use to pay for goods—rent, food, clothes, entertainment.

An exchange. Not necessarily of equal value, but an exchange nonetheless. It bears repeating: Money is nothing more than an exchange of currency for our precious nature's resources: time, creative energy, stamina, and emotion—which are our life's energy reserves.

The best, most life-changing definition of money I have

ever read is from metaphysical writer John Randolph Price in his tiny treatise *The Abundance Book*. He asks us to think of money as:

My Own Natural Energy Yield.

Money. Your own natural energy yield. Dr. Price explains it this way:

> What does **my** mean? It relates to me or myself as a possessor of something. What about **own?** It means belonging to oneself. And **natural?** It means God-given, genuine, normal, an essential essence. **Energy?** The word was first coined by Aristotle to express the concept of "vigor of expression." The Mystery School in Alexandria then began using the word to describe "cosmic forces"—the Power and Force of Omnipotence, that which we are individualized. Each one of us is the very Energy of the universe personified. And **yield?** It's defined as harvest, return, payment, i.e. to bring something forth as a result of cultivation or as a return from investment.
>
> With the above understanding, let's now describe money this way: Money is my very essence, which when properly expressed, returns to me as an all-sufficiency of legal tender, to be used in exchange for goods and services.

In other words, Babe: You are your own money. Your life energy is the numbered account, and only you hold the key. You are your own bank, mortgage company, savings and loan, mutual or hedge fund, retirement plan, stock option, T-bill, gilt, greenbacks, punts, pounds, gold standard.

So if you want someone to show you the money . . .

Here's looking at you, kid.

The Road to Perdition

Prosperity is a way of living and thinking, and not just money or things. Poverty is a way of living and thinking, and not just a lack of money or things.

— ERIC BUTTERWORTH

We don't just fall into the bog of lack in our life, we stumble our way there when we stop seeing money as an *exchange* of many different, desirable experiences on our heroine's journey. We start to see money as an end unto itself, as a goal, as an entitlement. And when that moment comes, probably imperceptibly, it's the beginning of a detour down a dark country road going nowhere.

While I was juggling being a freelance writer and a mother and receiving $250 every two weeks from my then-husband as my "grocery" money, which also had to pay for our daughter's clothes, toys, amusements, lessons, and day care, I had ringside seats to watching a financial windfall when one of my college friends suddenly hit the peak of professional and financial success. I learned my first important lesson about what money is and what it isn't. It was blissful to live vicariously and watch a peer not have to budget or curtail her desires. It also could, if I dwelled on my friend's success and my apparent failure, get very depressing. I started feeling bad after I talked with her and listened to a roll call of "Gee whiz" moments, because the closest I came to being out and about was my weekly visit to Gymboree.

My friend had always had her brilliant sparks, but she had a difficult temperament—an unpredictable combination of abruptness, defensiveness, and genius—which came across as arrogance unless you knew her well. Then you realized that she was actually very shy and always scared that any criticism was a complete put-down of her latest project. She was a genius because she wasn't afraid to put herself out on a limb and took many creative risks. But she was difficult, and by the time she left school she didn't have a lot of close friends.

All of that seemed irrelevant when her very first play became a Broadway and Hollywood hit. Awards flooded in, accompanied by critical acclaim. Money flowed in as well, along with a plethora of job offers with companies and stars whose very names provoked awe. She was on her best behavior, delighted to have the opportunities, and determined to create and maintain an excellent reputation so that her career wouldn't be a flash in the pan.

Within a few years of her Tony Award–winning Broadway hit and Oscar-winning film, my friend owned five luxurious homes all over the world. Winters were spent skiing, summers were spent on the Greek islands, and the only interruption in her cosmopolitan life of glamour was an occasional meeting in Hollywood. She put off writing. She always had another idea, but it never seemed to come to life on the page. Money no longer meant product to her but power. My friend, increasingly convinced that her money and prior success affirmed her way of doing things, became more and more resistant to asking for advice or even taking notes on collaborative projects, being agreeable to considering working on someone else's project until she reverse-morphed back to her old ways, flying by the seat of her Armani pantsuit and then doing it her way. She simply could not commit and then follow through on anything.

Over time, new jobs were being offered less frequently, which only triggered my friend's old insecurities. She would watch other, younger talents starring in, writing, directing, and producing mindless megahits. It would drive her crazy and then I'd hear from her for the first time in a year.

It also became clear that even the vast sums of money she originally pulled in couldn't last forever, not without smart management or occasional moderation, neither of which my friend wanted to address, because that made her feel like she was preparing for possible failure.

Did you catch that? She didn't want to save or put money away because it seemed to her like defeat—*as if she were preparing for possible failure.*

With a mind-set and worldview like that, her sell-by date came and went quickly.

The downward cycle sped up, my friend's defensive behavior increased, and a decade after her glittering successes my friend became a has-been. She isn't poor, but she can't get a job in her field. Instead she gives workshops, coaching the entertainment careers of others. One by one the expensive houses have gone away. She still gets royalty checks and will never starve, but living on a small plantation in the South (which she originally bought for her mother) isn't what she'd hoped for. However, starting over again just seems like too much effort. She's not willing to go back to the "Great...when can I start?" phase of creating a life from scratch again.

In quiet conversations over a bottle of good wine, she'll let down her defenses and admit that starting over is the most terrifying thing she can think of at her age and stature. I tell her that yes, it is terrifying, but anxiety feels the same as creativity before it ignites (that's the source of so much "stage fright" in show business), and all she has to do is push through the fog. I tell her I know this because I have no choice. It's start over or stop dead in my tracks, and I have so much I want to live for again.

My friend claims that the lesson to be learned from her story is that Hollywood is shallow and success never lasts. Well, that may be. The lesson I have learned up close and personally as well as once removed is that no matter how successful you are at any given moment, life-long success is ultimately the knack of working well with others, the ability to consistently deliver exceptional product, and the realization that success and failure—including profit and loss—come, like the bear and bull markets of Wall Street, in successive and repetitive cycles. When the money's coming in, sock it away for a rainy day—it's always raining somewhere in the world. When the money's not coming in, sock away even more. You are investing in yourself. You are your own natural energy yield. You are an AAA blue-chip investment. You'll never know what you could have done after everyone else said you were through if you don't squirrel away your nuts with an eye toward preparedness. And nothing, nothing, nothing beats doing what the world told you was impossible to do, the first time or once more with gusto.

As the writer Gertrude Atherton said in 1923, "Success is a great healer."

Follow the Money

I've been rich. I've been poor. Rich is better.

—SOPHIE TUCKER

Do you know how much money you need to live every day? This isn't a trick question. What I'm asking you is a deeply personal prompt and one that I've only recently started to gently ask myself. Or rather, try to answer. It costs so much more than I remember to start over, especially while trying to dig myself out of debt. I'm baffled by the fact that my initial few weeks' stay with my sister has become a yearlong sojourn as I'm caught in between the hard places of financial circumstances, paying for the past's foolish decisions and bad choices.

Meantime, while I realize intellectually I'm making important changes each day and can see a reassuring pattern of small solvencies, the path to peace and plenty nudges along at the soul's pace of grace. Think of a weight loss program: Experts insist that if you lose slowly, changing your eating habits and integrating new behaviors into your life, such as exercise, the weight will stay off. With money, if you stop spending and begin saving and budgeting, the money will accumulate.

But I long to see results from any self-improvement program immediately. So many days still start off with the sigh of struggle. You might be existing at survival level this morning (or feel that way), juggling to make this month's mortgage, health insurance premium, or car repair, paying down Christmas, stretching to cover an unexpected vet bill, books for a son's college semester, or coming up with the security deposit for your mother's new assisted living accommodation. You're still in shock from discovering that she's been making the decision between prescription meds and food, but closing the money gap isn't going to be easy. You're squeezed dry.

Well, whatever your expense is today, it's probably unexpected. I've discovered that when you're worried about money and can only focus on lack, debt, and what's missing in your life, that's all that seems to shackle you.

"I can't make headway," you say.

Neither can I.

Maybe it's because, literally, our heads get in the way. The way we *think* about money trips us up.

One thing is for certain: Money seems to be a shapeshifter, and holding on to it is a fine art. "I believe the ability to make money is a gift from God," John D. Rockefeller declared, and I'm a true believer, but managing money once you get it into your life is an even *greater* gift and that's what holds our interest right now. Becoming a "Good Stewardess" of my talents, resources, and money has become my soul's new prime directive. You're welcome to hitch your wagon to mine.

Years ago, my first (and much adored) editor at the *Washington Post Magazine*, Bill MacKaye, taught me the number one rule of any story was to "follow the money." When you followed the money, you could always backtrack and find out the *who*, *what*, *when*, *where*, and *how* of the story. That includes our *own* story. It amazes me as I make this connection personally. Perhaps part of the reason we are all caught so short is that we haven't been following where our own money has been going—and maybe we even got a bit careless about its coming into our bank account as well. We don't know the who, what, when, where, and how of our own lives.

A friend who works at a high-powered job in the entertainment industry just called me because she needed a sympathetic ear. Knowing I was sharing my own money mea culpas, she confessed to feeling like a "moron" because she'd just noticed an error in her salary direct deposit; she'd been getting a third less than her correct salary. It could be a clerical error; it could be a humongous new health insurance contribution or payroll tax deduction. Hopefully, the company owes her big-time. But this reduction or error in her net pay has been happening for six *months*. Now she's spending the rare weekend she doesn't have to work sorting this mess out before she brings it to the attention of the company's accountant. Since she's among the most intelligent, capable, clever, and detail-oriented women I know, I'm certain she will get to the bottom of this. But the fact that it's happened is a stark cautionary tale. Why has this error gone uncaught? Because she's been too busy caring for other people's money instead of her own: managing huge film production budgets, dotting the i's, crossing the t's, coming in *under* budget (an art form she excels at), working 20/7 most weeks. She's not had the *time, physical energy,* or *creative emotion* to reconcile her own bank account or even open the bank statements. She's not had the time to take care of herself. And the darker, more insidious reason for her lapse? She's also scared that taking care of herself financially is some secret signal to Cupid that she's given up on Happily Ever After. Did I mention that she's also single and thirtysomething?

"We are, I believe, fascinated by other people's financial issues because we all want to know the same things: *Is she like me? Is her life better? Worse? Does she have more than I do? Is what I have enough?*" observes Hilary Black, editor of the thought-provoking anthology *The Secret Currency of Love: The Unabashed Truth About Women, Money, and Relationships.* Several years ago when Hilary broke up with a very rich boyfriend, her friends were aghast.

"One of my friends actually said, 'Are you crazy? This guy could take care of you for life!'" admits Hilary. "These were thirtysomething women who would never publicly advocate marrying for money, yet they implied that I was making a mistake. It was interesting: It seemed a sign that women have a more complicated relationship with money than they let on."

As do you, and I, and my fabulous friend. So if you want to start over with me, with a little TLC instead of tongue-lashings, let's take the plunge and make a new commitment to begin taking care of ourselves properly, with kindness, compassion, and self-nurturance. There is a distinct connection between self-nurturance and self-esteem, and having enough money to take care of yourself, under any circumstance, is a basic instinct women seem to have abandoned.

We're going to have to start at the beginning, by counting our money as well as our blessings, acknowledging every cent received as an enormous blessing, and watching with fascination and deep respect where every cent goes. I know this makes you all fidgety and edgy—I know it because I feel that way, too. We all do. We may be in serious trouble financially, but we certainly don't want to be nagged by the Inner Bitch of the Bottom Line. However, not being willing to count where your money goes is how you end up on a first-name basis with the process servers, and Dog the Bounty Hunter is as far as I'm prepared to go.

All we're doing today is beginning to count. Counting is keeping track of our spending each day, especially those automatic purchases that we never give a second glance to but end up taking a great chunk out of any day's disposable money. Remember how to count? One, two, three. Did you realize you're paying practically $5 for a cup of coffee? Or $4.95, to be precise, for a tall, nonfat, sugar-free hazelnut latte. Let's say you do that Monday through Friday; that's $24.75 each week. Really? $6.99 for a pint of organic blueberries. Really? $10.49 per pound for pan-roasted turkey in the deli? Really? $14.48 for three skimpy magazines? *Really?*

Really. And just by paying attention, you are starting to make it count.

Starting Where You Are

The way to achieve a difficult thing was to set it in motion.

— KATE O'BRIEN

One of the hardest things about starting any-thing—cleaning a room, updating a résumé, beginning that blog, going on a diet, or even planning something pleasurable, like a vacation—is that no matter where we are, it feels like either it's not the right time to begin, or there's not enough time to finish properly. And the hardest task to start of all? Beginning to sift, sort, and make sense of your financial affairs—setting in motion your solvency.

It's as though we feel that our puny efforts—the one hour we have free this entire week—can't possibly pay off unless we find the "perfect" starting point from which to launch our whole new life, so let's not waste what precious time, emotion, and creative energy we do have available. Let's take a nap instead. *With everything swirling about, you have no idea how exhausted I am.*

Oh, sweetheart, yes I do. That's because right now we both feel lousy about ourselves, our lives, our finances, and anything else that comes to mind. Procrastination is the most effective tool of the devil, the biggest energy drain conceivable (except for meetings that require conference rooms). We want a respite from all the crises. Just a little breathing space. A sip of water. I wonder, is your chest constricting as tight as mine right now?

Having the confidence and courage to boldly set out toward finding the oasis of financial serenity that comes from taking the best care of ourselves because we're taking the best care of our money is a little like an excursion in search of ancient Moroccan desert communities or the Kasbahs. Oases are in the middle of the desert journey, not at the starting point. Right now you just have to get the stubborn camel going when the ornery beast of burden is more interested in chewing his cud. "The charm of camel trekking is that it will help you gain insight into how ancients traveled through the desert for centuries before," a travel brochure pulled from my Contentment Chest this morning tells me. Charm. Insight. Luxury. Camel trekking. Ah, the wide and wondrous things that can distract us from our tasks. Don't be surprised if you suddenly find yourself insatiably curious about beekeeping, backgammon, or learning how to microbrew your own beer in the basement. Learning anything is preferable right now to discovering what you need to know about your financial situation.

So don't worry about perfection, just take the Next Step.

The amazing thing is that taking the Next Step is always (for now) the perfect personal prompt, the perfect response, the perfect gesture, the perfect nudge. Having that sense of the Next Step is the life force in action, and you can trust it. Like the light coming up in the morning or the calm, quiet stillness of twilight, the Next Step never rushes but is always moving forward in slow motion to take you where you want to go. Think of a camel ambling across the desert. Now, these dromedaries (one-humped camels) can fly like the wind—faster than horses. But their preferred speed, like my own, is slow and steady. They make it every time, and so will you.

The Next Step may seem too small (like collecting all your unopened mail from around the house) or overwhelming (like opening all the envelopes at once) or scary (like calling the mortgage company to discuss why you can't make a payment this month). But the very fact that the prompt comes from deep inside you, that it floats up to your awareness, is an intuitive sign that you are ready to do it. Long before you have insight or clarity, a plan or a goal, you can start to put your foot down in the right direction on the path of peace and plenty, if only you will take the Next Step.

Cents and Sensibilities

Wisdom is harder to do than it is to know.

—YULA MOSES

The who, what, when, where, and how (or how much) of our story are its facts, and the facts of our lives change, as do our circumstances. But our circumstances can change *only* through choice or crisis.

For many women—and this certainly includes me—most money choices have been unconscious. That is, until they lead to a crisis. Since my most fervent prayer for the last few months has been a respite from all the crises, we're going to start making conscious choices to count our cents and save our sensibilities. Heaven likes to help those trying to help themselves.

The amount of money currently in your bank account is a fact. The amount of money you spend today is a choice. And the way you reconcile both is through clarity.

"Counting is the most basic tool for gaining clarity. When we spend, we count the amount. And when we make money we count that too. Money in—money out," Julia Cameron and Mark Bryan reassure us in *Money Drunk, Money Sober.*

Counting shows us how much—or how little—we take care of ourselves. For many of us, life's proportions are off; we overwork and underplay. We overplay and underwork. We binge on new fashion but starve ourselves intellectually. Or we are gluttons for books but won't give ourselves a nice shirt.

We throw away money on expensive dinners but never use the cash to buy a good mattress/a decent reading chair/some new sheets. These discoveries about our misdirected spending can frighten us at first. We are often shocked by how poorly we have been treating ourselves.

Several years ago I had my eyes checked, and the optometrist said my prescription was fine. And it was, for five years. Then gradually, almost imperceptibly, my eyesight started to worsen. Finally, it got to the point where I wasn't comfortable reading the back of boxes, menus, the newspaper, books, or anything, for Heaven's sake, because frankly I couldn't. I started to doubt my perspective: Was it me or was the point size of print becoming smaller? Since I worked at a large-screen computer, my work wasn't affected, and so I did nothing to remedy the situation. Still, my daily round became a series of frustrations. I couldn't read the fine print, was continually oblivious to my intimate spaces, and suffered continuous eye scrunching and head throbbing. When I moved in with my sister, she noticed immediately. "You know you can get reading glasses at the drugstore," she said, offering the kind of sound advice that sisters give best.

"I don't need reading glasses. Maybe you need better light in these rooms," I rationalized. So I went out and bought lamps for her apartment. Now I could see brightness but not words.

"Just try them," she urged as we headed out to the drugstore for flu shots. "You'll be amazed at the difference." Coincidentally, there was a long line at the checkout counter and an abundance of reading glasses on display. I fiddled around for a few minutes while I was waiting and lo and behold, the seas parted. My miraculous recovery set me back $9.95—about $150 less than the bevy of lamps I'd thought so necessary. Why hadn't I listened to her sooner? When I stopped to examine my choices, I remembered the last time I'd purchased glasses was on Madison Avenue in New York. Of course, that hefty tab had included several pairs of designer spectacles. The only unknown is how much an eye exam would cost now, because that would have meant my taking the time to learn the facts (I might have discovered that they give inexpensive eye exams at Costco and Walmart). But when you're existing at survival level financially, fact-finding doesn't make it to your to-do list.

Providence is very patient. How long do *you* want to continue living in lack, bitterness, regret, and frustration, struggling through every minute of your life, discontented and envious, as the darkness encroaches? It's been my experience that with spiritual lessons, we can learn the easy way or the hard way. Choosing to live in lack rather than abundance is the hard way. So is choosing the path of least resistance over the path to peace and plenty. It's our choice. It's always our choice. The angels, by the way, call this magnificent fact "the gift of free will," and our habit of ignoring our own free will probably explains why celestial beings must spend a great deal of time shaking their heads in bewilderment.

So let's start counting. Here's a very old budgeting trick. Grab a few index cards (or a small notebook), a small pencil, and a ziplock bag. Starting today or tomorrow, write down everything you purchase, from breath mints to groceries. Put the receipts in the bag. You could also use your debit card instead of a credit card for every purchase, again putting all the receipts in the bag. At the end of the day, total the spending and record the amount in your *Journal of Well-Spent Moments*. You'll pledge to do this for one week. But you'll want to keep doing it for another, and then another, until you get to a month of keeping track. Don't tell yourself that you're going to do it for a month, however, or you won't even finish tomorrow.

It's also very important not to censor your spending in any way. If you buy magazines every time you go to the supermarket, don't stop this week; the point of this exercise is to see how your rote choices add up. Cameron and Bryan advise, "Don't judge yourself or your spending. We are just looking. Don't be surprised if this is hard to do at first."

I've tried counting several times before I got it to stick. I'd do it for a few days and then forget one purchase. Being a perfectionist, I'd beat myself up and then give up the whole effort. Stick with it. Not counting, especially after you're conscious, is a sophisticated form of self-sabotage. "I've discovered you never know yourself until you're tested, and that you don't even know you're being tested until afterwards," Marilyn French consoles us. "And that in fact there isn't anyone giving the test except yourself."

The Margin of Happiness

*Annual income twenty pounds, annual expenditure
nineteen, nineteen six, result—happiness.
Annual income twenty pounds, annual expenditure
twenty pounds and six, result—misery.*

—CHARLES DICKENS

The margin of happiness was the euphemism Victorian literary domestics used when referring to the household budget. As Charles Dickens pointed out in his novel *David Copperfield*—published in 1849 and based on his own childhood, when his father was sent to debtors' prison—the difference in life between happiness and misery can be as little as six shillings of overspending. Because overspending never stops at six shillings! I think creating a "happy margin" in our financial affairs is a splendid way for us to begin to reframe the concept of household budgets.

Heaven knows I wished I'd kept to a budget when I had (or so it seemed) limitless resources. But in fact I didn't, which is why I'm right with you, sweetie, as we figure out our sums together.

The first step of creating a workable budget is to understand both your income and your expenses. Remember, what money you have coming in must be enough to pay for money going out. Most of us are paid on a bimonthly basis, with income to work with every two weeks. If you are self-employed or on a fixed income, you will want to design your budget with that in mind. As you begin this process, ask yourself: *How can I live below my means?* The desired outcome is to keep creating a buffer of more and more savings to pay down debts and keep yourself protected from want—your own margin of personal happiness.

Before we go further, we need to remember the power of our words. If we call what we're doing a budget, it feels horribly restrictive, punitive, like we've just been tied to a chair and left in a dark room. Hmm, it seems like Charles Dickens isn't the only one still feeling the long, chilling shadow of shame.

"The word budget seems to frighten some people. They think of it as of a beast which will devour, or as a tool by which the homemakers arbitrarily, almost automatically, cut themselves off from all possibility of ever obtaining the things they want," the home arts magazine *Modern Priscilla* told readers in January 1928. "On the contrary, it does, if well made and well used, prevent careless expenditure for things outside the scheme of life. It prevents wandering thoughtlessly into debt. It insures the purchase of many things which, however desirable, would have been counted among the impossibilities or extravagances, if the careful survey demanded in making the budget had not shown them to be possible."

In other words, a budget is an instrument of possibility; it is your margin of happiness waiting to be created. You'll feel different about budgets if you believe you're an artist of the everyday, actively creating tangible happiness.

Now that we've taken some of the sting and stigma out of the word *budget*, let's get down to it. It is easiest to look at your finances on a monthly basis. Add up your monthly income and your expenses. If your balance sheet doesn't balance, don't worry, you'll get there. You may be using your credit cards more than you would like in the short term, but you'll change that in time. In the beginning it may require some strategies to get ahead of the game, but it will be worth it in the long run.

BUDGET BASICS

When creating the areas you want to focus on, keep in mind the way you actually live today.

Expenditures can be divided into four categories to start:

- **Fixed:** Those that remain the same each month, including bills for rent/mortgage, health insurance, car payments, telephone, cable, cell phone, student loans, margin of happiness (your savings—and I did put savings in this category on purpose; it's time to make this a priority).
- **Flexible:** Medical expenses, dental expenses, medicine, heating oil, electricity, groceries, child care, donations, lunches, entertainment, eating out, car maintenance, household maintenance, gas, parking, education savings, retirement savings, clothing, tithing, special offerings at church, fund-raising in the community, gifts.
- **Occasional:** Regular payments that may come quarterly, semiannually, or annually: life insurance, car insurance, homeowner's/renter's insurance, and fees — bank fees, finance fees, convenience fees. Track them all. They make a difference.
- **Clubs:** Yes, we're going to begin an old-fashioned Vacation Club and Christmas Club, just like our grandmothers and mothers did. Let's say that beginning January 1, you put $10 a week away for Christmas; come next December 1 you'll have $480 (not $520, because you'll want that money in December) to spend on the holidays with no guilt. Oh, I can see you shaking your head. It's not enough, is it? Would $1,000 feel more festive? That

will be $20 a week (about four lattes, as I remember). Now, isn't this fascinating: You're making a choice to have a stress- and guilt-free holiday, prepaid. I'm having fun already because I can feel the margin of happiness at work. You'll be amazed at the power of a focused amount that accrues.

Of course, each category can be broken down into more specific subcategories, such as insurance: car, home-owner's/renter's, flood, health, life, disability, if that feels right to you. But I think you should keep it simple when instituting a new behavior or good habit—I don't want to set myself up to fail anymore. The key is just to account for all your necessary expenditures and get a handle on where you have some flexibility.

One of the best ways to handle budgeting your bills is to create a fixed payment each month for the majority of your expenses. For example, if your car insurance is payable every six months, you want to calculate a monthly payment that can get you ahead of the game. Let's say the total payment due for six months is $730. If you double that, your car insurance is $1,460 for the year. Round up the amount to $1,500 and make a monthly contribution for car insurance of $125. At the end of the year, you will find yourself with an extra $40—contingency money should the rate unexpectedly increase.

Play with the categories and expand or collapse them to fit your family's needs. It is also helpful to consider everyone in the family in the budget as well. Your spouse may want to have lunch out or a night out with friends, and your children may need birthday presents, school supplies, field trips.

Once you have created all your categories, revisit them and mark them NECESSITY or DESIRABLE. This is all part of your distinguishing between wants and needs and gaining clarity in your spending patterns.

Your budget comes alive in two places: in your book

of household accounts and in your soon-to-be-explained budget envelopes. I know you can do this on the computer; you may already be a wiz at it. But I chose an old-fashioned black-and-red ledger book from an office supply store. It's solid like my idea of the ground beneath my feet and my financial future. No more fantasies or illusions. I figure if it's in the account book and the money in is greater than the money out, I've got more of a chance at contentment. Try it. At the end of every month, you can move any excess funds to any other expenditure or saving category as you wish (this is how Christmas and Vacation Clubs grow). You can borrow from any variable account but not from the fixed accounts or those labeled NECESSITY.

Are you still with me? Good, we've taken in quite a lot today then. Time for some fun. We're going to balance the books!

How to Cope
When Money
Makes You Mope

Many people think money is something to be set aside for a rainy day. But honestly, how much money do you really need for a dozen or so hours of inclement weather?

— MISS PIGGY

Coping days and moping nights are all part of our spiritual and financial journey. Just as patience and perseverance are necessary to bring our financial lives back in balance, so is a bit of comic relief, especially if we've sunk deep in the bog of gloom. Solvency takes time. It also takes creative energy, a finely wrought sense of irony, and extra dollops of wry humor to get us through the gnarly getting-over stage.

When we're deep in money-pit dumps, life as we've known it is out of control. Like a beautiful secret garden that's overgrown with weeds from neglect, we have lives that need nurturing, acknowledging, and appreciating as we prune back and pare down. We are entitled to make our lives as pleasant as possible. Instead, we automatically forfeit any kindness, contentment, and pleasure that come our way because we're feeling guilty and unworthy. So we turn down a friend's invitation to attend a covered-dish supper, a concert at our community church, a talk at the bookstore, or a night of improv at a local college.

This gloom is difficult to shift, because after you've toted those sixteen tons of financial guilt, regret, and contrition all week long (and possibly for months), getting your groove back for the weekend is almost impossible. That's why I came up with my imaginary financial advisers—all of whom make me smile, especially when I'm a serious mope.

Do you remember the comfort and joy of an imaginary playmate when you were a child? Just because the rest of the world couldn't see your constant companion, it didn't mean he or she wasn't real. Reassuring companion spirits can be an immediate presence in our daily round—guiding, inspiring, guarding, and loving—even if it's been a long time since you made mud pies in the backyard. I remember when Hillary Rodham Clinton became the object of ridicule because it was revealed that she held fantasy conversations with Eleanor Roosevelt. "She usually responds by telling me to buck up, or at least to grow skin as thick as a rhinoceros," the former first lady responded. Wonderful advice, but so is the practice of seeking advice from imaginary counselors. I keep reminders of them in my Contentment Chest; you can, too.

My first financialista is Miss Piggy, who can always be counted on for sound money advice. In *Miss Piggy's Guide to Life*, she confides, "It can be very depressing to run low on money. Nevertheless, it is bound to happen to everyone sooner or later, and you should know how to handle it." She suggests a budget divided between "Necessities" and "Luxuries," and then in each category five different levels of liquidity:

Very Stingy
Just Right

Oh-Oh!
Very Careless
Naughty

This is a brilliant concept and one that actually works amazingly well. "Note that necessities and luxuries are separated. It is up to each person to decide for herself which is which, but some things, like a bare minimum of ten dresses, a good color television set, and at least one movie a week, are clearly necessities, while excessive visits to the dentist, library membership and savings bonds are typical luxuries."

Think of Miss Piggy's method as an imaginary Geiger counter; before you spend, just register where this purchase will land. We all know that if we psychologically stay in the "Just Right" stage of spending, we'll feel balanced. Buffering our buying binges is the "Oh-Oh" meter reading. Once we start to stray into the "Very Careless," we start to feel woozy and unsteady on our feet. Besides finances, Miss Piggy tackles diet, fashion, beauty, exercise, romance, and success and offers scintillating business tips that make more sense than anything you'll hear on the evening news.

"Business sense isn't being able to predict the price of peppermint, or knowing when to get out of tea cozies and into doilies and little dishes, or being able to tell in advance that there is going to be a glut of maraschino cherries in Umbrellastan," the super pig reminds us. "You see, the longer money is held on to, the more likely it is to suffer from what is technically termed cashosis or decashification. But never mind the nomenclature. I know that you have seen the awful results. Two or three crackling clean ten-dollar bills folded neatly in a purse and left for a week or two turn into seven greasy ones and some nickels and pennies. Large amounts of paper money are also a fire hazard, and the prudent individual sees to it that major accumulations are avoided. Although purse blazes are a relatively uncommon occurrence, there is just no reason to be smug or complacent about the potential threat."

Admit it, you're smiling. I know I am, which is why I'm doodling in my Comfort Companion, a version of Miss Piggy's Balance Sheet that takes into account our intangible but very valuable assets before our liabilities. She wisely suggests we include:

Looks
Valued Friends
Talent
Health
Winning Personality
Sense of Humor
Brains
Fans

With million-dollar looks and brains, a priceless sense of humor (carried for accounting purposes at 1,000,000 laughs with a $1 par value each), and 100,000,000 fans, it doesn't at all seem too bad that her "Cash on Hand" is $7.23.

Regrettably *Miss Piggy's Guide to Life* by Miss Piggy (as told to Henry Beard) is out of print, but a used-book store excursion is one of the best cure-alls for whatever ails you, if the Pig isn't. I got mine for $2 — and it was a steal.

One last question, Miss Piggy. Should a woman have financial secrets from the man she loves?

"Should chocolates have cherry centers? Should satin pillows have fluffy stuffing?"

Any investment tips?

"Pork futures."

("It looks like a self-help book ... it reads like a self-help book ... but what a difference a pig makes!")

And the Envelope, Please

Life is a luminous halo, a semi-transparent envelope
surrounding us from the beginning.

—VIRGINIA WOOLF

There's a good reason that entertainment award shows put each winner's name in an envelope. Envelopes are powerful symbols—in fact, many of our most cherished events involve envelopes. Imagine a love letter or wedding invitation with no envelope or news announcing the blessed birth of a new baby on a postcard. What would an acceptance to a much-desired university be without the satisfying heft of a fat envelope? Unfortunately, envelopes can also be unwanted, like the thick thump on the floor of an astronomical telephone bill. In England, bills and re-minders come in cheap brown envelopes, as second-class mail, which soon begin to attract a parsimonious pile of their own on the kitchen counter.

For centuries, envelopes have endowed the daily round with ceremony, custom, and ritual. The envelope acts as a "Messenger of Sympathy and Love, Servant of Parted Friends, Consoler of the Lonely, Bond of the Scattered Family, Enlarger of the Common Life, Carrier of News and Knowledge, Instrument of Trade and Industry, Promoter of Mutual Acquaintance of Peace and Goodwill Among Men and Nations," according to the English poet Charles William Eliot (1834–1926), whose beautiful words encase the roof of the National Postal Museum in Washington, DC.

The envelope held another place in our history: It was the budgetary tool of many a household from the Great Depression through World War II, and it's high time for its comeback. Now, you might think I'm trying to turn back time—and mostly I am—but until you try this vintage bliss art form, you will never know what respite from a stressful day holding your cash in your hands may bring.

In her recent book *Payback: Debt and the Shadow Side of Wealth*, Canadian author Margaret Atwood reveals her family's Great Depression envelope stories.

> My mother had four envelopes, into which she put the money from my father's pay cheque every month. These envelopes were labelled "Rent," "Groceries," "Other Necessities," and "Recreation." Recreation meant the movies. The first three envelopes had priority, and if there was nothing left in the fourth envelope, there were no movies, and my parents went for a walk instead.

In my family, my grandmother was the envelope budgeter. My mother was more a *How much is there in the checkbook* budgeter, and this slipshod practice led her astray. Growing up in the 1950s and 1960s, children were admonished to remember that money didn't grow on trees. But what about money that now comes out of machines in a convenience store or the side of a building, or shows up as a mysterious green filament on our computer screen? The way money is exchanged today via computers, whether it's online banking, bill paying, or purchasing, pushes its true value away from us and into the hands and keystrokes of strangers. There's no real way to make a positive emotional connection with money, which is something I'm convinced we're all seeking.

The Irish proverb "Money goes where she's welcomed" was one of my Irish Nana Rose's bedrock beliefs.
She was not only the ultimate budgeter and envelope jug-
gler, she was a master at hiding her household money from
my grandfather Joe. To Nana, the category of "Household" money included any money she found around the
household along with whatever money my grandfather
gave her as "the grocery money." Now, Joe had a couple
of vices that drove Rose crazy. He loved poker and the
ponies. Friday nights were devoted to playing cards or the
ponies with his pals. Joe was actually pretty good at it,
too, although mysteriously his winnings kept disappearing
and he could never understand why.

The explanation? Grandpa Joe always came home
from a night with the boys tipsy and tired but determined
to hide his winnings from Rose, who only pretended to be
asleep upstairs until he was snoring beside her. Before he
flopped onto the bed, there was always some loud clang-
ing and fumbling with furniture, and like sonar equipment
she'd mentally fix on the part of the house the noise came
from. One weekend I stayed over with my grandparents
and was awakened by all the brouhaha. Nana tucked me
back in bed and told me we'd go on a treasure hunt the
next day. The first thing my grandmother did at 7 AM on
Saturday was a sweep of the house. You'd have thought
the woman was an international spy the way she rooted
out every last one of Joe's hiding spots while the old man
was snoozing on his day off.

Her first stop was the ceiling fixture in the living room.
It had an old-fashioned frosted-glass dish to diffuse the
light, but the funny thing was when Nana turned the light
on she could see the outline of the dollar bills through the
glass. Nana was savvy; she confiscated only 90 percent of
his winnings, leaving just enough so that if Joe remembered stashing his dosh there, he'd think he hadn't really
won as much as he remembered.

For the next hour or so that morning, I followed Nana

around the house as she searched for my grandfather's winnings with a big smile on her face and a few giggles from me. She checked all his favorite hiding places: inside the piano, in the light over the dining room table, in the window seat, and under the rug. Grandpa Joe tried to outsmart her each week, but she bragged that she always found "her" money.

Once she had recovered the weekly winnings, Nana took the cash and divided it in her envelopes according to category, then stored them in a locked box. She wore the key around her neck, beside her cross, until the day her earthly cares ceased.

Nana Rose's scavenger hunt was equal parts amusement and profit and led to truly dexterous financial maneuverings. For those of us learning the way to financial serenity and solvency, the envelope system teaches prudence, patience, and perseverance with a dash of fun, beginning with making our own envelope system.

And while the envelopes are old-fashioned, they can work in tandem with modern technology. "What if I pay my bills online?" The answer is to simply create a new online account called Bill Pay. Once you have saved up your payments, make a deposit directly into your Bill Pay account and pay your bills. Don't forget to factor in the fees for all your bank accounts.

The envelopes are the only way known to womankind to keep from overspending your budget. ATM cards and balancing the checkbook in your head or from your online statement are devices of the collective consciousness of the banking industry to keep us in debt. With the envelope system, you can only spend what you have. This is such a simple concept, but somehow the tangible feel of those envelopes keeps our impulses in check better than any accountants and monitors. One rule, though: You can *never* borrow from rent, utilities, car payment, or insurance envelopes, but you can go without a pedicure to go to a movie. However, here is an important caveat. Like the

Simple Abundance Gratitude Journal, in which you have to write out five things for which you are grateful each day, you must do the envelope exercise with real envelopes for a few months to have the magic work. The envelope system isn't as overwhelming as keeping a budget, which I'm asking you to commit to week by week, since it only takes once or twice a month to keep it going.

Now, just to prove how this system works, go get a new envelope and mark it JUST FOR ME. Take your loose cash and change, put it in the envelope, and hold it in your hand. Doesn't it feel good just to be back on Life's list? Imagine how good it will feel when your debts are paid down and you can increase the amount that goes in the JUST FOR ME envelope each month. Don't worry, you'll get there with the *Peace and Plenty* plan—with a smile on your face and relief in your heart.

The Thrill of Thrift

Every Woman's Secret System

There are the stories that never, never die, that are carried like seed into a new country, are told to you and me, and make in us new and lasting strengths.

— MERIDEL LE SUEUR

What is a budget, anyway? Is it something complicated and technical that few persons can understand and use? That seems to be the impression many people have," *McCall's* magazine columnist Isabel Ely Lord asked her readers with cheerful élan in January 1930, two months after the collapse of Wall Street in the Great Crash. She set out to charmingly demystify the B-word by pointing out all the good qualities of budgets, rather like trying to set up a friend on a blind date.

"First, a budget helps us get the things we want. It brings us peace of mind and the confidence of knowing what we are doing. But it cannot work by itself."

Readers were to write in with ways to bend the budget. "These appetites haven't noticed the depression. My budget has. On half our former allowance, I have to provide exactly as much food—and just as good."

Mrs. Lord tried her best. "You are not limited by a budget, as so many seem to think. What limits you is your income. A budget frees you since staying within it limits what you can spend with a good conscience."

I imagine that the eyes of readers seventy years ago began to glaze over, as mine do now, reading her myriad suggestions for our "readjustment" to life on a budget. Which is why the story passed down from generations of women suits me just fine: Envelopes. Cash. A match made in Heaven.

The financial television and radio commentator Dave Ramsey has done wonders for spreading the good word about his grandma's envelope system and has even gone so far as to develop a product line of envelopes and binders available on his website and through the Financial Peace University. However, they have a distinctly business feel or "guy" appeal. I think the real thrill of thrift is developing your own set of envelopes, something that reflects your feminine sensibilities, similar to finding or making the perfect box for your Contentment Chest and Comfort Companion. Remember, these are insight tools to trigger feelings of peace, plenty, and pleasure. Visit a party store and you can find colorful opaque transparent envelopes (for invitations). At San Francisco's amazing Bell'occhio (www.bellocchio.com), you'll find a delectable supply of vintage glassine envelopes, gossamer French carnival gauze envelope bags, and more. Collections of pretty labels (French General, Susan Branch, and Cath Kidston) let you add an elegant flourish. Personally, I've taken to clear file folders with a snap, which give me room for receipts as well as flashing my cash and holding on to clippings of items I'd like to read in the future. All are enclosed in a gorgeous box file with a handle, space enough for the files, bills waiting to be paid, my accounts ledger, stamps, calculator, and card sets. I call it my *Peace and Plenty* Portfolio and every girl should have one. It will change your life.

And here's why.

"Every woman loves a system, in her heart of hearts,

because she loves feeling comfortable and safe," an anony-
mous contributor to *Girls Own Annual* confessed in 1919 as
she revealed "how a married woman made her husband's
income buy just what she wanted." This system is so much
fun to set up, it sparks your creative energy, and it calms
you down. Which is, after all, our entire raison d'être. A
century later, it's our own money we want to take care
of—much as we would take care of a lover. Remember,
Miss Moneypenny not only goes where she's wanted, but
stays there.

The Courage to Be Rich

*It takes courage to live with financial hardship, and
unbelievable as it may seem, it takes courage to be rich.
Why? Because choosing wealth as a goal requires facing
everything about your money bravely, honestly, with
courage — which is a very, very hard thing for most of us
to do. But it can be done.*

— SUZE ORMAN

Do you remember the television program *Lifestyles of the
Rich and Famous* (1984–1995), hosted by Robin
Leach? With all the movies, glossy magazines, gossip
tabloids, and blogs that have come since, providing entic-
ing glimpses of a golden world of beauty, luxury, and
comfort, it would seem easy to fantasize about the joys of
being rich. However, I know that "visualizing" wealth
makes some women feel uncomfortable, even anxious. Because as we grow, reinvent ourselves, and learn to
distinguish between our needs and our wants—which
change as often as we do—what being wealthy means
changes, too.

A few years ago, a friend received a tremendous promotion at work. She was in advertising, and her agency
in New York was merging with a British firm. She was
offered a bigger and better job than she ever dreamed possible, and while it felt wonderful, it also felt weird. "My
boss told me I could have my choice of any international
capital I wanted to make my home base. I was having a

hard time concentrating because I was feeling quite wob-
bly at such a sudden turn of good events. I kept wishing
I could be alone for just a few minutes when she asked,
thinking it would help me decide, 'If you could create your
dream life, where would it be?' To my horror, it was all I
could do not to cry."

Later that night my friend realized that she had never
allowed herself to think about attaining that level of success; her anxiety came from breaking through her own
internal "glass ceiling," which made her feel vulnerable
and exposed. "I always thought it would make me safe not
to know what I really wanted because I thought I'd just be
disappointed when I didn't get it. That night I realized that
by not knowing my dream, I had created a major handicap
that could cost me a great deal more. I had to teach myself
that it was safe to dream."

Finding a safe place to dream is what I was seeking
when I created my *Peace and Plenty* Comfort Companion.
Starting my life over from scratch at sixty (which I'm
assured is the new forty), I've discovered that it takes
tremendous courage to distinguish between your needs
and your wants; enormous energy to claim your right to
happiness. I flip through magazines and can't tell you what
my dream home looks like anymore. This feels very scary;
I've always had such clear visions. So I've been concentrating on what qualities I want to have and experience in
my home rather than what it needs to look like.

Comfort. Safety. Space. Light. Warmth. High ceilings.
Beautifully proportioned large rooms. Decorative cor-
nices. Built-in bookcases. Wide, deep-set windows. Shut-
ters. Window seats in every room for pillows. Beautiful
floors, hardwood, wide planks throughout except for tiles
in the kitchen, slate in the pantry and mud room. Working
fireplaces. Wide staircase, wide steps, narrow risers to
make it comfortable to walk. Pale shades: putty, gray,
sage, buttermilk, cream. Pinewood. A large, spacious entry hall, big enough for a large round table. Mullioned

windows in some rooms. En-suite bathrooms with bed-rooms. A dressing room. An art studio with a skylight. A library. A kitchen wing: eat-in kitchen, pantry, freezers, larders, study alcove for cookbooks. A sewing room with a walk-in linen closet upstairs, airing cupboards. A laundry room...a kitchen garden surrounded by a white picket fence.

Well, I guess I know more about my preferences than I thought I did. This comes as a wonderful surprise since most of the time I feel so dazed and confused, I can't pick out an item from a dinner menu. But you see, each of these descriptions came one at a time to be kept safely in my Comfort Companion until, like the mystery of compound interest, they add up to a new chapter, if not an estate! And I never had an estate at the height of my wealth.

"Can you remember the courage it took to endure a setback or overcome an obstacle in your own life?" the in-comparable Suze Orman asks in her groundbreaking book *The Courage to Be Rich: Creating a Life of Material and Spiritual Abundance.*

> You know, I know, it takes tremendous courage just to keep going, to work hard to pay the bills every month, to meet the next financial or emotional chal-lenge that comes along. The courage to be rich, how-ever, goes beyond the chains and limitations of our minds and present-day circumstances, and it brings tomorrow—when yesterday's defeat will be long past us—into every today. This kind of courage is vision and it refuses to let today's defeat block our path into the future.

We all need to dream, to become conscious of our deepest yearnings and give ourselves permission to make those dreams come true. If we don't allow ourselves to visualize the lifestyle we want to be living—one of peace and plenty—we create a major handicap for ourselves, a more perfect prison than any enemy could devise. For when we deny our imagination scope, a clean slate, another chance, we limit Providence as well.

But we develop courage one step at a time, by doing anything that is difficult at the moment but also the next easy task. Courage is a habit. My favorite kind of courage turns our dreams into a daily dose of destiny. "Courage can't see around corners, but goes around them anyway," the writer Mignon McLaughlin tells us. "The only courage that matters is the kind that gets you from one moment to the next."

Part Four

Down for the Count

I think somebody should count to 10.

—FRANKIE DUNN, *MILLION DOLLAR BABY* (2004)

On Losing Your Job

*Her work, I really think her work
is finding what her real work is
and doing it,
her work, her own work,
her being human, her being in the world.*

— URSULA K. LE GUIN

If we put the death of a loved one to one side, there aren't many occurrences that can rattle us like the loss of a job. In one fell swoop, we lose our sense of security, our livelihood, and our self-esteem. Even if you've hated your job for years (and if that's the case, then you're not the only one who's known about it), the pink slip triggers shock, fear, and uncertainty.

Perhaps you thought you were at the top of your game, but then on the day after Labor Day, you arrive at your office and find out that the company is divided into two groups—Group A will be meeting in the Penthouse Conference Room in fifteen minutes. Group B, report to the cafeteria. The CEO and CFO draw straws. Next they toss a coin. Heads it's A. Tails it's B. The CFO heads to the cafeteria; the buck-stops-here man heads to the Penthouse Conference Room where some of his best and brightest are gathered. You're among them.

There's a long sigh. He rubs his eyes with his hands and shakes his head. "I'm sorry," he says, and he really is. Some of you have been with him for fifteen years, from the start-up days in a loft. "This isn't about performance. It's about money. We've run out. We can't keep the buzzards at bay any longer, and we can't keep you. There's two weeks' severance, but please clean out your desks in the next hour." Later as the wildfire of gossip sweeps through the corridors, bathrooms, pavement, you'll hear that it really wasn't about performance. It was the luck of the draw. Everyone in the cafeteria has kept their job. For now.

If you've just lost your job, I am so sorry for your pain. I've lost two that hurt; one because I really needed it and the other because it was my first bylined newspaper gig. However, they both led to better opportunities and brighter days. Still, I know the sharp visceral blow that accompanies the pink slip. I also know how difficult it is right now to even think of the concept of "reinventing" yourself. But when you can step back from the drama for a moment, taking stock of that pitiful brown box you carried out holding all your worldly work possessions is a good place to start.

You probably have a calendar in there. Take it out and count the days, the hours, and the minutes you contributed to your employer's bottom line, including the time it took you to commute, the unpaid or paid overtime, the mandatory meetings or "parties." This may take awhile, so make yourself comfortable and use a calculator. Now take all the time that you have actually expended in the pursuit of your employer's wealth and look at what you got in return. When you compute your hourly wage against the real time you committed to your job, you'll be surprised at the real cost to you.

Now turn to your box. What was really important enough to take to the office with you? Maybe you have a picture of your loved ones, a drawing by a preschool admirer, your favorite fountain pen, a coffee mug that reminds you of a great vacation. Do you have books you purchased that inspire you? As you take inventory of the important things in your life, the ones that bring you peace

and plenty, most likely you won't find anything of importance from your employer. You won't need that nameplate
anymore, either, unless it states, as it should, QUEEN OF
ALL SHE SURVEYS.

You see, a job, unless it is your calling, your sacred
work in the world, is a means to an end. The end is not
your identity, it is not your security, it is not your life. It
is only one of many vehicles of transportation to get you
where you're headed out of thousands available to you.
Think of all the end-of-the-world disaster movie scenes
where people are fleeing the city. A pickup truck is hand-
ier than that stretch limo. Pull back for a wide-angle shot
of your life and see where you actually want to be headed.

There are some occasions in life when the Universe
gives us the opportunity to revisit how we are spending
the most precious commodity we have of all: our time. If
we are not spending the majority of it doing what we love
and being with the people we love, we're going to get a
wake-up call that we can't ignore. If you are one of the
few who lost a job you really enjoyed, then you probably
have outgrown the position with your former employer.
You've been given the chance to spread your wings a little
wider and this time, you'll seek out an employer that has a
mission and an attitude toward its employees that you can
align with. If you were lucky enough to be relieved of duty
at a job you didn't love, congratulations, you now have the
cosmic space and Divine Blessing to do what you really
love, or at least explore all the options.

See this shock of job loss for what it really is: a reminder from the Universe that the most important things in
life are carried in our hearts and represented in the little
box you just took from your former office—not in the office itself.

"Work is a world apart from jobs," Alice Koller writes
in *The Stations of Solitude*. "Work is the way you occupy
your mind and hand and eye and whole body when they're
informed by your imagination and wit, by your keenest

perceptions, by your most profound reflections on everything you've read and seen and heard and been part of.
You may or may not be paid to do your work."

Oh yes, you will be, eventually, because this time
you're going to start doing what you love. When you give
to the world with all your heart, money is the energy the
world pays back to you. That's just how it works. Of
course, learning how to handle all the abundance with
your name on it isn't simple, but that's why I'm here now.
We'll take it one cup of tea at a time.

Losing the Future, Gaining Your Life

Occasionally the impossible happens; this is a truism that accounts for much of what we call good luck; and also, bad.

— FAITH BALDWIN

For an author each book is like a child with its own tale to tell about conception, confinement, and birth. So is each job. This is the story of how my first book, *Mrs. Sharp's Traditions*, came into the world in 1989—but only after I learned the truth about claiming what was mine and protecting it. It is a story of blessings in disguise, handy because so many times, especially now with such a difficult, tumultuous economy, what seems like bad luck can, with faith and fine-tuning, turn into your good.

Such as losing your job.

After my daughter, Kate, was born in 1982 my freelance articles, written regularly for the *Washington Post* Style Plus section, began to center on families, children, and lifestyle instead of the arts. But this was the 1980s—the harsh, brash, self-indulgent decade of "the Me Generation." We "dressed for success" with big hair and even bigger shoulder pads, watched prime-time soap operas like *Dallas* and *Dynasty*, and headed to shopping malls for recreation. Madonna was the Material Girl and Gor-

don Gekko's mantra that "Greed is Good" in Oliver
Stone's movie *Wall Street* gave the Baby Boomers permis-
sion to behave badly, just as the Jazz Age of the Roaring
Twenties became the catalyst for the "Lost Generation."

In the 1980s the Mommy Wars, which began between
Betty Crocker and Betty Friedan in the 1950s and 1960s,
went nuclear. One of the reasons we're all so crazy about
Mad Men is that women wear chic white gloves, pearls, and
hats as they use their perfect manicures to claw their way
to the corner office. But in the 1980s the gloves really came
off, and women started slugging it out with briefcases
and diaper bags. Like a lot of women torn between having a career and being a stay-at-home mom, I forged my
own compromise by working from home. But the harder
I worked, the less I seemed to accomplish either way, and
the more stressed out I seemed to get.

I longed to be part of a simpler time when women
didn't appear to be conflicted about their role. I found it in
the late nineteenth century.

I truly believe that we attract what we long for, becoming magnetic to our good by constantly focusing upon it.
In the last few years, there's been quite a lot written about
the Law of Attraction and money, but you can set the Law
of Attraction in motion for anything that you madly desire
in this world. For me, answered prayers came in the form
of a treasure trove of vintage women's and children's periodicals chanced upon on an excursion to a Maine antiques
shop during a family vacation. I remember that moment
with iridescent clarity; I felt instantly transported, like
Lewis Carroll's Alice, emerging from the rabbit hole and
surveying enchantment in Wonderland. For more than an
hour I was rooted to the floor devouring the pleasures of
"Rainy Day Occupations" and "Cozy Home Circle Eve-
nings." The writing was so quaint, yet very moving, the
sentiments it stirred within me reassuringly familiar, yet
fresh. It was a magic-carpet ride back to the Victorian era,
when life seemed so ordered, so serene, so blissful, and so

completely unlike my own. I bought the lot. The Victorian era became my passion, and I began to develop workshops on reviving Victorian family celebrations; I wanted to write about it as well. I wasn't alone in yearning for simpler times. The "Victoriana" boom in antiques was just beginning, and Hearst began publishing an exquisite women's magazine called *Victoria*. For frazzled women like me, it was a spiritual tonic and an inspirational revelation. I convinced the *Washington Post* Writers Group to take me on as a nationally syndicated columnist with a weekly feature called "Mrs. Sharp's Traditions."

What a heady adventure was about to begin! I had arrived at that blissful intersection where work becomes elevated beyond craft to art because you're doing what you love. When the Writers Group sent out the gorgeous mauve-colored announcement of the column to potential newspaper subscribers, I tied every one of the matching mauve silk ribbon bows on them with as much care as if we were sending out wedding invitations.

The economics of nationally syndicated newspaper columns and cartoons work this way: The syndicate charges newspapers a small fee depending on circulation; let's say $25 per column, and in those days that was a very real number—mine, in fact. You and the syndicate split the revenue fifty–fifty. The only way to make any money is to increase the number of newspapers carrying your feature. So in the beginning, nobody expects any real money—but nobody goes into business convinced it will fail. I was on the crest of a wave. Timing is everything. I knew intuitively that the Victorian craze was just starting, so I had only one request—I wanted a two-year contract. This meant in essence that I'd be working full-time for two years for free, but I knew in my heart that it would probably take that long to find my audience.

Not surprisingly, my then husband thought very little of this arrangement. But he was supportive, and so "Mrs. Sharp's Traditions" was launched in October 1987.

Nine months later, we returned from a beach vacation to find a letter from the Writers Group waiting for me. They said that the column had failed to attract the number of newspapers they required to break even and they were closing it down immediately. Essentially, I was fired.

My entire world fell crashing around me. Granted it was not a loss of current income, but it was a huge blow to my expected income. Gone were my platform, my product, my dream, and my prestige. Being a member of the *Washington Post* Writers Group had clout. It was my Holy Grail. I knew it got more people interested in my work than just being a freelance writer would have.

I had failed utterly and publicly. I was ashamed and embarrassed. My notion of my self-worth was completely tied to that byline. "As subjects, we all live in suspense, from day to day, from hour to hour," the novelist Mary McCarthy tells us. "In other words, we are the hero of our own story. We cannot believe that it is finished, that we are 'finished,' even though we may say so; we expect another chapter, another installment, tomorrow or next week."

The pain—physical, emotional, psychic—became so harrowing that I descended into a very dark cave, an abyss from which I didn't believe that I could ever crawl back. "The planet is full of hurt people, angry people, lost people, confused people, people who have explored the vast cartography of trouble, and people stunned by a sudden grief," admits Diane Ackerman, the prizewinning poet and author, in her brilliant book *A Slender Thread: Rediscovering Hope at the Heart of Crisis*. And there are certainly a lot of people hurting because of the current financial crisis. People hurting so much and worrying so much over what will happen next—the disgrace of bankruptcy, the terror of lawsuits and losing their home, the horror of being homeless, or the fear that they will never, ever get another job to support their families—that they've dropped off the unemployment rolls, off the radar, and into a bog of despair.

We are individually shattered and collectively frightened and frail. But what you don't realize is that the moment you feel so close to giving up, to being swallowed by your adversity, you are only one choice away from a miracle, your answered prayer.

In my case, I arrived at that choice after I sought help for my depression. While working through all the conflicting emotions with my therapist about what had occurred, I "remembered" that my contract was for two years, not nine months. I couldn't legally be dropped. But I would have to say something. I'd have to speak up. Did I have the moxie to do it? They weren't going to be particularly pleased about this contractual footnote, but what choice did I have?

So here's when the currency of chance turned my bad luck to good fortune. I told the Writers Group, in the nicest possible way, that I wanted to get a book contract before I left and that I felt I had a better chance to get one as a syndicated columnist than as a freelance writer. Standing up for myself—no lawyer, no agent at this time—was one of the most difficult things I have ever done. But they reluctantly agreed—egos and column inches aside, it was a matter of contractual law, and nobody wanted a fight. We parted amicably after I got a book contract and advance of $65,000 for *Mrs. Sharp's Traditions* with Simon & Schuster.

At forty years old, after failing at a lifetime of jobs, I was about to begin my brilliant career.

When a Girl Gets Fired

Work...has always been my
favorite form of recreation.

—ANNA HOWARD SHAW (1915)

There are some things that happen in life that never feel good, and getting fired is one of them. Even though it may sting, however, sometimes it is the best thing that could happen to you. As with any other loss, you need to take some time to process your feelings, reboot your interests, pick yourself up, and start over. Here is some vintage advice that has brought me enormous comfort. I'm delighted to pass on these words of honest wisdom from the 1938 inaugural issue of *The American Lady Magazine* on "Why a Girl Is Fired" by Helen Woodward:

> The little demon that sits by the side of every girl who works for a living is the fear of losing her job. And by a kind of spiteful indirection that very terror spoils her work and adds to the chance of losing the job.
>
> If you can get rid of a little of that fear, your life will be easier and you will do better work. And you can get rid of much of it by understanding some of the reasons why girls lose their jobs. These reasons are many and some of them are mysterious and incalculable. But there are five clear major reasons. Keep these in mind. They may be of help to you. They are:
> 1. Personal dislike.

2. Poor work.

3. Untidiness of person.

4. Wishing to lose your job.

5. Lack of work.

Of course lack of work makes more people lose their jobs than any other cause, but it may not make you lose yours, unless one of the other reasons also exists. Suppose five girls were laid off in your office because things were slack. Twenty others were kept. The ones laid off were chosen for one of the four reasons here given. In other words, when things slow down, the girls who are fired are those whom the boss dislikes, who do poor work, who are not clean or who wish to lose their jobs.

Next to this you probably expect me to give incompetence as the most important reason. But I really do not believe that poor work is as important as personal dislike, dislike that may be apparently without basis, but very strong nevertheless...

In the course of my own twenty-two years of working in offices I was fired from jobs four times. The first time was because the woman for whom I worked did not like me, the second because I was incompetent, the third because my boss and I disliked each other, and the fourth because business was bad and there was no work for me to do, the whole department was being abolished.

So you see that out of four times, I lost a job twice because somebody did not like me. The first time was peculiar. I loved books and thought I should be happy working in a library. Great was my joy when I got a job in one. But it only lasted one day. At the end of the day, the librarian, a disappointed, sad sort of person, told me that I had not asked enough questions. In other words, my personality grated on hers and she wanted to get rid of me.

The second time I lost a job for similar reasons, I

was working for an advertising agency. I was doing the kind of work which later on in other organizations I did without difficulty. But here my employers said my work was impossible and it probably was, because they did not like me and I did not like them. We annoyed each other continually. Everything I did was wrong. For instance, my boss found me always too slow. Yet one of the special qualities I have is great speed. I often do things too fast. I never do them too slowly. Yet these people found me too slow. When we dislike people we see them through strange spectacles.

Where personalities do not harmonize the situation is hopeless, whether it is in love, in marriage, or in business. If you don't like your employer as a human being, the chances of holding your job are slim. No matter how competent you are.

The next best reason for losing your job, I should say, would be bad work. It is exasperating to have some one working for you whom you like very much, but who does poor work. You put up with it for a long time but after a while you cannot stand it and you find an indirect way of discharging the girl, no matter how much you like her. Sometimes you get her another job.

The next reason for losing a job is an unpleasant appearance. It is amazing how many girls look untidy, or—what is both more common and more disagreeable—carry an unpleasant attitude with them. The number of competent women who have lost jobs for this reason is too terrible to think about.

The fourth reason for losing a job is that you want to lose it. You may not realize that you want to lose it. But often the truth is that your mind is always on something else you want more. You haven't the courage to leave, but there is something else so dominant in your mind that you do your work absently until your employer is forced to let you go.

There are many ways in which this hidden desire to lose your job may show. One is a combination of always arriving late for work and leaving too promptly at night... If you come late in the morning and hate to leave at night, then your lateness is not due to dislike of your work. But if you come late in the morning and rush off promptly at night, it means that you hate your work, and that you should, if possible, be doing something else...

Now those are the five reasons—personal dislike, incompetent work, untidiness, the unconscious desire to quit, lack of work. About the last you can do nothing. But about the others you can do a good deal. Understanding a problem often helps solve it.

Sometimes we are so unhappy in a job that we talk ourselves right out of it. No matter what the reason, take it as a sign that you have overstayed your welcome. Trust that the Universe has a new adventure with your name on it.

Claiming Your Own

Nothing succeeds like failure.

—REBECCA WEST

Sitting in the rubble of your dreams? Now what? Well, first you'll need to pull yourself together so that you can keep calm and carry on as you collect your personal belongings.

There's no denying that pink slips stun like a taser—you're not dead but you're certainly not moving. And being let go stirs up all kinds of unsavory emotions that seem incomprehensible (for now), uncomfortable (for a while), and contradictory. You're so embarrassed, you want to slink away from your own life. As you walk down the hall toward the elevator with your brown box, waves of shame, embarrassment, fear, and anger roll over you like a tsunami.

Later tonight, after the crying, the wine, and the recitation of how it happened and feeble attempts at why; after the house is dark and quiet, you'll crawl into bed exhausted. Maybe, though, just as you close your eyes, you'll let out a big sigh. And guess what? You'll feel a brief sense of relief.

A *thank you, God,* might cross your mind. *I didn't ask for this, but thank you.*

When I was first fired as a legal secretary during the 1970s, it was because my heart wasn't in the job and I guess it began to show in my work. I was keeping my day job while trying to build up my portfolio as a theater critic, and the more reviews and features were published with my byline, the more nervous my boss became. It seems the firm had landed a big client with a thorny lawsuit that could take years to win, lose, or settle. His nightmare scenario was losing an experienced secretary and bringing in someone new who didn't know the background or the shorthand vital to this important case. He saw that I wasn't a true "team member"; I didn't seem committed to being a legal secretary for the rest of my life. It was too much risk for him, so I was out the door. I was utterly flabbergasted, especially because I was a darn good legal secretary.

On the way out, one of the other partners called me into his office and suggested that I apply for "unemployment compensation." I didn't know which shocked me more, being fired or told to sign up for the dole! I explained I needed to find another job. I came from a working-class Irish family and I was "skilled"—in typing and shorthand (sort of). What that meant was that I would apply for another job on Monday. In my family, collecting anything remotely like "benefits" from the government was seen as being feckless. I felt my cheeks burning at the very thought of it.

He told me to calm down; this was not the end of the world, but probably the beginning. (Just like I'm telling you.) He also wanted me to realize that I was entitled to unemployment benefits and there should be no emotion connected to it. "You paid into the Unemployment Fund with every paycheck. Claim what's rightly yours."

And so I did collect—for sixteen weeks while trying to find another job and working hard on my writing. During this time, I applied for and was selected to receive a National Endowment for the Humanities Critics Institute Fellowship. It was one of the most fruitful, creative interludes in my life. But it was difficult for me to overcome my own prejudice concerning unemployment benefits. Getting out of our own way is the hardest job we ever take on.

Moral of this tale: Don't feel guilty about collecting any benefits you have been accruing in your job. They are meant to be a safety net for your next leap. And if you haven't yet started looking out for number one, this would be the perfect time to rethink that concept. But that, as they say, is another meditation for another day.

The next job I got was as a newsletter copywriter for a Washington trade association. This was definitely a step up, or so I thought, but it turned out my secretarial skills were called on far more than my writing. I held this job for about nine months and vowed it would be my last dip into the steno pool. After I was fired, I went to the unemployment office immediately, no hesitation this time, and met a caseworker who called me a week later and asked me if I wanted to go out for a cup of coffee. Two years later we were married. In the two decades we were together, I became not only a published writer but the mother of a beautiful baby girl.

Moral of this tale: When one sliding door closes, the next one to open may not look like one you want to go through. Stride through it anyway, for some of life's best gifts arrive in plain brown paper.

It can be hard to get objective about ourselves, especially when external financial pressures are asserting their own urgency and we simply can't wait until we "get our head together" before we start to rectify our financial woes.

On the other hand, we must realize that there are deeper rewards to our work in the world other than just paying down our credit cards; this knowledge can eventually provide the motivation to move to our next unfolding. So many times the money pressure squeezes out our soul's need for work that is fulfilling.

And sometimes a woman meets her destiny at the job she took to avoid it.

Your Lucky Break

The Great Escape

Be consoled, Nadine. The situation is trying, I grant, and what is worrying you, far from growing less, is going to be more of a problem from year to year. The new vibrant spirit that animates the mode is taking possession of it. A catastrophe? Or a blessing?

—*VOGUE* (JANUARY 4, 1930)

Somehow it seems to defy common sense, maybe even sanity, to stand in the middle of what looks like the collapse of your life, with your dreams, your achievements, your very sense of self in tatters, and say aloud, "Oh, lucky me, I get to reinvent my whole life! I get to downsize like Goldilocks, to find the perfect fit between my reduced circumstances and sense of well-being. Happy day!"

Yet if you look around, time and again you will see that with a strong sense of survival and a determination to find your authentic path, lucky is exactly what you are. I will never forget a conversation I had with Marianne Williamson, who told me the most dangerous prayer was praying that the Divine Plan would now take the place of the life I had planned. "You'll be standing in rubble before the week's out." And how right she was. I've known it to happen in a day. One minute you're on top of the world, and the next the world has crashed around your ankles. When you look up calling for God's help, you might discover the wrecking ball descending upon you from Heaven.

Having enough money, basking in that really tenuous sense of security, having your life work out pretty much as you planned it can be great, but it can also be seductive. Why would you stop to think about whether or not you are on the right path, if the path seems to be paying off? There's something about that step-by-step rhythm of things—it's the psychic equivalent of munching on one potato chip after the next. We enjoy continuous progression and therefore derive a positive sense of accomplishment that comes from an uninterrupted march through everyday life.

Sometimes this sense of accomplishment is real. Sometimes it's every bit as positive and productive as it seems; an honest expression of your true dreams, goals, and values.

Sometimes it's not.

After a few years of unstinting time, creative energy, emotion, and effort, a good friend found herself a top television network executive, living on the thirtieth floor of a New York apartment building with a 180-degree panoramic view of the skyline. It literally seemed that she had the world at her feet, and in some ways she did.

Then came a shake-up at her company that reverberated throughout the industry. She was initially consumed with exactly the kind of panic, shame, and desperation we all feel at times. But as the ax fell, she confessed that, to her amazement, she secretly felt...relieved.

She'd been so busy burning herself out at both ends as a "success," she hadn't allowed herself to realize that she really wasn't enjoying it. She didn't like the pace, the superficial lifestyle, the corporate politics; every fiber of her being was screaming No as she considered other job offers from other networks. She forced herself to examine this intuitive negative response and realized that while she might have had the talent for her line of work, she definitely did not have the temperament.

Without the kind of money she was making, she had to find a cheaper place to live. One decision led to another, and now, ten years later, she is living in a lovely small university town and teaching, happier than she has ever been in her life, having found a way to express both her talents and her personality in a way that finally feels "right."

As much as we hate to admit it, often the lack of money pushes us where we really wanted to go, but didn't have the courage to go on our own.

I always love finding the continuing thread of failure preceding success in life when I unravel the colorful skein of famous women's lives. *Jane Eyre* and *Wuthering Heights* would have never been written if the Brontë sisters hadn't lost positions as governesses or failed miserably in opening a small school. Louisa May Alcott was a wretched failure as a writer of adult fiction and reluctantly agreed to write a children's magazine serial called *Little Women* so she wouldn't have to move back home to her family after enjoying independence in Boston.

Can you think of a financial problem that forced an issue you can now see needed to be dealt with? Did you ever have the incentive to turn your passion into a business because you were let go at the office? Did a painful divorce challenge you to begin to take care of yourself financially? Did you ever get a speeding ticket that forced you to slow down and avoid a highway pileup? Strange as it may seem, more blessings come to us unbidden than we know.

"The success or failure of a life, as far as posterity goes, seems to lie in the more or less luck of seizing the right moment of escape," Alice James wrote in 1891. And Babe, no matter what has happened to shake your confidence, suspend your disbelief for a moment and consider that you may have just found your great escape.

The Thrill of Thrift

Sleep Is Your First Defense

*I reached for sleep and drew it round me like a blanket
muffling pain and thought together in the merciful dark.*

— MARY STEWART

Fancy an early night, dear? Oh goody, me, too. That's
because I've learned that an early night will temporarily ease just about whatever it is you're supposed to be
facing and can't yet. Beatrix Potter described feminine fatigue as being "worn to a raveling," and I don't know a
woman today dealing with her own economic crisis who
isn't feeling raggedy and threadbare.

There is something pleasant about the kind of physical
tiredness that comes after an afternoon of cleaning closets
or planting rosebushes, but financial fatigue is so emotionally draining, no amount of sleep at night seems to refresh
or revive you. Dealing with debt, day after day, is debilitating. What's more, this kind of emotional exhaustion is
laced with just enough distress and desperation that it poisons you slowly but doesn't kill you off. Which is why I
was delighted to discover that the editors of *House Beautiful*
advised their readers in 1942,

> Your value as an American woman [or civilized
> woman] depends on how you slept last night. If you
> slept badly, it is very likely that you are discouraged

and pessimistic about the future. If you woke this morning unrefreshed, chances are you didn't do very good work today, that you weren't as efficient as you should have been.

You know all of this is so. You know it the sure way—from all the practical experience of observing that your good days are preceded by good nights. So it is no stretch of the imagination to claim that sound sleep is our first defense. For in the months, and maybe years, that lie ahead of us we cannot fall prey to fatigue. The life that stretches ahead of each of us offers no place for pessimism, irritability or inefficiency.

This is great stuff, because it's so true. What impresses me about women's editorials in the first half of the twentieth century, through two world wars and the Great Depression, is that the morale of women was deemed to be *very* important. I've often said that women are the emotional thermostat for their families and that when Mama ain't happy, ain't nobody happy. Nowhere is this more certain than when a woman is worried about money. Financial fretting is so dangerously depleting of a woman's natural resources because you've got the major body circuitry in overdrive: Your mind won't stop racing over the bills and future, projecting what will happen; your heart is heavy because you feel inherently that somehow *you* have failed those you love who depend upon you; your body is physically drained of its vitality because you're probably not eating very healthily, or taking vitamins, or exercising. You're the walking wounded, one crisis away from crashing and burning.

So it behooves all of us to take care of Mama in the most immediate way possible, which means at least three nights a week, in bed by 9 PM. If you can make this a priority, everybody's going to feel better, especially you.

And this is the way you do it—by creating a personal

bedtime ritual, just as you did for your children when they were little. Begin with a long, lingering perfumed steam soak in a dimly lit bathroom. When you return all warm and glowing, it should be to a welcoming room, the bed pulled down, with a hot-water bottle in between the layers. Now don your rosebud jersey jammies or comfy nightgown and sleep socks. Prepare a lovely warm drink. Rabbits did not suffer from insomnia, as Beatrix Potter pointed out in her Victorian adventures of Peter Rabbit, because "the effect of eating too much lettuce is *soporific*." I love that wonderful old-fashioned word, which means "inducing drowsiness." Victorian mothers knew that a nighttime sip of lettuce tisane works wonders. Here's what to do: Take a few washed leaves of any lettuce variety, bring to a boil in a saucepan filled with a cup of water, then take the mixture off the flame and let it steep for ten minutes. Add a drop of peppermint extract, or stir with a sprig of fresh mint, and hippety-hop, sip your way to dreamland. I keep a small pitcher on my night table, to sip in the middle of the night if I wake up.

On early nights, I try to limit the reading to twenty minutes, just enough to get me drowsy. If you share your home with others, it may take a bit of rearranging to get an early night, but everyone benefits in the morning.

"There is a fatigue so great that the body cries, even in its sleep," the choreographer Martha Graham confessed. But it's the muffled sobs while awake that break the spirit. If they're yours, time for a little snooze.

There's a reason they call it downtime. It's so we can get back up. Blessings on your blankey, baby.

Million Dollar Baby

FRANKIE DUNN: You forgot the Rule. Now what
 is the Rule?
MAGGIE FITZGERALD: Keep my left up?
FRANKIE DUNN: ...is to protect yourself at all
 times. Now, what is the rule?
MAGGIE FITZGERALD: Protect myself at all times.
FRANKIE DUNN: Good. Good.

— *MILLION DOLLAR BABY* (2004)

Have you seen the 2004 Academy Award–winning movie *Million Dollar Baby* starring Hilary Swank as Maggie Fitzgerald, a thirtysomething "white trash" waitress who dreams of slinging punches instead of hash as a professional female boxer? Director Clint Eastwood is her reluctant but eventual trainer and mentor, Frankie Dunn; and Morgan Freeman is Eddie "Scrap-Iron" Dupris, the ex-champ philosopher who now runs Frankie's shabby gym. (All three won Oscars, and the film won the Best Picture award.) This cinematic Holy Trinity holds a special place in my cinematherapy collection because they've taught me that it's not the times you're beat, bloodied to a pulp, and down for the count that matter, but the times you get up again, with legs like jelly, dazed and dizzy at what life can throw at you. But, sweet Lord, at least you're standing in between the sways and swoons.

I love Maggie Fitzgerald because she's so honest.

Stripped to the marrow and heroic in her determination to make a better life for herself:

> I'm 32, Mr. Dunn, and I'm here celebrating the fact that I spent another year scraping dishes and waitressing which is what I've been doing since 13, and according to you, I'll be 37 before I can even throw a decent punch, which I have to admit, after working on this speed bag for a month, may be the God's simple truth. Another truth is my brother's in prison, my sister cheats on welfare by pretending one of her babies is alive, my daddy's dead and my momma weighs 312 lbs. If I was thinking straight, I'd go back home, find a used trailer, buy a deep fryer and some Oreos. Problem is, this is the only thing I ever felt good doing. If I'm too old for this, then I got nothing. That enough truth to suit you?

This is what crushing debt, foreclosure, and the threat of bankruptcy feel like as you weigh your financial options and try to get clear on what's possible, what's probable, and, finally, what isn't. Past-due notices, threatening letters, and phone calls come at you like phantoms, ready to knock your lights out, and every day you know that it's coming for you. "Frankie likes to say that boxing is an unnatural act, that everything in boxing is backwards," Eddie tells us. "Sometimes the best way to deliver a punch is to step back . . . But step back too far and you ain't fighting at all."

The biggest backstep that any of us can take is the thought of bankruptcy or foreclosure. The word *bankruptcy* used to be one of those whispered words we always caught the tail end of when we walked into the kitchen when the extended family came visiting and all the mothers huddled together as they were cooking. But bankruptcy didn't happen to anybody you knew; it was always Aunt Mary's friend. Now everybody is trying to reorganize their financial lives (which is what bankruptcy actually is, after all), including forty-six states and General Motors, by whatever legal means available. For years, GM's motto was "What's good for General Motors is good for America." We might want to think about that for a moment.

Actually, bankruptcy is the last thing that any woman wants to think about. But we need to woman-up to the truth.

According to a study done by Harvard's Elizabeth Warren and her daughter, attorney Amelia Warren Tyagi, more women will be fighting for their fiscal lives this year by filing for bankruptcy than will graduate from college, suffer a heart attack, or be diagnosed with cancer. The greatest number of the newly bankrupted will be single (or divorced) women with children. The other large percentage of personal bankruptcies are families devastated by the medical costs of a chronic illness.

"Sometimes things don't go according to plan. Sometimes, even when you are doing your best to put everything together, the pieces just don't work. Maybe you get laid off, and it takes months to find another job. Or maybe you get divorced, and your ex leaves you with a cranky cat and a pile of bills. Or maybe your business partner takes off to get in touch with his inner wildebeest or maybe a refrigerator falls on your foot. We get it," Warren and Tyagi reassure us in their wise and compassionate *All Your Worth: The Ultimate Lifetime Money Plan.* "There are times when bad things happen to good people, times when it seems like you just can't catch a break."

And when this happens, the one thing you need to do is practice the Million Dollar Baby's first rule: Protect yourself. Deciding to declare bankruptcy's not an action to be taken lightly. Bankruptcy is not the easy, painless fix to your financial problems. In fact, it is considered one of the five most negative "life-altering" events that can happen in a person's life, along with disability, divorce, and a death.

In her unflinching memoir *On the Couch*, Lorraine Bracco describes what it was like landing the part of Dr. Jennifer Melfi, the mobster Tony Soprano's psychiatrist on the legendary HBO drama *The Sopranos* in 1999. This was also the year she filed for personal bankruptcy, which she describes as the lowest point of her life. Lorraine had been fighting for custody of her daughter Stella with actor Harvey Keitel for five years. Although she won custody, the legal fees beat her to a pulp. The surreal juxtaposition of praise and shame simultaneously was a nightmare, and Lorraine fell into a deep clinical depression. "It was horrifying and embarrassing: getting foreclosure notices, lawyers knocking on your door," Lorraine explained in an interview with the *New York Times* (January 1, 2006). "It was basically, who do you pay at the end of the month. You have to pay the mortgage. You have to pay the taxes, food and electricity and the lawyers."

If your back is truly against the wall and there is nowhere else to turn, here are a few things to know before you begin considering your future. There are two types of bankruptcy: Chapter 7, which is an exoneration or relief from the obligation of paying your debts; and Chapter 13, which is a reorganization of your debts and payment plan. A Chapter 7 bankruptcy stays on your credit report for ten years; Chapter 13, for seven. But really, the truth is that filing for bankruptcy is a life sentence, for the next time you apply for a loan, a mortgage, or a credit card you will have to check the box that says "Have you ever filed for bankruptcy?" Skipping that box is a criminal offense, so get ready to explain your situation.

"I went to go lease a car, and it became a trauma," Lorraine explains. "I said to the rental car people: 'This is a done deal.' And they said, 'We are sorry. We are great fans, but we are not going to lease you the car.'"

Not everything is covered under the bankruptcy laws, so if you pay spousal or child support, some student loans, back taxes, damages owed as the result of an accident, criminal fines or penalties, or new charges to credit cards forty days before filing, you will still be obligated for these debts.

Much like the question *Should I marry him?* asking *Should I file for bankruptcy?* does not have an easy answer. Pray about your finances. Ask for Guidance and Grace to stay on the path of peace and plenty. Seek the advice of a professional bankruptcy attorney and research the topic. Money speaks its own language. Look for advice that you can use and *understand*, and consider the source. In their comforting and easy-to-understand book *All You're Worth*, authors Warren (a chaired professor at Harvard Law School and the chief adviser to the National Bankruptcy Review Commission) and Tyagi (a respected financial consultant and journalist for American Public Radio's *Marketplace*) tell us to "never trust a bill collector" and "stay away from Credit Counselors." But most important, don't hide in shame.

"If financial troubles come your way, you may find yourself feeling isolated, overcome with feelings of embarrassment and shame. In a society where people speak publicly about everything from their struggles with alcoholism to their efforts to get pregnant, financial trouble remains the great last taboo."

But the authors reassure us that in these difficult economic times, "a person is now more likely to file for bankruptcy than file for divorce! You may not know, but scattered among the folks in your grocery store, your office, your church or synagogue, and even your own family, are men and women just like you—people who have done their best and who are now in financial trouble."

So when you're down for the count, pray for the strength to just get back on your feet, and retreat to your corner to lick your wounds until you hear the Divine Trainer whisper the most important rule of all: Protect yourself. As Scrap-Iron Dupris puts it: "There is magic in fighting battles beyond endurance."

Bleak House

When Foreclosure Looms

I gave my love to the house forever.
I will come till I cannot come, I said,
And the house said, I will know.

—LOUISE TOWNSEND NICHOLL

The phone keeps ringing. The official letters keep coming and the e-mails flood in.

The bank wants its money, or it wants your home.

Again, the shame, the panic, the rage. Confusion courses through your body and crushes your soul. Your heart is pounding. You can't think. You can't stop thinking. You've failed and now the whole world will know it.

Twenty years ago, the word *foreclosure* conjured up Dickensesque images of the dastardly landlord in black hat and cape, twirling his handlebar mustache, laughing and rubbing his hands together with glee. Today it is the fresh face of your friendly mortgage banker, who assured you that an interest-only loan was the way to go. Or your bank manager, who won't return your calls for help while you are being dunned by the bank's collection department. If you and your family are facing foreclosure or the threat of foreclosure, you probably feel like the damsel being tied to the railroad tracks. Take heart, dear one, for facing these circumstances will be the bravest thing you have ever done, and remember, bad bank deals happen to both the wealthy and the good. Only the crooks seem to know how to stay one step ahead of the law, but don't get me started.

So know that you're not alone. The statistics are staggering: 10 percent of all homeowners are behind in their mortgages. FOR SALE signs are everywhere even though the nightly news is filled with stories about how no one can get a loan to buy them. Houses are "underwater" or "upside down" or in "negative equity" and other vivid phrases meaning that the house is worth less than the mortgage, so there's no hope of refinancing or paying off the debt even if you sold it today.

Losing a home feels like the end of the world, as stark as the command to leave Eden. I'm facing this challenge as I write. My divorce to the Englishman is final, but it was so expensive that I don't have enough money to pay for a new start here and continue to hold on to my English cottage dream.

Now is not the time for putting your head in the sand; now is the time for action. Right now you need to keep your wits about you, to use every aid at your disposal to save your house—or, if the worst has already happened, to find a new place full of love, hope, light, and space for your family to dream again. "If I were asked to name the chief benefit of the house, I should say: the house shelters day-dreaming," the French philosopher Gaston Bachelard tells us. "The house protects the dreamer, the house allows one to dream in peace."

A few years ago, a dear friend of mine was going through a very sad and acrimonious divorce. Her husband was playing hardball and put their house at risk for foreclosure. She desperately wanted to keep her children in the only house that they had ever known. Every inch of her house displayed her creativity and passion. The top borders of the white kitchen walls were stenciled with strawberries and vines; I remember Sandy telling me how her arms ached as she precariously perched on the ladder just one foot shy of being tall enough to do the job without pain. She decided to leave the blue-and-white gingham-checked custom curtains with the deep country ruffle that she had labored over with love and the 1950s stove with the griddle/broiler pan on top. When I asked her how she could leave what she had poured her heart and soul into, I'll never forget her answer; it has brought me a sense of calm concerning my own need to leave my beloved Newton's Chapel:

> The Universe comes knocking at our doors from time to time. Most often it brings us gifts of lasting joy: baby giggles, puppies that scuff the floor, and the laughter of friends around the table. Sometimes the gifts are temporary in nature, for a certain phase of your life, like your first home. We don't lose most things we love without warning. Fights over money, spending indiscretions, or the loss of a job or marriage are the warning signs that it is time to move on.
>
> I was so tortured about losing the house that I prayed night after night that the tug-of-war would end. One night I had a dream and in the middle of the tug-of-war with my husband, I heard a voice that said, "Just let go of the rope." If we recognize the signs we can move on peaceably. It is only when we hold on too tight that we exacerbate our own pain.

From the moment we were banished, daughter of Eve, loss has been part of the human experience, and relentless change is our only constant. Do everything you can to save your home. Remortgage, talk to your banker, your pastor, your family, and a lawyer. But first and foremost, have the courage to hold an intimate conversation with your heart. These are the questions that I asked myself to help me make my decision:

• How long has the stress of trying to hold on been taking a toll on my health and spirit?

- What percentage of my resources is being consumed by my mortgage?
- Can I sell my house and start fresh?
- Have I done everything I can to hold on?

If you can answer these questions for yourself, you should be able to find a clear vision for the next moves for yourself and your family. But let me sound a warning bell here: *It is very important during the process of foreclosure not to ignore the warning letters from your mortgage company.* At some point after you have received notice of the foreclosure, the bank can come in and evict you, and you have to leave within an hour or so. If the foreclosure is in process, make sure that you move your belongings to a new apartment or storage unit so they do not become the property of the bank.

If your next move is to move on, embrace it as an adventure. God knows I'm trying to follow my own advice. Change the image in your mind from Hester Prynne in *The Scarlet Letter*. The FOR SALE sign could become an emblem of a woman who is taking control of her life and walking away with dignity.

With regard to your new dwelling place, start with a realistic budget. Experts say your housing costs should be no more than 33 percent of your income, but that's a lot of money. Can you scale down and still be comfortable? If you have children and a spouse, get them all involved in creating your new life together. Most of all, when you leave the home you once loved, don't look back. The angels knew what they were talking about when they told Lot's wife not to look back at the home she was leaving or she'd turn into a pillar of salt. This wasn't a Divine rebuke. The salt was from her tears because she couldn't let go.

Taming Shame

Courage allows the successful woman to fail—
and learn powerful lessons—
from the failure—
So that in the end
She didn't fail at all.

—MAYA ANGELOU

During the nights when I rewind the internal movie in my head of where it all went wrong financially, trying to retrace the steps that led me here through impetuous choices, avoidance of choosing, blind faith, benign neglect, self-sabotage, naïveté, stubborn decisions, bad timing, stupid mistakes, bitter failures, deliberate detours, unexpected derailments, bungled efforts, whims of fate, perfectly plausible outcomes that were anything but, rejections, romantic fantasies, blasted good intentions, and just plain bad luck, it's enough to drive me stark raving mad. And it does. On those nights, the one thing that can soothe my soul like nothing else is imagining that Dr. Maya Angelou comforts me with her honey-dripped voice of Mother Courage: "You did then what you knew how to do. And when you knew better, you did better."

And with that thought, I can breathe again and sigh deeply into the pillow, pulling the covers over my shoulder as I return to sleep.

I thought a lot about that wisdom and shared it when a friend of mine came over for coffee the other day. She was

clearly nervous at the beginning, but soon I was struck
by her candor when she revealed that she wanted to get
my advice on reversing an irresponsible financial decision
she'd made years ago, the memory of which has followed
her like a black cloud and made her feel deeply ashamed.
She admitted that she hated telling anyone about her actions but after years of turning to food, alcohol, or com-
pulsive shopping to distract herself from the burning sensation of guilt, she knew that it was healthier and more
healing to deal with the feelings directly. I was writing a
book on finding financial serenity: What did I think of her
situation?

I had many mixed emotions during our talk. I am
hardly a financial expert, but I could be a comforting
sounding board for my friend and bear witness to the
process she was going through to get to her money truth. I
was deeply moved by her courage and the wisdom she had
learned the hard way, and I felt compassion that she was
in so much pain. Then, in an instant, I turned on myself
inwardly with a viciousness that shocked me; I got furious
at myself, because once upon a time I could have just written her a check to help get her out of her difficulty. We
would have broken open a good bottle of wine, toasted to
better times, and abracadabra, problem solved. Once more
smiles all around.

I used to write checks, for the whole world it seemed,
all the time. If there was a problem, either mine or anyone
else's in my intimate circle, including more than a hundred
charities or complete strangers on the phone with heart-
wrenching stories that got passed up the line to me, with a
wave of the hand I became Lady Bountiful. Money solves
so many problems, especially if you don't have any. And if
you do, money creates problematic situations you're meant
to solve with your other precious natural resources—time,
creative energy, emotion, as well as money. As soon as
there is money available, we forget that.

Ironically, the one really strong emotion my friend was

sure I'd have—disgust at her action—never occurred to me at all. I was too busy being disgusted with myself. I understood immediately why she had been tempted to make the mistake, and I was sorry to see how much extra suffering she was putting herself through by labeling it as so heinous rather than a relatable temptation.

By the end of our talk, my friend felt better, even though her external situation hadn't changed at all. By having the courage to talk honestly with someone who wouldn't judge her, she gave herself a chance to see that other people wouldn't automatically assess the situation the way she did. She also discovered that she was not the freak, the outcast, or the failure that she feared. By the end of the talk, my friend was using different words, less punitive and explosive phrases to describe her situation, and she had started thinking about actions she could take to minimize the damage to herself and others. We began damage-control brainstorming together; by late afternoon we had an action plan on reams of yellow legal pads, along with plenty of moist crumpled tissues as we cried our way to financial clarity. She cried from the sheer relief of no longer holding an untold story within her, and I cried from grief and self-loathing that had festered in the secretive money heartache I've kept buried so deeply; I'd done my best to keep my despair hidden from the world because I'd been so ashamed of the trouble I'd gotten myself into. I didn't know how or where to begin, but I knew the moment to start doing something had arrived.

"You did then, what you knew how to do," Maya Angelou reassured us both, and perhaps today this truth speaks to you as well. "And when you knew better, you did better."

The Thrill of Thrift

The Poetry Prescription

Poetry connects you to yourself, to the self that doesn't know how to talk or negotiate.

—RITA DOVE

We rarely see poetry anymore in women's publications, and yet women's lives are the stuff of poetry. Years ago, I remember discovering in a vintage *Good Housekeeping* (October 1925) an article called "The Poetry Cure." It suggested that when we're frazzled and frantic, meditating on a line or stanza of poetry can spiritually induce a sense of calm; I wrote a meditation on it in *Simple Abundance* (August 22). Being my own spiritual research-and-development guinea pig, I try everything I recommend to you—and I'm thrilled to remind you just how powerful the Poetry Prescription can be for you today. Well-spent moments that cost you next to nothing and bring a hush to your harried heart are waiting for you in your local library's poetry section. It's been a passionate palliative for me for many years. However, while trying to make sense of my money history, I found myself actually writing notes about my journey to sanity, serenity, and solvency using poetry in my accounts ledger. At first, I thought they were just word doodles; moodlings to release the inherent tension that budgets and account keeping triggered. Then I started listening, in between the lines.

Through poetry, the reading of it, but especially the writing of it, I've been able to slip past the conscious mind's sentries of fear and intimidation barricading my memory vault. With a pen and a few choice words, I signal *the way is clear* to the guerrilla truth squads, sent to bring me in from the cold, like a rogue spy. As with any task we might be putting off, we just need to distract our conscious mind long enough for us to begin. It's been my experience that only five engaged minutes primes the creative well and sends procrastination packing.

Many of us resist the power of poetry to illuminate our lives because we have such bad *"I heard a fly buzz when I died"* memories of high school English class (with apologies to Emily Dickinson). Get past it. You're cutting yourself off from one of life's sublime bliss triggers—and it doesn't cost a dime. But even more of us have an inferiority complex about poetry that we need to dispatch: We view it as an esoteric art that only the well educated, literate, and erudite can appreciate, preferably with an upper-class English accent. Interestingly, poets are the first to disagree, seeing themselves as everyday alchemists—for they know life's hours of lead are base metal waiting to be transmuted into wisdom's gold. The Russian poet Anzia Yezierska tells us, "The real thing creates its own poetry," and we know all too well how true this is.

But back to poetry as a prescription for whatever ails you.

Reaching for a poem to meditate upon when life gets harried is the reassuring remedy London-based television producer and presenter Daisy Goodwin recommends for all of us. Even a brief glance at her marvelous poetry anthologies will make a believer out of you. Take a dip in *101 Poems That Could Save Your Life: An Anthology of Emotional First Aid*; *101 Poems to Keep You Sane: Emergency Rationing for the Seriously Stressed*; and *101 Poems to Get You Through the Day (and Night)*. You'll feel better for them. These books are so addictive because Daisy Goodwin writes witty and insightful narratives linking the poems that are in turns upbeat, tongue-in-cheek, and serious, which makes you feel as if she's selected the perfect antidote for your particular crisis. I think when we are broken by life, we need to know that we're not alone. And to find someone's description of our sorrow in words arranged on a page is one of the most wondrous experiences any of us can have. Unless it's writing through our own sorrow until we discover a new voice that we recognize as our own.

A marvelous place for you to start exploring the idea of writing your own poems is with Pulitzer Prize– and National Book Award–winning poet Mary Oliver's *A Poetry Handbook*, which teases the poet in all of us to come forth. She explains many mysteries about poetry, reinforcing the truth that poetry is a craft as much as an art, and notes that revision (she revises her own poems forty to fifty times before they're finished) is the secret to not only good poetry but living authentically.

"Because poets feel what we're afraid to feel, venture where we're reluctant to go, we learn from their journeys without taking the same dramatic risks," the poet Diane Ackerman reassures us. "Think of all the lessons to be learned from deep rapture, danger, tumult, romance, intuition. But it's far too exhausting to live like that on a daily basis, so we ask artists to explore for us. Daring to take intellectual and emotional chances, poets live on their senses." Sometimes, "we need to be taught how and where to seek wonder, but it's always there, waiting, full of mystery and magic."

Try God

No one would remember the Good Samaritan if he'd only had good intentions. He had money as well.

— MARGARET THATCHER

Flipping through the TV channels recently, I heard the question posed by a televangelist: "Does God want you to be rich?" On another channel there was a Hollywood telethon to raise money for the ravaged survivors of the earthquake in Haiti. That really got me thinking about the spiritual life and whether God does want us to be wealthy. Well, I've been both rich and poor, and I can tell you I did a lot more good in the world when I was rich.

The question of whether God wants us to be rich makes most of us feel anxious, and I'm no exception. Has God graded me on how I handled my talents, resources, and gifts? Well, the truth is God doesn't have to because I already have. I wasn't a Good Stewardess—I was too scared of money, too scared of people's expectations of entitlement, too scared of the jolt that came from being a freelance writer one day and a millionairess the next and feeling as if I should know instinctively how to behave because I was a good, trusting woman with a big heart and a generous spirit. You know the expression "God won't give you any more than you can handle." Well, I discovered that goes with the good things in life as well as the crises. If you can't handle the money, fame, and success (which by the way are among the most difficult karmas, according to Buddhism), then you won't hold on to them.

The thing about backward glances is that they won't provide any insight if you're not going to be ruthlessly honest with yourself. And the truth is, I didn't go to the Almighty to ask for guidance in handling my wealth. It never crossed my mind because I was financially helping more than a hundred different nonprofits with the Simple Abundance Charitable Fund. I gave away over a million dollars and I could see the tangible evidence of good I was doing, whether it was a new home built by Habitat for Humanity or meals delivered to housebound patients with AIDS.

My not consulting God with the handling of my wealth was an enormous aberration for me. I begin and end each day in prayer and meditation and have for my entire adult life. I wouldn't think of writing a word without asking the Great Creator for assistance. I can't write on my own. What made me think I could become or stay rich on my own? It boggles my belief, and yet I did it. I conclude that this flouting of my intimate relationship with my Creator must be a vital part of my cautionary tale.

Let me go back and examine how things went for me in the wealth department when I was regularly consulting with God. When I was in my thirties and juggling being a freelance writer and working mother of a small child, I saw an advertisement from Tiffany for a gold pin that said TRY GOD. It was a fund-raiser for breast cancer, and I think it cost $25. Whatever the price, it was a lot of money for me then. But that pin spoke to my desire to help others, my dreams of wealth and reliance on Providence to steer my course. So I bought it and when it was delivered I was so enamored of it, you would have thought it was as costly as a twenty-four-carat diamond ring. It was beautifully packaged in the familiar tiny robin's-egg-blue box with the white satin ribbon. I stared at that packaging for a long time like a young child at Christmas. When I opened it, there was a blue pouch with the magic word imprinted on it in black. TIFFANY. I felt like Truman Capote's heroine Holly Golightly, who believed in the spiritual power of the most famous jewelry store in the world much the way the British believe in the soul-sustaining powers of tea and Irish Catholics in the miraculous healing powers of Holy Water from Lourdes. As Holly said on those days when life got her down: "What I've found does the most good is just to get into a taxi and go to Tiffany's. It calms me down right away, the quietness and the proud look of it; nothing very bad could happen to you there."

And truly that's how I felt whenever I opened my egg-blue felt pouch and took out my tiny golden TRY GOD pin—it became an emotional talisman of Grace, power, and wealth for me. I kept it on my desk and would finger it during the writing of *Simple Abundance*. I was convinced that someday I'd have the money to buy anything I wanted in Tiffany's, and that unshakable belief came true—though it took many years.

So why did I put the pouch away when I became wealthy? I must admit I'm still searching for the definitive answer to this question. Did I feel I didn't deserve this success so I didn't want to admit to it in the eyes of God? Did I fear God would disapprove of my behavior once I found wealth and take it away?

Maybe the question that makes us all so nervous isn't *Does God want us to be rich?* But *How do you want to learn the lesson that God does want you to be rich?* All alone through hardship, struggle, poverty, debt, and lack? Or through gratitude, prosperity, wisdom, financial serenity, joy, and Divine Grace?

"God is no White Knight who charges into the world to pluck us like distressed damsels from the jaws of dragons or diseases," Nancy Mairs observed in her memoir *Ordinary Time*. "God chooses to become present to and through us. It is up to us to rescue one another."

And money helps. So if we are ready to rescue, and be rescued, God really does want us to have more than enough money to do so.

In God We Trust

God does do finances. In fact, turning our finances over to God's care has often been a route not to poverty but to prosperity. God is an expert at husbanding resources. God is an expert at increasing the worth of what we hold. To involve God with our finances is to ask that source of all abundance to have a hand in our affairs.

—JULIA CAMERON

You're a little past the panic state. You've grieved, you've surely railed, and maybe some things have become a little clearer as your anger's settled and the fog of denial has lifted.

However, you're a long way from having a real plan or having the peace of mind that a realistic plan, based on the life you really want, can provide.

So what do you do now?

Well, this is where "Good Orderly Direction"—or God—comes in, as the brilliant, compassionate writer Julia Cameron has shared in her groundbreaking work on creativity as a spiritual path. If you're uncomfortable asking a Higher Power to help you with your finances, the idea of Spirit as good, orderly direction is very reassuring. "It is during hard times that we come to rely on God and that is a reliance that we can encourage in ourselves at all times. We do not need to be broke to ask God to help us with our money," she writes in *Faith and Will: Weathering the Storms in Our Spiritual Lives.* "We can ask God to make us attuned to our financial seasons, to cue us when we are free to spend and when we should curtail our spending. We can ask God to take away our fear of financial insecurity and to direct us as to where, from what corner, our prosperity might come from."

Many women acknowledge that their spirituality is a great part of their life and yet, when being frank, will admit they don't feel comfortable mixing money management with God. It just feels unseemly. Cameron admits, "This is an area where I do not want to let God run my life for me. I am afraid lest his will for me be less abundant. And so I say, 'Sure, God, you can run the seasons and the planets and this green earth, but you cannot run my financial affairs.' You see where my faith has holes in it." However, what is faith without gaping holes? Perhaps I chafe at increasing the flow of money in my life—instead of asking to learn how to successfully manage the money I have and increase it with loving diligence. For that I need more wisdom. And to achieve more wisdom, I need to ask for it, to pray affirmatively that good, orderly direction is my daily bread, and then to give thanks.

It doesn't seem to make sense that sitting down and figuring out exactly how much money you have—and how much money you need—is the way to feel more peaceful, even prosperous, but ironically, that's just how it works. Somehow until we know, down to the last copper cent, what we have, what we owe, what we need, what we earn, what we can save *before* we decide what we can spend, anxiety increases in direct proportion to our imprecision no matter what the balance is in our checkbook.

No woman I've talked to about this reckoning ever felt worse off after doing this, and almost all of them felt tremendously better. No matter how bad the situation is, at least now they know what it is. We derive an enormous sense of pride and relief from looking in all the dark corners and realizing that we have survived the shock. No matter how bad the situation may be, knowing the facts allows us to stop the hemorrhaging of our emotional energies. We've heard the age-old aphorism "God helps those who help themselves" since infancy, but now we can see its evidence. When we frankly assess our situation then ask Spirit to help us, our creative problem-solving abilities kick in. We may think we'll never get that blockage flowing again on our own. But after we ask for the grace, the wisdom, and the next step, possible solutions begin to float through our minds—and our budgets. Our deep breath becomes a sigh of relief.

When we invite good, orderly direction into the handling of our financial affairs, we find that the mundane is endowed with a spiritual arc of synchronicity and serenity. As I move my hand across the big yellow pad, writing columns of numbers, I begin to feel a sense of safety. "We begin to feel that God is doing for us what we cannot do for ourselves," Julia Cameron shares. "We must believe that we are being cared for and very carefully. We must believe that we are being watched over, that there is a Divine plan of goodness for us."

Getting the Hell Out of Dodge

We shall hardly notice in a year or two.
You can get accustomed to anything.

— EDNA ST. VINCENT MILLAY

The really *amazing* part of our human journey is that we *can* get accustomed to anything if it's part of our daily round long enough—thought patterns, schedules, intimidation, abuse, misery, anger, neglect, worry, hopelessness, illness, clutter, cowering, self-loathing, dirty dishes piled up in the kitchen sink, first drink of the day at noon, junk food because it's fast and cheap, shudders when the phone rings, bills that go unpaid until the collector pounds, or shipping off that charm bracelet with all the kids' and grandkids' names in a lousy prepaid envelope to pay for a vital prescription.

Getting used to whatever rotten circumstances we find ourselves in is a cunning coping mechanism when we're overwhelmed by lack and loss. It's also a convenient coping device if we're in a chain gang. But it's not a very pleasant plan; nor is it a creative, inspiring, or spiritually uplifting strategy. Still, everyone here has had moments when the only plan we want for the day, week, month, or the rest of our lives is the sure thing.

To coping. Many thanks, and may we give you all the credit you so richly deserve.

Now let's get the hell out of Dodge.

My God, as I write this essay I'm forced to realize that I've been here at this desk, in this corner of a living room that's not my own, for eleven months, having to regain every morning the one foot of lost ground yanked from beneath me while I slept. One fire gets put out and another section of wild brush takes flame. I save up for an apartment of my own and the divorce attorney needs to be paid; you know the drill. Through it all I have tried to remain calm, upbeat, positive, because that's who I really am, but you know what I also am? I'm itching for a showdown at the OK Corral, because things are so not okay anymore.

Today might not be the day you feel like exploding and throwing this book across the room. But that day might come, so put a Post-it in place 'cause when you get there it's better to rip off a Post-it than half a head of hair, your own or otherwise.

Take a deep breath. Simmer down, now. Simmer down. This is all good. We know that there's still a pulse — and thank goodness, because to tell the truth I was getting a little concerned at how resigned we both were getting with our fate and our place. But this anger is the life spark continuing, pressing forward. Anger is as much a spiritual grace as her sister, passion. It helps me to think of my emotions as women — Anger's nearly six feet tall, with flaming red hair, a gorgeous Pre-Raphaelite nymph. She's stunning, in the fullest sense of the word. And most of the time, she's not all fired up; she's as contained and on target as a heat-seeking missile. In fact, Anger's part of your own personal nuclear deterrent system. Start to think of her differently, as the blessing she is. Anger will move you onward and upward.

Anger is the Divine Energy that fuels the growth spurt. If you've been around small children, you know that every so often they just have a meltdown; they cry and yell, stomp and scream for no apparent reason. Tantrum over, they eat like crazy and then drop like a stone and sleep all night long. Next morning you go to put the snow-suit or shoes on and they've grown two inches. Growth spurts hurt. Your legs ache and your back feels like you've had a yoke of oxen pulling you down. Your Authentic Self, your soul made visible, is stretching now and looking for the first wagon train out of Dodge City, doesn't matter if it's heading to Deadwood in the Dakotas or Tombstone Territory. What matters is that she is in motion.

It's the same way with Anger. Making peace with our past in order to prepare for the plenty in our future and trigger serenity in our present may require a little fury. When we had our personal economic meltdown, we were first in shock; then we grieved, took stock of our situation, maybe got really depressed, and now we're angry. How did we get here? How did this happen? What were we thinking? Today (or whenever you want to read this meditation), past verb tense *only* is permitted.

"I don't know if fury can compete with necessity as the mother of invention," the extraordinary Gloria Steinem tells us. "But I recommend it."

So do I. This much I know for sure: I've *never* had a hissy fit that I've regretted, but I've had plenty of regrets because I pushed that redheaded hussy down when all she was doing was covering my back. So try it, don't deny it. Get real, get angry, and get going.

Part Five
All About Eve

Eve. Eve the Golden Girl, the Cover Girl, the Girl Next Door, the Girl on the Moon. Time has been good to Eve. Life goes where she goes. She's the profiled, covered, revealed, reported. What she eats and what she wears and whom she knows and where she was and when and where she's going. Eve. You all know All About Eve. What can there be to know that you don't know?

—ADDISON DEWITT, *ALL ABOUT EVE* (A 1950 FILM BY JOSEPH L. MANKIEWICZ)

Tomorrow Is Another Day

Child, it is a very bad thing for a woman to face the worst that can happen to her, because after she's faced the worst, she can't ever really fear anything again.

—MARGARET MITCHELL

Fiddle-dee-dee. Which shall it be? We've agreed, we're getting out of Dodge, but where are we headed, Deadwood or Tombstone?

Now, there's a choice. It's not exactly the fresh start I was thinking about, unless you consider six feet under the right direction. Still, you know that's how it feels when you are rock-bottom broke. You may have been looking for a job for the past year and your benefits have run out. Perhaps you're now faced with such extreme measures of "relief" as food stamps, foreclosure, bankruptcy, borrowing money from family, selling all your possessions, or discovering you have no place to live but in temporary housing.

In our hearts we're already standing at the grave site hearing the minister intone, "In the midst of life we are in death," and grabbing a fistful of dirt to throw upon the coffin of everything we've worked so hard for, a life that we cherished.

But wait a minute. While it may be true that in the

midst of life these days all of us are in debt, may I suggest that you do something else with that fistful of soil? Raise it to Heaven and declare an oath that you are a survivor. Here's how another heroine put it (with poetic license) when everything in her life had turned south, in the truest sense of the expression.

> As God is my witness, and God is my witness, the Bankers and Bailiffs aren't going to lick me. I'm going to live through this, and when it's over, I'm never going to be hungry again. No, nor any of my folks...if I have to outsmart the devil himself, as God is my witness, I'm never going to be hungry again!

Gentle Reader, you've met Katie Scarlett O'Hara Hamilton Kennedy Butler, haven't you? The heroine of Margaret Mitchell's 1936 Civil War epic *Gone with the Wind*, which became the 1939 blockbuster starring Clark Gable and Vivien Leigh as the star-crossed lovers who battle the Yankees with as much determination as they battle each other. *GWTW* is one of the most beloved films of all time. Why did it strike such a chord? Yes, we admired Scarlett's sixteen-inch waist. Yes, we loved that kiss, but this movie exploded into our national psyche for far weightier reasons. Coming at a time when the Great Depression had devastated the lives of millions of families, who had nothing left but their breath, people needed iconic heroes and heroines to show us how to put one step in front of the other—even if it was at a bread line—and pledge to the Almighty that they might be down but they were not defeated.

When I was younger, I took these moments at face value. I yearned to have Scarlett's "gumption" and "true grit" to make life become the way she wanted it to be. I admired her unyielding intensity and was convinced her strength sprang from her stubborn refusal to submit to unpleasant realities, such as seeing the man she had set her heart upon, Ashley Wilkes, marry his cousin Melanie and not her.

However, I recently re-read the novel (what a bathtub treat!), and now I see her through slightly different eyes. Near the very end of the story, there is a moment when all her emotional defenses fall away. She fully realizes that she actually never loved Ashley, that she had really loved Rhett because he loved her truly, madly, and deeply in all her glorious contradictions, and that this fundamental mistake had caused all of the "optional" suffering for herself and so many other people that hadn't already been imposed by the war.

Facing those kinds of truths really takes guts. Acknowledging them takes grace. Getting up the next day and starting your life over from scratch takes even more than courage—it takes gumption, a potent blend of perseverance, patience, and persistence. If you're like me, there are big mistakes to admit to, and even if most of them were made with the best of intentions, now in hindsight you see how these devastating choices resulted in ripples of remorse and ruptures of the landscape of your life.

The area I have struggled with most is money. I used to think it was love. But now I know that if I had understood money and the impact it has on our everyday lives, I wouldn't have made the wrong choices in affairs of the heart. And I have to tell you, best-selling self-help author I might well be, but I've been unable to help myself. You have no idea how terrifying it is to rerun the reel in my mind of the money I wasted, opportunities I didn't take, truths I refused to acknowledge, personal dreams always put aside for other people's preferences. The reel of regrets is in Technicolor, and all the good I've accomplished fades to black. Perhaps the reason I am so passionate about your taking care of yourself and getting yourself on the top of the list of your own life and understanding that your happiness is not a frivolous yearning is that I have not been able to do that for myself yet. But I'm trying.

Each day brings a new set of circumstances, challenges, and changes. We meet them with true grit, amazing grace, gumption, guts, and gratitude. In these fraught economic times, trust me, these feminine natural resources are more precious than gold. They are the sweat equity for your financial serenity on the path to peace and plenty.

Still, as Scarlett says, "I can't think about that right now. If I do, I'll go crazy. I'll think about that tomorrow."

Going crazy won't help us win this private civil war between our wants and our needs. So when you sense you need a break from all the hard work you've been doing, know that we all need to think about some things tomorrow, not today. Instead, think about this image, courtesy of Rhett Butler: "He had never known such gallantry as Scarlett O'Hara going forth to conquer the world in her mother's velvet curtains and the tail feathers of a rooster."

The Second
Mrs. de Winter

*She was, or so it seemed to me, bathed in a strange
mystery. She held a secret — not one, not two, but many
that she withheld from many people but would give to one
who loved her well.*

— DAPHNE DU MAURIER

Last night, knowing that I would be writing about England and forced to fit memory to the page, it's not
surprising that in my troubled half sleep I returned to
Newton's Chapel, standing outside the gates, mystified by
the loss of my happiness there, so abruptly cut short, much
the same way the nameless heroine of Daphne du Maurier's mesmerizing 1938 novel *Rebecca* returns to one of the
most famous literary settings, seeking to unravel a spellbinding mystery of a house, a marriage, and a haunting:

> Last night I dreamt I went to Manderley again. It
> seemed to me I stood by the iron gate leading to
> the drive, and for a while I could not enter, for the
> way was barred to me. There was a padlock and
> chain upon the gate. I called in my dream to the
> lodge-keeper, and had no answer, and peering closer
> through the rusted spokes of the gate I saw that the
> lodge was uninhabited...

No smoke came from the chimney, and the little lattice windows gaped forlorn. Then, like all dreamers, I was possessed of a sudden with supernatural powers and passed like a spirit through the barrier before me...

Now, if you haven't read or seen Alfred Hitchcock's film version of *Rebecca* I'm not going to spoil it for you, but it's an incredible jolt, especially when viewed as a parable of a woman's relationship with money.

Cue lights, music, and popcorn. A shy, socially awkward young woman (Joan Fontaine) working as a paid traveling companion to a rich, odious American meets a handsome, wealthy, sophisticated widower twice her age, Maxim de Winter (Laurence Olivier), in Monte Carlo. He proposes to her within a week. She accepts (who wouldn't?), and then they return to Maxim's stately home known as Manderley on the Cornwall coast of Britain. Suddenly the second Mrs. de Winter finds herself swept into the glittering world of English upper-class money and luxury—yet living in the palpable shadow of her husband's dead, beautiful first wife, the exquisite Rebecca, whom everyone adored, including the Gothic housekeeper Mrs. Danvers, who loved Rebecca as if she were her own child.

I could see she despised me, marking with all the snobbery of her class that I was no great lady, that I was humble, shy, and diffident. Yet there was something besides scorn in those eyes of hers, something surely of positive dislike, or actual malice?

Are the hairs on the back of your neck standing up yet? Just wait. A fascinating footnote to the making of the movie, which was the English director Hitchcock's first Hollywood film and was named Best Picture in 1940, was the battle royal between the director and the producer,

David O. Selznick, over the point of view. In one of Selznick's memos to Hitchcock, he emphasizes that every "thing that the girl does in the book, her reactions of running away from the guests, and the tiny things that indicate her nervousness and her self-consciousness and her gaucherie are all so brilliant in the book that every woman who has read it has adored the girl and has understood her psychology, has cringed with embarrassment for her, yet has understood exactly what was going through her mind...'I know just how she feels...I know just what she's going through...'"

And it's true. Most of us do identify with "Daphne de Winter" (as Hitchcock called the character) and her emotional struggle as she tries to feel at home in an unfamiliar world.

We all have dreams of wealth, success, or professional acclaim, and much of the appeal is in the very fact that achieving those dreams would help us create a world completely different from our current humdrum everyday life. But what I've learned to my great shock is that the initial adjustment into the fairy-tale lifestyle is much harder than I could have ever imagined.

This might be because none of us imagine what daily life will be like when we start our own café, move to the coast, open that bed-and-breakfast. One of the best pieces of aspirational advice I know is to imagine what your ideal day looks and *feels* like from morning to night. Who are you with? Where are you eating breakfast? Do you love to cook? How high do you want the island in your kitchen to be? What is the view from your porch or upstairs deck? Do you like to garden? Are you getting tired of the maintenance that goes with the joys of homeownership? Do you prefer big windows or cozy nooks? Once you start reimagining your life, you'll see that Heaven really is in the details.

No one ever tells us that two-comma successes and six-zero sudden windfalls bounce us out of our comfort zones at warp speed and push us into a new world that requires courage as well as clarity, confidence, and calmness in order to make the unfamiliar choices so necessary to protect ourselves. Not having our dreams come true immediately may drive us crazy and seem unfair, but the pace of peace and plenty is a blessing much to be desired. We need to learn how to read the fine print and have the time to build a team of wise advisers.

When the world suddenly changes, when our old habits don't quite fit and we haven't had time to make new ones, it can be very disconcerting. I went from writing a book by myself at home, in between school runs, to overnight being expected to run a small company. But nobody's expectations were more impossible to live up to than my own. If we are not prepared for the transitional phase of success, it's easy to interpret our discomfort as a sign that we really don't belong in this new world or at this level of success. We believe we don't deserve it, that it's a fluke, we're a fraud, and it will all disappear tomorrow.

And you know what? As long as we secretly think that way, even if we appear polished on the surface, our subconscious mind will set in motion circumstances that make sure it does all disappear, whether through bad advice from others, or following our own bad advice because we don't know better and are embarrassed to ask.

But the reverse is just as true. When we become comfortable with our authenticity, when we respect the woman the rest of the world sees and honor her, our ability to self-destruct diminishes, too. That's why I love the moment when Joan Fontaine announces: *"I am Mrs. de Winter now."* That's the moment when she claims her power, her right to be there, and redefines what being Mrs. de Winter really means for her.

Thrills and chills await you, my darling. Your Mrs. de Winter moment is waiting in the wings and mustn't be missed.

She Who Must Not
Be Named

*She had the loaded handbag of someone who camps out
and seldom goes home, or who imagines life must be full
of emergencies.*

— MAVIS GALLANT

To write the truth about women and money is to write about fear, loneliness, abandonment, and shame. These are awfully difficult companions to hang out with—more tequila (with the worm) shots in a dark dive at noon than canapés and champagne on a beach at sunset. More than a decade ago, I spent an entire year meditating on the secret wounds of a woman's soul—betrayal, marital indifference, and self-loathing—in my book *Something More: Excavating Your Authentic Self.* It wasn't fun, even if by the time I finished it I was astonished by its truthfulness and my unexpected courage. As I remember I was on a tight deadline, the clock was ticking, the editor was pacing, and the editor's assistant needed to know how many galleys she should be ordering.

I remember saying to myself: *Just tell the damn truth, Sarah, and get it over with.*

So I did. However, to my surprise there's not one word about money in there. Was that because I had millions of dollars when I wrote *Something More*? This is now: Money is very much on my mind. More exactly, why don't I have any of it left to take care of myself?

How about fear, loneliness, abandonment, and shame?

"Life has a way of bringing you back to places you thought you had left for good," concedes the psychologist William Bridges, author of the groundbreaking book *Transitions: Making Sense of Life's Changes*, with the irony, wisdom, and grace that come only when you suddenly discover that you're circling back upon yourself. For decades, William Bridges had been a pioneer in the study of personal and business transitions. But when his wife of thirty-seven years, Mondi, died from breast cancer, Bridges felt not only bereft but purposeless, unable to help himself. "All the things that I had written about transitions—the very things that people had said were so helpful to them—now felt strangely unreal to me. I wondered, *How could I ever have tried to pass myself off as an expert on transition?* I felt now that my words had totally failed to match in depth the *experience* of actually being in transition."

If a change is deep, the ripples of transition can be far reaching, lasting for years. William Bridges explains that a person can feel not only that a piece of reality is gone, but "that everything that had seemed to be reality was simply an enchantment. With the spell broken, life can look so differently that we hardly recognize it."

Or ourselves. Consider the aftershocks at either extreme of life's financial spectrum—losing your home in a flood or winning the lottery. Both events strip you of the familiar. Whether the change of clothes you put on comes from an emergency shelter or from a chic boutique you never felt entitled enough to browse in before, the result is the same. We do not feel or look like ourselves. Even if we still answer to our names, we begin a wrenching process of separating from our previous identities. Think of it as psychic identity theft. We've been snatched, mind and body, from all that was customary, from the person we were just yesterday. The only entity who knows what's going on is your Soul, and when was the last time you had a good long chat with Her?

And the specter who haunts us all? She who snatched our personalities, our accomplishments, our money, our past contentments, comforts, security, our home, peace of mind, complacency, the source of all safety? She whom we turn away from in disgust and revulsion and yet secretly entertain in the dark shadows when we think no one else is watching. She who must not be named. Oh, let's call her bluff. Come out, come out, wherever you are: Cruella de Vil. Our inner bag lady. And baby, if she don't scare you, no evil thing ever will.

I was amazed to read this morning that 90 percent of women feel financially insecure and almost half of them harbor fears about our inner Cruella; with the failing economy and our diminishing confidence about the future, we're becoming dangerously agitated as well, triggering both flight and fight responses at the same time. And these statistics come from an Allianz Insurance report from 2006, well before the world economy tanked. So you can imagine how we're all feeling this morning. We fear losing our money, our independence, and becoming forgotten and destitute.

Now, you might be surprised, as was I, to also discover that this fear is an equal-opportunity phantom; half the women surveyed earned over $100,000. Women as successful and wealthy as Jane Fonda, Lily Tomlin, Shirley MacLaine, Katie Couric, and even Oprah Winfrey have confessed to having had "bag lady syndrome." I read somewhere that Oprah has put away $50 million to handle her bag lady fears, which should definitely be enough to make sure that she doesn't end up alone, friendless, and pushing a shopping cart of her belongings on the street. But as you see, the distressing truth is that women of all ages and incomes have Cruella looming in the dark recesses of our lives.

All of us can relate to some degree to the fear that at any

moment the financial security we had counted upon could vanish, especially since that's exactly what has happened in the last couple of years. Our reaction to these unsettling occurrences and very real traumas is to become almost miserly in our determination to make sure this fate doesn't befall us—or we ricochet in the opposite direction and become hoarders. Some women are denying themselves necessities in an effort to safeguard their future, while others are stocking up on every discontinued item they can buy at the dollar store that might be handy someday. Yet no matter what extreme measures we implement, our serenity seems to be diminishing rather than increasing.

I think that's because the real source of our pain is not worrying about the future but making sense of the past: the emotional mistakes we made, the relationship misjudgments, the money mismanagement. The core of the bag lady pain comes from the assumption that we have not or cannot truly own the achievements, income, professional expertise, and life lessons that we have realized at some point in our lives. Instead, on some level many women choose to believe that our success was because we were "lucky," "in the right place at the right time," or the recipient of other people's kindness.

Although at first glance this point of view might seem modest and humble, the truth is that by choosing to see ourselves as passive recipients of whims of fate, it is all too easy for us to imagine that bad fortune is taking over control of our lives in the same way. We become convinced that we don't possess the wisdom to help us redeem our lives and get us to a better place.

"Was there no one over thirty-five who had not some secret agony, some white-faced fear? Half one's life one walked carelessly, certain that some day one would have one's heart's desire; and for the rest of it, one either goes empty, or walks carrying a full cup, afraid of every step," the writer Helen Waddell wondered in 1933 when everyone was afraid of what each day would bring.

So the next time you are haunted by Cruella, try to look at your life and career objectively and see what you have achieved. Is it truly realistic that a woman with these accomplishments, skills, knowledge, creative energy, and experience would end up on the street? Think about Jane Fonda, Lily Tomlin, Gloria Steinem, Katie Couric, and Oprah. I'm sure their internal anxiety feels as real as yours does, but do you think that these women will end up eating cat food in an alley? I suspect that someone looking at your life would have the same confidence that one way or another, you will find a way to take care of yourself with grace and wisdom.

Borrowing Trouble

When life knocks you to your knees ... well, that's the best position in which to pray, isn't it?

— ETHEL BARRYMORE

Back in the early 1970s, during my single/white/female days (pretending to be a grown-up in the Big City, but only as daring as *That Girl*'s cutesy Marlo Thomas and perky Mary Tyler Moore), there was a homeless woman who regularly stayed in the lower stairwell of my apartment building. Her name was Mrs. Lester, and she roamed around Capitol Hill in a man's overcoat and slippers. Her hair was matted, her face was dirty, and she smelled. Mrs. Lester was a familiar sight on Capitol Hill in Washington, DC. As the story goes, she had once lived in a town house until she couldn't pay property taxes and she ended up on the streets. Every so often her extended family from Maryland would come and get her and she'd disappear for a week or two, but then she'd be back with her shuffle, slip-sliding along the currents of life.

Just as we have our own bag lady fears, we also have memories of "there but for the grace of God" phantoms we've all looked toward and away from in morbid fascination. "I remember the time when I was six, holding my mother's hand, and I saw an old woman using her stuffed and tattered shopping bags to shield her face from the arctic air near our home. Her bare ankles were red-veined poles stuck into cracked black shoes with torn newspaper sticking out at the heels. Her layers of shredded sweaters were held together with safety pins. Even when I was a kid I somehow knew she didn't have a place to live, that she was frightened and alone," Alexandra Penney shares in her absorbing memoir *The Bag Lady Papers: The Priceless Experience of Losing It All.* Like many other successful women, Penney, the former editor in chief of *Self* magazine and beauty editor of *Glamour* as well as best-selling author of *How to Make Love to a Man,* feared ending up as a bag lady.

"For many years, I've feared that one day I'll wake up and be destitute and alone. I won't have enough money to feed myself or pay the medical bills. I will have to hole up in a rusted-out car or a closet-size room with peeling green paint and a single light bulb swaying from a frayed greasy cord, or I will end up trudging the streets, cold and abandoned, with a shopping cart filled with tattered bags full of god knows what," Alexandra confides as she begins her tale of losing all her savings in the Bernard Madoff swindle and the steps she took to regain sanity and serenity after her worst fears were realized. And though she felt betrayed, she was keenly aware that she was not alone in her distress. On a deep level, each of us has a pivotal "reckoning and recalibrating of money, class, status and society. We've all had to make adjustments and transitions."

And while we're all having our own financial shakedown, when it's your shakedown somehow it feels different. We learned how to support ourselves, we've done our best to prepare for the future, and now just as many Baby Boomer women are beginning to face retirement, it feels as if the whole game is changing. We are all having to find our way from scratch.

It's easy to feel scared and it's tempting to panic and more mornings than I care to admit have arrived, even while writing this glorious book that's saved my life, when I barely have the energy to turn over and put a foot on the floor, never mind untangle my financial mistakes, deal with the fallout of the divorce, create new work, or figure out where I want to live and how I'll do it. But you know, when I start this "litany of loss" it has a negative power energy of its own—it starts feeding on whatever precious natural resources are available: time, creative energy, emotion, vitality, and money, until, depleted, I achieve nothing and another day that could have been spent in reinvention slips away.

Even if we had the energy to start all over, we also don't have control over our outside circumstance. Since the economic downturn, people who have never had serious financial problems in their lives are facing tough choices and hard times. I have good friends who are losing their houses, having cars repossessed, and getting dunning calls around the clock. I had the bill collectors pounding at my door making a list of what can and will be collected unless they're paid and all I can say is that unless you've been two months behind on your mortgage, and I have been, you don't know how lost and forsaken—by fate and Heaven—you can feel. As unexpected as the actual financial problems are, the worst aspect of our situation is the tremendous sense of shame and self-loathing. So many friends of mine have seen a lifetime of payments in pension funds erased in the last couple of years—and this might include you. I would have been with everyone if the Englishman hadn't raided my pension on his own years before. But in the end, does it matter whether we blame Bernie Madoff, Lehman Brothers, Goldman Sachs, or Mr. Big for the empty retirement fund?

Some of this severe emotional pain has to do with the assumption that these kinds of problems—bankruptcy, foreclosure, unemployment, repossession—only happen to "bad" people; if they are happening to us, it must prove that we are beneath contempt. It becomes difficult for us to separate the external disgrace from our internal sense of unworthiness.

Once we're in that mind-set, things can spiral down

and out of control quickly. We don't believe that we are worth saving, so we lose the motivation to take control of the next step. We believe that people will think the worst of us so we don't ask for comfort, advice, or help.

Almost every woman I know well enough to talk with frankly about money has had at least one very hard period. And they tell me that they learned some of the most important life lessons during that period, lessons that have deeply enriched their lives later on. I know that this is true with me. If it's true that we are spiritual beings in a human body and that "this" life is just a sojourn for lessons, then I have gained countless insights into the human experience by having a financial windfall, losing it, and then regaining financial serenity.

While we can't force the housing market to improve and we can't force the banks to increase their credit lines, there are some things we can do. Being as careful with our money as possible is clearly one. Facing difficult choices, if they are necessary, is another, because nothing good ever comes out of denying the truth about our situation.

Once we realize that having a financial problem, even a very public one, is not a judgment on our authentic, essential selves, but part of Real Life's curriculum, we can begin to take an inventory of how many spiritual resources we have to meet these challenges, inner gifts that we often take for granted. Imagination, for instance, is often dismissed as an asset because it's not grounded in reality. Organizational skills are dismissed because they're too boring. But we need to soar above our reality right now, and the ability to get a larger view of our possibilities, to bring order out of chaos, clears not just our desks or overdue bill piles but our minds.

What else is in our bag of tricks? Creative brainstorming. Try this today. Write a letter from your happy, serene, contented (yes, I'm certain of it, you will be) Authentic Self five years from now, and let Future Self give today's inner gal a heads-up about choices she'll make, where she'll be living, and the work that she'll be doing, which she loves.

This is the most amazing blues and inertia blaster. I write letters to my Authentic Self asking questions at night; in the morning, I let my wiser self make suggestions after my prayers. With my first cup of tea, lo and behold, "spiritual solutions" appear on the page before me.

Wisdom is another precious asset we need to own and value—the wisdom that only comes from hard-won life lessons, such as how to stand up for ourselves, how to make and protect boundaries, the wisdom to make new financial decisions. We have a richer understanding of what really matters in life, and we have untapped creativity just waiting to be asked to assist us.

For example, one of the latest housing trends is female friends moving in together—à la *The Golden Girls*. Some do it as roommates, some do it as part of a large group, but the great thing is that they pool finances and emotional resources to create a new definition of *family*. Some women have chosen to remain single, some are divorced, and some are currently married but are thinking ahead to a time when they may be left on their own and they have a future "time share" for either a vacation or a reinvention place.

One friend has recently moved to Dallas to live in the same neighborhood with three other friends whom she has known and grown close to over the years. They started as workplace friends, eventually began to vacation together occasionally, and now, twenty years later, they have become family with the view that "whoever loves you when you need them" is your family. At this point all the women are living in separate homes, but they have talked about the future and are contemplating moving in together in some type of resort apartment complex or small beach cottage collective when they are ready for the next chapter of their lives to unfold.

I love this idea. Women bonding together in new ways

to face new challenges, not merely surviving, but thriving. Just as we have always found ways to face obstacles in the past, we will continue to find ways to take care of ourselves and the ones we love, learning the art of choice and chance, and closing in on serenity as we go.

The Thrill of Thrift

Goodness Has Nothing to Do with It

A man has one hundred dollars and you leave him with two dollars, that's subtraction.

— MAE WEST

Before Madonna, there was Mae. At first glance, the incomparable Mae West may seem the unlikeliest of money mentors, but that's only because we associate blond curls and soft curves with vulnerability. However, when it came to cash — making it and keeping it — Mae was sharp as a tack and could teach us all a trick or two.

Why not today?

"Mae West was a 'financial whiz,'" authors Annette Lieberman and Vicki Lindner tell us in *The Money Mirror: How Money Reflects Women's Dreams, Fears, and Desires*. In 1935, at the height of the Great Depression, the flamboyant blonde earned $480,833, more than any other woman in America that year and second only to newspaper magnate William Randolph Hearst, who earned $500,000.

Mae (originally Mary Jane) West was the embodiment of Sheconomics — a Broadway star, movie siren, comedienne, scriptwriter, director, producer, costume designer, and a brilliant publicist for the brand Mae. Her career began at seven when she won a talent show as

"Baby Mae," leading to a string of smash-hit vaudeville appearances through World War I. With each new venue, Mae pushed the bawdy boundaries of censorship, publicity, and sexual mores and became the Roaring Twenties symbol of a sexually liberated woman. In April 1926, Mae starred in her own play—*SEX*—which received critical acclaim and packed in audiences for more than a year. This only incensed the uptight New York police commissioner, who raided the theater company and arrested the dazzling star for "lewdness," obscene language, and the indecency of her own "coochie dance." Sentenced to ten days in jail, Mae was a model inmate, wearing only her silk underwear and reading business reports in her cell comparing the earnings of the different film studios. She emerged head held high (two days early for good behavior) and decided to follow the money out to Hollywood.

"Once in Hollywood, Mae, who proved adept at studio politics, convinced conservative producers to do her kind of film. Eventually she earned $300,000 a picture—the highest salary paid to a star until then—portraying a lusty woman who knew what she wanted and always got it, and was never dependent on or at the mercy of men," Lieberman and Lindner tell us. "She was soon involved in writing and helping to produce her own films, in which she also starred delivering unforgettable lines like, 'Is that a gun in your pocket or are you just glad to see me?' She also learned judo, how to fire a six-shooter, and insisted on entering the lion's cage herself when a stunt man got sick during the filming of *I'm No Angel,* which grossed $85,000 in the first week of its New York run." That movie costarring a young Cary Grant and its follow-up, *She Done Him Wrong*, became the films that saved Paramount Pictures from bankruptcy and established Mae's ascendancy as a business icon as well as a sexual bombshell. Powerful combination!

One of the most enjoyable pursuits to help reveal our hidden attitudes toward money is collage, especially around subjects we have strong opinions about. I never thought of Mae West as a money mentor. For a long time any collage I would create on authentic success or financial moxie would always feature very serious images of no-nonsense women in suits with barely a pearl necklace to flash. I needed to get past my own preconceived stereotype about what it means to be a woman who handles her money skillfully. That stereotype quickly collapsed after I read Mae West's memoir. Now I've created a personal homage to Mae West's financial savvy in my Comfort Companion. Sexual romps and one-liners we know, but Mae's empire also included million-dollar real estate holdings, racehorses, and ranches, as well as jewelry and furs. I will take spiritual enlightenment wherever I find it.

So I thought I'd see what I could come up with when I created my Mae West collage, with its silk ribbons, paper corselet, pink marabou trim, black-and-white photos, and her wit and money wisdom. It's an amusing but potent reminder that when it comes to women and money, we, too, can learn how "one and one is two...and two and two is four...and five will get you ten, if you know how to work it."

First the Gesture, Then the Grace

All we have to face in the future is what happened in the past. It is unbearable.

— MAEVE BRENNAN

I've been wondering about the soul's journey here and the belief that prior to birth in this life, we each choose the spiritual lessons that we'll try to master. In particular, I've been wondering about money as a spiritual lesson. Understanding the parallel realities of abundance and lack and how we choose each day which reality to live in certainly has been among my required life's courses. I don't think I'm alone, and there is comfort in knowing that there are millions of people who seem to have signed up for the compulsory course being taught by the Great Recession.

After *Simple Abundance* became a best seller, I thought that I'd learned the crucial money lessons, namely, eliminating thoughts of lack; practicing gratitude as a spiritual catalyst for material contentment; doing what you love and being paid for it; giving from the heart in all the work that you do and receiving money as the energy others pay back to you.

Clearly, however, I have many more to learn, and the lesson that seems to be presenting itself at the moment is understanding money as a sacrament. When we start to think differently about money—respecting, honoring, protecting, saving, and being grateful for money—it will manifest in our lives differently and (here's a miraculous thought) stick around longer.

Just so you know: I believe in reincarnation. This is the notion that after our physical deaths, our souls are born again in another time, another place, and another body to continue our journey to Wholeness by mastering spiritual lessons on the earthly plane. The ancients believed that this deeply personal authentic journey takes many lifetimes. But once the lessons are mastered, we get to move on quickly, promoted, in a sense, to the next grade. These lessons are learned in sickness and in health, in passion, romance, marriage, parenting, adultery, addiction, divorce, sibling relationships, friendships, business, moral code and choices, work in the world, and, oh yes, wealth. Money. Wealth is a treasure trove for the reincarnationist.

But I also believe in re-embodiment, which is what I call an accelerated spiritual tutoring during this earthly sojourn. I asked this question in my book *Something More: Excavating Your Authentic Self* and I still haven't answered it, so let's try one more time:

> Why can't we ask Spirit right now to teach us the particular lessons that we need to speed up our journey to authenticity? Perhaps we can reach a state of enlightened re-embodiment—here and now—in which we enrich and transform our lives by remembering and re-examining the dreams, loves, and fears of our own past.

> Yes, even the fears. I fully believe that we can alter the course of our destiny in wondrous ways when we invite into our lives the very lessons that frighten us most. This is because spiritual law transcends the laws of karma. We are meant to work our way through the fears; that's our karma. But we

overcome them through Spirit. When we extend an invitation to meet our fears, even as our knees are knocking and our stomachs are churning, Heaven admires our mettle, applauds our audacity, and gifts us with Amazing Grace. Always remember, never forget: first the gesture, then the grace.

Being first-generation Irish American, my Belfast-born father found it disappointing that I never wanted to make Ireland my home once I started traveling around the world in my twenties. But my first port of call had been London, and it took very little time for England to feel like a safe haven—afternoon tea, country lane stone cottages, lambs gamboling in green pastures. Yes, I know, all of these things were available in Ireland. If I knew then what I know now, I might have chosen my homeland, but there's no accounting for how or when the chords of contentment reveal our sacred sense of place.

"Home is a place in the mind," the Irish short-story writer Maeve Brennan (1916–1993) tells us. "When it is empty, it frets. It is fretful with memory, faces, and places and times gone by. Beloved images rise up in disobedience and make a mirror for emptiness." For Maeve—it was said that she "looked like a fashion model and wrote like an angel"—home was the *New Yorker* magazine for more than forty years, from the exhilarating heights of being a regular contributor and darling of its legendary editor, William Maxwell, during its heyday, to finding herself, penniless and broken, living in a small cubicle beside the ladies' room on the nineteenth floor, down the hall from where she had once been a star.

Other women's stories can be inspirational or cautionary tales; for me Maeve Brennan's has been both.

The short of it: Maeve never knew how to handle her money, and she made a disastrous marriage to a man who knew how to spend for both of them until she sank deep into debt and the despair began to silence her words.

Although she wrote of the joys of domesticity, the life she was leading was utterly void of joy—and a house divided cannot remain standing. They divorced, but she could never get back on her feet. Life became a succession of moves between rented cottages in the Hamptons during winter and shabby residential hotels in Manhattan in summer.

When I trace any woman's story to where it all goes so terribly wrong, it brings me back to the blasted intersection of exhausted despair and unintentional debt with the road definitely less traveled—financial serenity. I'm gobsmacked by how enormously smart, gifted, clever, savvy, creative women are thwarted, stopped, silenced, betrayed, abandoned, neglected, lost to others but most especially to themselves; their talent obscured from the world, their generosity of spirit siphoned because of the holy terror that is not the lack of money, but the inability to learn and master money management. And then trust their instincts.

It's time to ransom our lives back, to stop cringing from the money mistakes we've made, however or wherever we were when we made them. The first step to sanity is taking responsibility for our mistakes. Come to me, all ye readers *beyond* nervous breakdowns, those of you done with stashing prescription drugs, empty sherry bottles, unworn clothing new with tags, shoe boxes, credit card receipts, and empty cookie dough ice cream tubs in a fruitless effort to deal with the stone of misery now weighing your soul down and stopping your life from going forward.

I see that I have reached the moment that inevitably occurs in each book I write. I call it "the Turning," the point of no return before the next sentence is written. It's now become much more painful to stand still, refusing to cross the mystical, transformative threshold, than to take the leap of faith. It's now more difficult to artfully conceal than it is to candidly reveal what Spirit is requesting of this book from both the writer and the reader. Heaven is giving me a Divine "Heads up, Babe." What about you?

To answer this call means that our daily round is about to get reshuffled big-time. This transformation will change me personally; if you continue reading it, it will change you, too. Go ahead, sweetie, I won't blame you; close the book, if you can. You don't have to come where I must go. Don't feel you have to finish what you've started. But I'm not running any longer. And I hope you won't, either.

Money and me. Money and you. Money and women. There's a sacred contract here unfolding with every sentence, every thought, every dollar earned, saved, shared, invested, protected for ourselves and those we love. Every money memory, every fiduciary flash of insight, every painful lesson endured provides us glimmers of truth—to create a new framework of financial wisdom, knowledge, savvy, experience, compassion, moxie, vision, and self-trust.

Let us try something really radical. Instead of cursing our luck, let us bless the Great Recession because it is helping us to be greater than we could have ever been without it. And if you're a man in a suit, better watch your back before you foreclose on one more house, call in more ruthless bill collectors, or send in the bullies, because we've been sitting around the kitchen table, just having a little chat, and we know there's a woman breathing over your shoulder—one of us—who's ready to take your place on our behalf. She will work with us as we pay our bills, honor our obligations, clean up our money messes. She trusts our integrity. She's had some hard times herself. And she knows other women who will help us all create new jobs, provide health insurance, nurse the sick, start new businesses in the spare bedroom and on Main Street, and fund new banks around the block and in a world we can believe in. We've got a lot to do. How about a little invocation to shore up our courage?

Mother of Plenty, Shield Against Want, hear the prayers of your Beloveds, who ask with a grateful heart that we might receive our daily portion of Heaven today, upon the hearth of our hearts wherever we may be living at this moment. Provide us with the blessings of light, space, warmth, protection, and solace. Gift us with the knowledge and wisdom to keep our wits about us. Give us, we pray, the next small step and the widest and wildest vision of our prosperous future. Thank you for providing for those we love and those who love us. Thank you that today, all we have is all we need. Thank you for the blessings of our health, which is the truest wealth.

As we sift, sort, let go, and move past feelings of lack and distress, help us distinguish between our needs and our wants. Help us to teach our children, as we teach ourselves, the sacredness of money. And the truth that money is Divine Energy that ebbs and flows in our lives as we create, release, and receive it. Restore in us serenity and common sense as we pay our bills and balance our household accounts.

Remind us that our Source of Divine Replenishment, our Simple Abundance, is not to be found beyond the reach of our souls and the holy desires of our hearts but on the path to peace and plenty. Thank you for the authentic gifts you have bestowed upon each of us, to make brighter the world and our place in it. If I am not fulfilling this birthright, if I have shied away because of failure, fear, or fatigue, give me the strength to honor my Sacred Contract to bring in the bounty for your glory and the greater good. Reveal to me one task that I might do today to increase both my faith and my fortune. And then give me the strength, vitality, and perseverance to pursue and protect my treasure, on earth as it is in Heaven.

Piercer of Doubt and Kindler of Courage, bless us, we pray, as together we grope our way out of the darkness and despair of debt and slowly make our way to the light of your peace and plenty.

First the Gesture, then the Grace.

The Slippery Slope
Taking Care of Our Inner Bag Lady

*I shall not tell you in this story about all the days when
nothing happened. You will not catch me saying, "thus the
sad days passed slowly by"—or "the years rolled on their
weary course," or "time went on" because it is silly; of
course, time goes on, whether you say so or not.*

—EDITH NESBIT

A year after the Englishman and I married, I invited all
the children to Newton's Chapel for Christmas. I have
one child, my daughter, Kate (who was then twenty-
three), and the Englishman has six children, then ranging
in age from forty-five to sixteen, from three previous marriages. I wanted to start a tradition for this blended family
that would honor us all as individuals but bring us closer
as a unit. Why did I think this would be a happy occasion?

I have no memory of what provoked him; all I do remember is that we were in the kitchen on Christmas Eve
and suddenly the Englishman was yelling at my daughter, "This is not your house anymore, it's mine!" I looked
at my stunned girl and I remember saying to him, "Don't
talk to her like that..."—and then he yelled at me. All the
rest is a blur, except I do remember crying all Christmas
Eve underneath the Christmas tree, until my eyes were

swollen slits, as everyone retreated to their own corners. The biggest mistake I've ever made in my entire life, after marrying that man, was not throwing him out of *my* house on Christmas Day, but his lovely children were also there and I didn't want to "spoil" Christmas for anybody even though my heart was broken.

It would take me another five years and a Court Order to do so.

To my great shock and delight, Kate surprised me at Christmas 2008. I had not celebrated the holiday since the debacle and so was utterly astonished by her visit. Bless her, she had told her father that she feared for me, and he advised her to come and see for herself how I was. Her instincts were right: I wasn't good. And while I might have been able to fool her during a telephone call, I couldn't keep up the pretense when we were together. My perceptive girl saw instantly what I could no longer hide: The atmosphere between the Englishman and me had become dark, menacing, fraught with hostility, anger, recriminations, episodes of rage, badgering, screaming, and bullying, usually about money or the lack of it, until I agreed to whatever it was he wanted me to do that day.

Kate stayed with me for a couple of days and then we went to London together before she flew back to the States. She took me out to dinner at our favorite London restaurant, Locanda Locatelli, where we ate pumpkin amaretto parcels with butter and sage sauce and compared glasses of Barolo Sarmassa with Sangiovese Reserve. We talked about my fears and the future. That night in the hotel I couldn't stop crying and held her hand as we went to sleep. She talked about how I would start over again. I told her I had nothing left to start over with. She assured me that I had helped millions of women change their lives, I could help myself. She would help me help myself.

The next morning I said good-bye to her at Heathrow. She lent me money to get back home because by then, the Englishman wouldn't give me personal money. From *my own* accounts! After I kissed her farewell, I started the journey back to Newton's Chapel, which was about two hours by train from Kings Cross station. I was going to use public transportation because taxis were too expensive to get to Kings Cross, but I became confused about what tube train I should be taking. I walked for hours between the terminals, crying, not knowing where I was headed or why I was going back, lost in a maze of underground tunnels and a labyrinth of sorrow, failure, humiliation, despair, and hopelessness. Finally, exhausted, I sat down at an underground café for a cup of tea. The café faced two directions and I looked out at two totally unfamiliar dark passages. I sat there nursing the cup of tea for an awfully long time looking at the two tunnels. And then the thought came to me.

Oh, so this is how it happens. The Slippery Slope. This is how you become a bag lady. You have no money. You don't want to go to where you live because you're afraid of who is there or what you'll have to face and you have no place else to go. It's not very dramatic, the slough of despond, is it? What about endings, then? How easy it is, really, to just slip away from one's moorings and get swept away in the fast-moving currents of nothingness, like white-water rafting without a raft...no one pays attention to you if you don't make a fuss. This is how women become homeless. They just sit quietly with a cold cup of tea until the café closes and then start walking or take the first bus to Mornington Crescent and get off and start walking until they come to a bench or the inside of a church...

This is how stones get placed in overcoat pockets to weigh down the world's Virginia Woolfs as they walk into the river until their despair becomes bubbles on the surface of the water. It must be over quickly, and how tempting to just step in front of an oncoming train, like the Anna Kareninas do...

I had forgotten how to pray for myself by then, but I must have called on God to help me.

For then she appeared before me, Mother Maeve, in her smart black suit with a rose at her lapel, her dark hair pulled back into a bouffant pouf, her red lips. "Get up now, we're going home. *Your home.* It's *your* home, Sarah. It doesn't matter what he's told you. It's *your* money, too. What's left of it. And when we get back to your home, you're going to make us a damn good hot toddy because it's bloody freezing in here, and a hot bath, lots of bubbles, and you're going to the bedroom at the end of the hall and you're going to lock the door and sleep. And then, when you wake up, you're going to plan. And then you're going to pack. And then, after you've planned and packed, you're going to leave and take the cat."

And in my hour of darkness, Mother Maeve, she came to me. Speaking words of wisdom. Let him be. But first, open up a new bank account in your name only.

The Thrill of Thrift

Handbags and Financial Serenity

I'm homeless! I'll be a bag lady! A Fendi bag lady, but a bag lady!!

— CARRIE BRADSHAW, *SEX AND THE CITY*

Cleopatra had one; so did Empress Josephine. Eleanor Roosevelt's attracted such attention that the *New York Times* felt compelled to report in 1945 that "it was of dark leather and of tremendous dimension, practically bursting with invisible contents. It clearly spoke of the activities of the First Lady. One glance and you knew the President's wife had a full-time job."

Michelle Obama has a full-time job but she's usually bagless, while the Queen of England is never seen without hers and even carried one to her coronation in 1953 before reluctantly handing it over to a lady-in-waiting so that she could accept the sword and scepter of her kingdom. Since then, her plain, unadorned, but well-made black leather handbag is her constant companion, even being carried from room to room within the palace; it begs the question: What is in the Queen's purse? Here are my carefully researched findings: a comb, a linen handkerchief, a gold compact given to her by Prince Philip as a wedding present, a lipstick, a collection of good-luck charms given to her by her children, photographs, mints, treats for her beloved corgi dogs, a crossword or two cut out of the day's paper, a gold pencil, and, on Sunday, paper money for the collection plate at church.

Oh yes. There's one more fascinating object the Queen is never without in her purse: an S-shaped metal meat hook, which is placed on the edge of furniture to hold the Queen's purse when she is dining. This is because there's a secret etiquette code used by Her Majesty and her staff in which her purse plays a starring role. If she moves it from left side to right, it indicates that she is ready to leave wherever she is; if she places it on the floor at a banquet, she is bored and wants to leave. If she places it on the table, she'll leave in five minutes. If it hangs happily on the left side of her arm, she's having a good time, and if her purse swings from the meat hook, she'll stay a bit longer as she's quite enjoying herself.

Some might think that the Queen of England has a purse fixation. Personally, I think Her Majesty's focus simply proves that real power is represented by an S-shaped meat hook. I must have one. Now. Actually, I have no idea how I lived before without one. Sound familiar? These are usually the first words out of a woman's mouth after purchasing a very expensive designer handbag...and she is beside herself with buyer's remorse.

"A woman without her handbag feels as lost as a wanderer in the desert. And she wants it large. If she cannot get it in leather—now growing scarce—she will take it in fabric, fur, or even plastic. The handbag is the movable base of her supplies—the depot of her expected needs," Anita Daniel wrote in the *New York Times* on January 21, 1945. "A woman's handbag is a mysterious dungeon. It's the key to her real self; the prosaic answer to many poetic conceptions."

And how do you empty a room full of women faster than a fire alarm? Announce that in five minutes every woman remaining must open her purse to be searched.

"A magician does not want to explain his tricks. There is an aura of taboo about a closed handbag. Every woman has an uneasy look if somebody glances into its sacred privacy," Miss Daniel continued, ratting out half of the human race. "Every woman's handbag is a lost and found department in itself. It is strange but things actually disappear there, as by magic. They finally reappear on the surface after three or four investigations and complete pell-mell of the contents. Every bus driver is fatalistically resigned to having a lady barring the passage while searching for a nickel in the depths of her handbag."

Who among us has not been whipped into a frenzy looking for lost keys only to discover the jangling is the long-dead dog's collar (don't ask). Not to mention a loose bank card, idly slipped in the side pocket you've never used before because it's too narrow to get anything in or out; or the damn cell phone with the ringtone "Don't Cry for Me Argentina." Missing. Vamoose. Gone. Madonna at the top of her lungs says it's not, but you'll never find it. That's because it's buried, for time and all eternity, underneath coupons, cash register receipts, an empty plastic water bottle, painkillers, a candy bar wrapper, as well as an uneaten diet protein bar, pens with no ink, three pairs of glasses (close, far, and sun), a parking ticket from six months ago, a zinc cough drop stuck to the lining, crumpled tissues and a $20 bill, hand sanitizer, an overstuffed wallet (can't go there), a moldy lipstick-smeared makeup case, a fold-up umbrella with two bent spokes, which is why it won't fold up properly, one glove, several Starbucks cardboard coffee cup heat protectors, sweetener packs, paper napkins, two dead AA batteries, heart attack aspirins, an empty Rescue Remedy vial, and the portable hard drive that has the only copy of your ex-husband's hidden Cayman Island account files.

May we have a quiet word? This purse weighs over 6.9 pounds and is one of the reasons you're prematurely developing a dowager's hump, only a slight one, to be sure, still time to get rid of it but not if you cannot stand up straight and you can't with that horrendous carryall, in the truest sense of the word.

Let's be ruthless. Other than the hard drive, heart attack aspirins, $20, hand sanitizer, and painkillers, everything else has got to go, including Evita. What is needed is a complete throw-out and reorganization of the purse, my pet. Because you are not homeless, never will be, even if at this moment, like myself, you feel adrift. But when we sling sloth over our shoulders, we become very unappealing to money magnetically. Do you think money wants to be carried around in a trash bag? As we inch our way from pain and panic to peace and plenty, we need to become aware of the blatant and the subtle energies we are always projecting, which come back like a boomerang to deck us. It does not cost us a cent to carry a bag that's worthy of carrying, and I'm not talking about the outside.

So how about a simple ritual. Clean out your wallet and your purse on Sunday evening, before the week begins. Here's a list of what a prepared-for-anything woman might have in her handbag to aid her as she's out and about:

Small wallet (including driver's license or identification and one bank card)
Coin purse
Small toiletries bag (blush, lipstick, comb)
Packet of tissues
Mints or breath spray
Small emergency clear bag (Band-Aids, safety pins, nail file, tampon, moist cloths, full bottle of Rescue Remedy)
Eyeglasses neatly in their case
Hand sanitizer
Small pill bottle (aspirin, painkiller, any medicine you might need during the day)
Clear envelope for cash and receipts (Get in the

habit of placing your parking ticket in it when
you enter a garage.)

Small notebook, rubber band with pen attached
(to keep track of purchases)

Small full bottle of water (no bigger than eight
ounces)

Keys, attached to a small pocket flashlight

Cell phone in its case or appropriate purse
pocket (Get in the habit of always replacing it
where it should go.)

A slender clipping file (Clip articles from magazines and put them in this file so you always
have something to read when waiting.)

Weather-related: The smallest fold-up umbrella
(I've seen them about six inches) or old-
fashioned rain cap; a scarf tied fetchingly to
the handbag handle can cover your head in
case of rain.

Oh, and don't forget the S-shaped meat hook. When
power beckons, you'll be ready.

Becoming Your Own Heroine

A lie hides the truth, a story tries to find it.

— PAULA FOX

Recently I had an interesting conversation with a professional screenwriting coach. She told me that you can tell if students are developing a truly authentic voice by investigating how they develop the central character of their story.

Apparently, one of the most common problems of novice screenwriters is that they write heroes by default, characters whose names are on almost every page but who are actually only the leads because of their frequency of appearance. They're presented as victims of circumstance or malice; they are "done to" or react to the actions of others. But they aren't driving the story through their choices. They only react. Often writers don't realize it, but they're scared to let their "heroes" make mistakes, so they create a straw figure for a hero and focus all their creative energies on the bad guys and continuing escalation of crises.

I find this fascinating, particularly because I think the same holds true in our personal stories. We think by putting the emphasis on our trials and tribulations—the ex-husband who cheated with our best friend, the broker who betrayed our trust, the bank that failed, the thief who stole our identity, the relatives who disappointed us, the nasty boss who fired us, the scam artist who ripped us off, the acts of nature or, worse, "the acts of God"—we are protecting ourselves from being wrong.

Because if we didn't make the choices that got us where we are at this sad moment, then it can't be our fault, right? And if it's not our fault, then we shouldn't bear the blame or the shame. Am I creating enough wiggle room for us? I'm trying my best.

But the sorry truth is, and you and I both know this, we are where we are today because sometime, somewhere we made a bad choice. We may have been asleep at the wheel when we took that detour, we may have glazed over the fine print when we signed that mortgage, we may have had the best of intentions, we may have said "I do" when we should have said, "Let me sleep on it," but no more excuses, Babe. Excuses are unbecoming to a woman coming into her own strength, grace, and wisdom.

And you are, and beautifully, I might add.

So as of today, let's agree: There's no one else to blame. No more mitigating circumstances. No more copping a plea or copping out. For when we choose reacting instead of acting for ourselves, not only do we give up our chance to be the heroine, but we also surrender every ounce of our creative energy, our vitality, our passion. We become a windup doll in our minds, sitting in the closet waiting for someone to come in and take us out to play.

Perhaps the mistake that young writers and younger women make is in thinking that heroines have to be perfect. They don't. We don't even want heroines to be perfect, we just need them to try. It's the attempt that both inspires us and makes their story intriguing whether they ultimately succeed or not. In fact, if a person doesn't have real challenges to face, she can't possibly be heroic. Who sees triumph in an Olympic long-distance runner crossing the street? But in the cold dark, running those laps at 4 AM? I'll tune in to that movie.

When you're embroiled in a personal financial crisis,

you can't cut through the thicket of fear, benign neglect, and confusion all at once, but you can make a gigantic spiritual leap by simply acknowledging that you don't want to live anymore crippled by fear. At the very moment that you choose the forest path to find your way home, rather than being chased into the thickets by the bad guy, you become the lead character—the heroine—of a whopping good yarn. A legend, shall we say, in your own mind, which is the best place for legends to practice their winning moves.

It can't be your life until it's your story. But I promise you, by claiming one, you begin to own the other.

Here's My Movie

The Way We Were

The change of life is the time when you meet yourself at the crossroads and you decide whether to be honest or not before you die.

—KATHARINE BUTLER HATHAWAY

When we're reconciling our relationship with money, it's necessary to travel back to life's major intersections—which at the time might have only seemed like a mere speed bump or two. These are the places where you made a decision that took you in one direction rather than another. It might have been a quickie marriage or a lengthy, acrimonious divorce. It might have been the rescuing of a grown child you could help or accepting the incomparable loss of one after years of trying to save her. It could be the decision to move your mother-in-law into an assisted living community when you would have made accommodations for your own mother at home. It could be the novel you talked about for years but never finished, which becomes the subject of someone else's best seller; or ignoring due diligence before you buy part of a friend's business because, after all, she's your friend.

It could be the hunch that keeps you out of harm's way; or ignoring an intuitive prompt that something's not quite right because you so desperately want it to be otherwise.

Red-flag alert: If you're unwilling to discuss a certain choice with your nearest and dearest, there's a reason for this.

Probably because you shouldn't be even considering taking this action.

Believe it or not, in each one of these scenarios, money plays a part—if not in Act One, then certainly in the finale. That's the irrefutable fact we can't seem to get our heads around: Money influences everything, and the afterlife of money choices can linger years, decades, generations. "Long afterwards, she was to remember that moment when her life changed its direction. It was not predestined; she had a choice," the English author Evelyn Anthony tells us in her novel *The Avenue of the Dead.* "Or it seemed that she had. To accept or refuse. To take one turning down the crossroads to the future or another. But this would be hindsight, and time always mocked truth."

At some point in your money reconciliation, an unruly mob of memories will rush out from both sides of the road seeking your attention. Every memory wants to have her own quiet word with you, a plea that she won't be ignored, forgotten, dismissed as folly, but when everyone's shouting, you can't distinguish the true whispers from the din. Don't even try. Do try, though, to remember the way it happened in real time, in a sequence. And the way you do that is slowly, with gentleness and with compassion. The same way you'd like to be heard.

Here's one of my money memories, which I've had to explore with tenderness in order to get at the truth. It's taken me nearly a decade but now I understand and have moved on. I've forgiven myself and found serenity where once I felt pain and shame.

In the late 1990s, I had a beautiful, large, luxurious prewar apartment on one of the most glorious boulevards in New York City. The walls were thick, the ceilings high, the windows enormous, and the rent exorbitant. But I fell in love with the beauty of the space the moment I crossed the threshold, and I justified paying more per month in rent (it wasn't available to buy) than I had earned annually as a freelance writer for the previous twenty years, as a well-deserved perk of my new, successful life. This was also not in the least sensible, or what you'd expect from the woman who wrote *Simple Abundance*. It was, in fact, reckless from a financial point of view. Maybe that's why I did it; at the time this apartment represented something far more than shelter: To my eye it was what success looked like.

But that was then and this is now. The question you're probably dying to ask is: Would I have kept paying such huge rent checks if I'd had a crystal ball and could view my financial future? Of course not. This truth is uncomfortable because when we make choices today, they will influence the tomorrow of a year from now, five years, a decade, or forever. And what's more chilling is that sometimes we must go on living far longer than we'd like with the choices we made before we knew better. Honoring transitions that come after cataclysmic change is how we maintain our equilibrium and preserve what's left of our sanity and our savings account.

On the plus side of life's ledger, I had more fun decorating that space than I've ever had, before or since. The furnishings were elegant, sophisticated, comfortable, witty, and sexy. Few places in the world have ever gifted me with as much profound pleasure as opening the door of this apartment. The spiritual psychologist Robert Sardello believes that "each room contains a mythic universe," and my Central Park West cosmos was the fulfillment of every art deco fantasy. The memory of it aches. Whenever I walked into that apartment, I blossomed into every woman I'd ever hoped to be. The siren in every film, the hostess of every sought-after soiree. The transformation was hypnotic and powerful. To tell you the truth, I couldn't believe it was mine. I couldn't understand how I was living there. I wonder if that isn't one of the reasons that it's no longer mine. It's hard to hold on to what we don't believe we deserve, whether it's money, love, or success.

Hold that thought.

Choosing Serenity
One Truth at a Time

Many a truth is the result of an error.

—MARIE VON EBNER-ESCHENBACH

So there I am, renting a beautiful apartment on Central Park West, and I love it. I adore how I feel in its presence. However, the problem is that I also have hot flashes, guilt surges because this apartment was really a very expensive pied-à-terre. I actually *lived* out of several suitcases in New York, Washington, and London. The apartment remained regrettably empty for lengthy stretches of time; looking back on the first year I rented, I'd be surprised to find I spent more than six weeks there. I know, I know—bad girl. See how easy it is to attach emotional and moral judgments to our behavior patterns with money? Note to self: That's got to go. Note to reader: Try to do the same. Pretend you're a forensic accountant, just following the money, not the emotion that sent it on its way.

In my rationale, I was going to let it go when my lease came up for renewal (with a hefty rent increase, naturally). Instead, I held my breath and *chose* to stay. I'm highlighting that word because its selection is very precise, although I've managed to squirm around it for a long time. I *chose* to spend my money this way, even if I was oblivious to the implications.

How about a little refresher on the spiritual gift of choice. It's so convenient to forget. Well, at least it was for me. Decisions like choosing to stay in an expensive apartment, when I really needed a smaller place, happen because we think of all the negatives first (*Oh God, I can't move now, I have a work deadline. I can't go through that upheaval so soon after the last. The time, energy, emotion, staff, and money it will take to find me another place will end up costing the same...*). Instead, I should have made a list of all the positives about moving to a smaller apartment, beginning with saving money. But now I also realize that I was depending on people's advice, people who didn't necessarily want me to move and were telling me I was so lucky to have this apartment. Not my accountant, obviously, but a personal assistant in New York who was comfortable with the arrangement; we had just moved two years earlier and it had been hard on both of us. Well, I never like to make anyone uncomfortable, especially people who work for and with me. Moving is hell, yes, but so is unemployment.

That's why I call decisions like this "coma choices," because they are always followed by "amnesia awakenings." When you finally come to, you say, "I don't know what I was thinking." I do. You *weren't* thinking. You may have been dreaming, fantasizing, having a rapturous reverie. But you were definitely not thinking—or using both sides of your brain, the creative right and the logical left—to discern the truth in your error of judgment.

Coma choices are also a bit like gambling for those of us who don't play the ponies, indulge in bingo, pick lucky numbers, pull the fruit handle, or scratch out gold crowns.

Perhaps the reason we use so many weasel words to get ourselves off the hook about *choosing* paths, partners, possible realities, and probable outcomes is that many women don't think about choice as a gift of Grace from Spirit. Rather, we think that choices are burdens to be endured, not embraced. One of the reasons could be that choice involves commitment of some kind: commitment of time, creative energy, emotion, and money.

Money. Lord have mercy, there's that word again, sneaking into every few paragraphs. Just when we've lost sight of it, it bounces back because of insufficient funds or attention. So because we commit to our husbands, partners, children, bosses, sisters, brothers, mothers, in-laws, friends, acquaintances, staff members, and anybody else who wants to add us to their Facebook page, we just want a little slack. We just want a little breathing space. We just want to be left alone.

Ha! This is how our cunning feminine wiles work against us. It is the art of self-sabotage, at which we all excel. You see, we think if we "sort of " avoid this choice (refusing to acknowledge that not choosing is definitely a form of choice), we can take a flier on the margin. Sneak under the Soul's radar.

You may not realize it or want to believe it, and neither do I, but our lives at this exact moment are a direct result of choices we made once upon a time. Thirty minutes, thirty days, thirty years ago, or somewhere in between.

So here it is, the Gift of Spiritual Choice recapped. Our choices are either conscious or unconscious. We must choose to choose consciously from now on. Unconscious choice is destructive, dangerous, and the heel of self-abuse. Never again, so help us God. Unconscious choice is how we end up living other people's lives in apartments we couldn't afford then or ten years later in our sister's because we've got to find one we can afford now. When we follow the money back to our crossroads, we discover our unconscious choices morphed into the who, what, when, where, and how of our destiny, the reason we ended up letting other people manage, spend, invest, squander, steal, or lose our money while we weren't paying attention, weren't rocking the boat.

"It's when we're given choices that we sit with the gods and design ourselves," writer Dorothy Gilman sighs.

Oh yes, when we know what this choice will cost us—physically, emotionally, financially, spiritually, psychologically—and are prepared to pick up the check, then our gift of choice becomes one beyond measure.

Unfortunately, there's no sure way of knowing the tab until we've lived the choice; we can't see in advance whether the choice was a wise or wrong one. But at least it was ours to make. We own it, and in our financially troubled life, choices are one of the most valuable things we *can* own.

How quickly the phrases slip off our tongue: *I have no choice. You left me no other choice. What choice do I have?*

We can't really know where a choice will take us, although we might sense its direction. We're torn between the agonizing should and shouldn't. I love the way the English writer Jeanette Winterson describes our dilemma: "I have a theory that every time you make an important choice, the part of you left behind continues the other life you could have had."

So with the stakes this high, how do we make our choices? We do the work necessary to make a good one. Gather as much information as you can. Weigh your options. Ponder the possibilities. Brood. Write down the pros and cons on a large legal pad. Have fun creating a collage in your Comfort Companion. Probe the probabilities with your best friend. Ask your heart what she thinks. Ask your logic for her opinion. Pray for guidance—I ask for big letters, short words. No interpretation, please, just Divine direction by a pillar of clouds similar to the one the Israelites followed for forty years in the desert until they reached the Promised Land. When the pillar of clouds stopped, they made camp. When the pillar of clouds started moving, so did they. If the clouds don't seem to be doing it for you, then sleep on it for three days.

Then make your choice. Don't look back and don't second-guess. Live your choice. Eventually, with hindsight, if you land on your feet with a smile on your face, a well-insulated roof over your head, and a private stash of cash, you'll see what it was, a wise or wrong choice. And if it was a wrong choice, you'll have the means to make amends and move on.

But wrong choices should never be confused with *bad* choices. Bad choices—and I have made some doozies involving men and money—happen when we embark on the smug stretches of self-destruction, usually with a smile or something to prove. Right now my head wants to declare that gorgeous New York apartment was a bad choice, slap my knuckles with a ruler, and say, "So there, missy!"—but to be fair to the woman I was then, the only thing that was bad about the choice was the furtive way I went about making it. I did not ask friends or my heart for advice. I did not ponder and I certainly did not pray.

Perhaps because on the deepest intuitive level I knew I shouldn't have been entertaining the thought of a two-year renewal. Perhaps I didn't want to feel that I had to keep asking for permission. I'd been "pretty pleasing" others all my life. I loved all the Central Park West home represented—that I'd made it against all the odds and the money was mine to spend however I damn well pleased.

And though it was inarguably frivolous, it served me well when I least expected it. Because the truest story and the richest life are always found between the lines of circumstance.

Take Another Look Around

The only real security is not insurance or money or a job, not a house and furniture paid for, or a retirement fund, and never is it another person. It is the skill and humor and courage within, the ability to build your own fires and find your own peace.

—AUDREY SUTHERLAND

In September 2001 my daughter was starting New York University, and while she would be living in a dorm downtown, she wanted to have a "home" base uptown for weekends. I was thrilled. Now I had a legitimate—even altruistic—reason for remaining a real estate spendthrift.

I'd moved her into her dorm just before Labor Day. Originally, I was going to leave the following day, as I needed to return to England to finish *Romancing the Ordinary*, but something made me change my flight to later in the week; an intuitive prompt "just to make sure" she had everything she needed. This was a huge adjustment for both of us, and I wanted to know she was settled before I returned to Newton's Chapel to write.

There were so many errands to do that gorgeous Tuesday morning. I was whizzing out the door when Kate called. She'd just left her dorm as the first plane buzzed low over Fifth Avenue and then flew into the World Trade

Center. It was 8:50 AM and she could see the gaping hole and smoke from the street. I couldn't understand what she was trying to tell me, so I immediately switched on the television; in the initial few moments after the crash, they were reporting it as a freak air traffic control accident. I told Katie, in that reassuring tone women have always used as a crisis is beginning to unfold, ears half cocked, that everything would be all right and she should just go to class, which she did. Within minutes I realized that things would probably never be "all right" in our lives again.

After her classes were suspended, Kate was walking back to her dorm with her roommates when the second tower collapsed in front of them. They fell on the ground screaming, covering their heads from the horror. Like millions of other people around the world, I watched as the unthinkable unfolded on television. For six frantic hours I tried to reach my daughter on her cell phone; around 4 PM she rang me. Thank God! She was walking uptown and was about twenty blocks away.

The sight of Katie as she stepped into the apartment foyer is something I will never forget; it was the Rapture for me. The hugs, the kisses, the tears, the enormous relief. The *feel* of her in my arms. The smell of loss clinging to her clothing. The taste of salt on her dusty cheeks. The sense of overwhelming gratitude.

Her dorm had been evacuated. Kate brought her three roommates with her; I told all the girls to just leave their backpacks on the floor, to go now, wash their hands and faces, and then call their families to let them know they were safe.

I went into the kitchen, put sandwiches on plates, and poured wine. I said more prayers. Blessed was I among women. How grateful I was to have this apartment, uptown and out of harm's way. How healing it was to be able to hold us all together, to guard these precious chicks in my nest.

And if I were given the chance to do it all again, not

knowing then what I do now, I would make the same choice today. It was worth every penny. Every tear ever shed. Worth every regret. Every reckoning.

"Painful as it may be, a significant emotional event can be the catalyst for choosing a direction that serves us—and those around us—more effectively," Louisa May Alcott consoles us. "Look for the learning."

Or for an alternative perspective. If you've made what seems like a horrible financial choice, be your own advocate and try to tell yourself the story from another view. Try a little tenderness. Take another look around.

The Thrill of Thrift

The Gratitude Garden

It is not graceful and it makes one hot, but it is a blessed sort of work, and if Eve had had a spade in Paradise and known what to do with it, we should not have had all that sad business of the apple.

—COUNTESS ELIZABETH VON ARNIM

Of course, it would all end and begin again in a garden. Love. Admiration. Adoration. Celebration. Devotion. Inspiration. Frustration. Obsession. Relinquishment. Redemption. Renewal. Restoration. The Divine and perennial passion to be reignited annually as long as humans lust on this earth. Not between Adam and Eve, mind you, but between Eve and Eden. Even women like myself, whose horticultural knowledge is limited to planting with the green bit on top, are apt to stir with basic instincts that make us feel like natural women when the sun shines, the earth grows warm, and the air becomes moist and soft with promise. Once again, we say with great conviction: "This is the year I shall *have* a garden." Once more with great feeling. I don't know about you, but this year I mean it.

"Musing on the strangeness of life, and on the invariable ultimate triumph of the insignificant and small over the important and vast," Australian writer Marie Annette Beauchamp wrote in her 1898 memoir, "the garden is the place I go to for refuge and shelter, not the house. In the house are duties and annoyances...furniture and meals, but out there blessings crowd around me at every step." These wry, witty, and very wise recollections would be published as *Elizabeth and Her German Garden*. This first attempt at writing became an instant and perennial favorite. It would be twenty-two years before she would write *The Enchanted April* as Countess Elizabeth von Arnim, or just "Elizabeth," after two husbands, five daughters, and a dozen books. But the story of the passions and profound peace she unexpectedly found and celebrated in her first German garden as a young bride would become a cherished volume for women of all ages and eras, whether writers, gardeners, or aspirants.

Many a day at Newton's Chapel I would head out, following Elizabeth's encouragement to forage for herbaceous or floral treasures to decorate the house, and I'd return with other gifts from the garden besides plants: forgetfulness, tranquility, serenity, the passage of time unfettered, hope springing suddenly, a salve for the sore and parched parts of my soul. Most of all, in the garden, I chanced upon new dimensions to the six principles of *Simple Abundance* as gardening transforms them into saving graces that grow before my eyes. Mother Nature is a patient tutor—she has all the time in the world—and when I'm ready to make Divine connections, a new lesson plan appears for Gratitude, Simplicity, Order, Harmony, Beauty, and Joy—and it's always right on time. I'm blooming where I'm planted.

Last summer, Gratitude arrived in a new guise. I'm always surprised by something new when I spend time in my garden, such as the spontaneous wild irises that have shown up this year fully formed and fabulous. How did they get here? It's the tenth summer I've spent here, how is it that I'm only noticing them now? Could it be because I know that next year at Newton's Chapel, another woman might be discovering them for the first time, might smile at first sight and then offer thanks for the garden's gifts? I wonder which woman's garden today, in what part of the world, I will call my own next year? And this summer, is she feeling as wistful as me? Thinking of our cosmic exchange encourages me to weed and edit with a bit more ardor, planning and plotting the new beholder's pleasure, as I hope she, in turn, plots mine. Moving gives new meaning to "Garden for others as they shall garden for you."

The garden's simplicity reminds me how little it takes to make women happy; often just a fistful of bright pink peonies or a jug of daisies will do the trick. None of the flowers in my little patch are exotic; they are instead the old-fashioned cottage variety, but the elegance and grace of arranging just one type in a vase or a jug has always seemed to me one of the best sources of glee available. Simplicity's taught me this valuable tip and given me the wisdom to grant each bloom her moment.

The desire for order in the garden was abandoned long ago; I'm always waging a tug-of-war between tidiness and mess in the house, so there's breathing space aplenty—and lots of room to exhale. Even the debris—tree limbs and roof tiles after a big storm, rose vines sheared from the walled garden—looks relaxed in its disarray, as if to remind me that any harmonious life needs room enough for temporary untidiness. "Accept your life as it is," the birds seem to twitter in a rhythmic pattern. Have you ever played the game of divination by birdsong? You sit quietly, or better yet lie, on a lovely blanket in the backyard with your eyes closed, listening to the conversation of the birds. Each song has its own repetitive beat and secret message as you pick out familiar "words." This morning a little winged choir sang, "Ready when you are...ready when you are...ready when you are..." alternating with "There she goes...there she goes...there she goes..." What personal Divine message is hidden in birdsong waiting for you today?

Order becomes Harmony when you're lying on a blan-

ket in the backyard. "All that was here—peace, and happiness, and a reasonable life—and yet it never struck me
to come and live in it," Elizabeth confesses, surely for all
of us. "Looking back I am astonished, and can in no way
account for the tardiness of my discovery that here, in
this far-away corner was my kingdom of heaven." And
of course, the wonder is that as soon as you find your
own faraway corner, you notice extraordinary, ephemeral
beauty constantly surrounding you—like bright orange
Japanese poppies with their tissue-paper petals and rav-
ishing sapphire eyes swaying in the breeze or Solomon's
brilliant daylilies—meant only to provide fleeting glimpses
of the Great Creator's generosity of Spirit and love of great
beauty, not to be gathered up for splendor in the vase. Just
like the manna that fell from Heaven each day for the Israelites while they wandered in the desert but couldn't be
saved, the garden teaches me that beauty, love, and life
can't be hoarded. Once in a rather overzealous experiment
I cut everything for bouquets, only to have my plunder
wither overnight. It was such a reassuring benediction to
greet them again the following summer, I simply basked
in their radiance. Yes, the garden and Mother Nature are
bountiful with their wisdom, especially gleaned the hard
way.

Hastened by overwork and underappreciation, the
pileup of little daily disappointments and financial skir-
mishes can grow until we're worn to a raveling. We lose
love or a friendship, we worry over getting the bills paid,
the sight of houses floating downriver in a raging flood
or foreclosed because of relentless debt stays with us during sleepless nights, becoming waking nightmares. I don't
know how it is affecting you, but I'm searching for an unexpected blessing here. Sometimes I'll be standing in the
backyard, arms on hips or head in hands, and suddenly realize after a few minutes that nobody's followed me. Over
the next five minutes my breathing steadies. So take ten
minutes, then fifteen. What the heck, while you're here,

take half an hour to call your own. Nobody will even notice you're gone until an hour's passed. You make note that the world doesn't stop spinning without your assistance, but thank Heavens, you do. There's one for the Gratitude Journal—yes, but also one for the Gratitude Garden. A private spot created for you, daughter of Eve, to experience viscerally the blooming loveliness of gratitude, the expansiveness of appreciation, the natural generosity of Spirit. The path to peace and plenty.

The summer approaching will bring a change. I won't be at Newton's Chapel, and I won't have a backyard garden of my own, either. Like many of you who live in the city or even suburban apartments, our patch of green may indeed be just a patch—the size of a balcony, tiny patio, or even window box. Fret not; what is important is that we plant something in the dirt and let redemption bloom in her loveliness. Sometimes when we are overwhelmed life prunes us back, but we do not have to become potbound, our roots tangled and our growth stunted. All that's needed is a larger pot.

And how do you redeem a solitary golden hour that shimmers in cool green? Being a woman possessed of her reason—a most valuable possession, indeed—do like I do and create your own "drama-free zone" with a spade, a plot or pot of soil, a packet of seeds, a little water, and sunlight. You'll catch on very quickly why it's called your Gratitude Garden: because you're always grateful when you spend a few minutes each day there. Or you're grateful because you've outfitted a basket by the back door with hand tools, a hat, sunscreen, gardening gloves, a bottle of water, so that you don't have to search for anything before a quick visit. Or perhaps you're grateful to handpick a few fresh salad leaves each night from pots on the patio—some tomatoes, basil, rosemary, or thyme, mint for iced tea, and a single rose for tomorrow's breakfast tray.

I know I'm grateful for the fresh reminder that every day it's our choice whether we'll wither from lack or thrive through appreciation. Because with gratitude, the more it is communicated, the more it is recognized and encouraged, the more it *does* grow. Do you remember the Victory Gardens that women planted on both sides of the Atlantic during World War II? Well, I have a dream of every woman in the world growing *Peace and Plenty* Gratitude Gardens. Growing flowers, vegetables, medicinal herbs, nourishment, contentment, and fulfillment. Reclaiming Eden one plant, plot, pot at a time.

"What a happy woman I am living in a garden, with books, babies, birds and flowers," Elizabeth von Arnim reminds us. "Sometimes I feel as if I were blest above all my fellows in being able to find my happiness so easily."

There's a thought worth remembering. Now grab that spade.

When Love Files for Bankruptcy

Divorce is the one human tragedy that reduces everything to cash.

—RITA MAE BROWN

I've been married three times to very different men. First came an Irishman, which lasted eighteen hours and ended in annulment, followed by an American, which lasted eighteen years and ended in a divorce. Both of those marriages illustrate the extremes of my personality: parts spontaneous and stubborn. But my last grasp of the golden ring, to an Englishman, is the one that has brought utter ruination to my heart—bankruptcy in the *truest* sense of the word. It was almost a complete financial wipeout, and the pittance that's left can't cover or even make a dent in my debts, at least not at this moment. But I believe with all my heart that understanding money and its meaning in our lives is a journey and that I will work my way back to strength, creativity, and solvency, one resolved debt at a time.

Why? For the first time in my life, I am as passionately committed to my financial recovery and independence as I once was to romance. Spiritually, however, I'm surrounded by such a cavern of loss and disillusionment that I can barely speak about it, just yet, other than to acknowledge that it's happened. "By such slight ligaments are we bound to prosperity or ruin," Mary Shelley wrote in 1818.

It was such a slight ligament, we'll call it, that brought me to glance upon Newton's Chapel for the first time in September 1997. I had come to England as a special correspondent covering Princess Diana's heart-wrenching funeral for *People* magazine and stayed an extra day to travel to the wilds of rural England to see a special property. The previous month while casually flipping through an English newspaper discarded in an airport lounge, I'd discovered a cottage for sale that had formerly been Sir Isaac Newton's private chapel. Ever since an English newspaper had described me as "the Isaac Newton of the simplicity movement," I'd developed a mad, passionate crush on Sir Isaac. It felt like a cosmic connection, so I read everything I could find about the object of my fascination. I was intrigued and captivated to discover that Newton wasn't only the first modern scientist, but the world's last sorcerer and a mystic after my own heart. And now his private refuge was for sale—I couldn't wait to see it.

Just one look, that's all it took. Just one look, and the earth tilted on its axis. "I am as susceptible to houses as some people are susceptible to other human beings. Twice in my life I have fallen in love with one," the early-twentieth-century English writer Katharine Butler Hathaway confessed for the two of us. "Each time it was as violent and fatal as falling in love with a human being."

The facts are these: I was newly separated from my daughter's father and shaky after our long-standing marriage ended abruptly; I didn't know a soul in England. I was feeling overwhelmed by the demands on my time that my new success brought with it. It was almost impossible for me to settle down and write in New York. But I gave no thought to the life changes this long-distance love affair with a house would trigger. I didn't call my best friend to ask for her opinion. I didn't ask my accountant for his advice. I didn't even tell my daughter until the deed was done. What does *that* tell you?

I didn't want anyone telling me how to spend my money is what it tells me.

Wait, there's more. The cottage was nine hundred years old and only had two rooms. It was barely big enough to hold me, and I'm just five feet. There was nothing the least bit practical in this real estate transaction. It would require extensive long-distance renovation across the Atlantic and could become a money pit. Recalling the exact moment my common sense went south—from the sublime to the ridiculous in a fleeting glance—only one word comes to mind: *home.*

From the moment I opened the garden gate, a strange enchantment took hold. "Enchanted places have the power to change us, to germinate and nurture that tiny seed of happiness...that each of us have kept so carefully concealed," the English writer Alexandra Campbell reveals in her novel *Remember This.*

I belonged here.

All my life, I've never felt as if I belonged anywhere; my harried heart was possessed by a mysterious "holy longing" that never seemed to be satisfied. But here, in the garden of this tiny ivory stone cottage with its huge, ancient apple tree, heavily laden with reddening and ripening orbs, I felt that there couldn't possibly be anyplace else more exquisite. The warmth of the September afternoon made the earth fragrant, yeasty, and fruity; bees flitted among the drooping pink hollyhocks. Wasps droned over sweetly decaying apples on the ground, drunk in delight. Doves cooed from the top of the red-peaked tile roof. Across the meadow, sheep grazed on a green hill bordered by hedgerows of blackberries.

Inside Newton's Chapel, the stillness was so luxurious, it took my breath away. The silence was lyrical; the atmosphere sensuous; the very air was intoxicating, an aura that was simultaneously serene and exhilarating. It also felt sacred; I knew I was standing on holy ground. Later I would be told by a geomancy master (who divines sacred spots in the earth) that the chapel had been built on the site of a holy well belonging to practitioners of the Goddess faith around the first millennium. This was a common occurrence during the early medieval times as Christianity replaced the practice of worshiping the Great Mother.

I could feel all of this sacred energy in this physical place. I was thrilled, and a bit dazed, as I tried to take it all in.

I'm sharing this story because I have identified buying this home as the moment when my seemingly random money choices changed my life. I also want to understand the battle I've had to wage this past year to hold on to my precious home. Perhaps you are having a similar difficulty. If you are, I want to fortify your strength and help you hold on if you can to what you cherish as well. Or help you to let go, as I must. For as you attempt to make peace with your financial past, second-guessing and a hundred turnings of the mind will bombard you in coming days, weeks, and months as you regain your clarity and shore up your solvency.

These are the kinds of comments you'll hear inside your exhausted and frazzled mind: *Why did you ever take such an action?* your Cruella de Vil will demand. *It was so rash, romantic, without logic,* you'll berate yourself, as fear and intimidation seek to undermine your confidence. *Whatever made you think you could ever create such a life in a foreign country?* Or, *Whatever made you think you were an artist? Whatever made you think you could open up a successful bakery in this economy, or work from home?* We need to prepare our hearts to stare down all the personal phantoms of darkness that descend when we are tired, doubtful that we'll ever regain a sure footing.

That September afternoon, I suffered from none of these doubts. The sunlight was strong, and against it the old dark wooden beams supporting the roof looked as sturdy as the day they were hoisted sometime in the twelfth century; the plaster walls were five feet thick; in one room stood a partially exposed but completely intact twelve-foot Norman arch. I rubbed my hand slightly against the grainy stone, and a hush soothed my heart and summarily dismissed my head from the negotiations. A palpable awe came over me; I was draped in a mantle of reverence as soft as cashmere. I felt so safe, so loved, so protected. So chosen. I knew I had been led there, step by step, by some mysterious grace. I knew that I had come home.

As I stood in Newton's Chapel, my past and future intersected. I didn't ever want to leave because I knew when I did I would be facing more expectations, deadlines, obligations, and responsibilities. I was still shaken from reporting on Princess Diana's funeral. I'd covered it from Hyde Park where hundreds of thousands of people slept, wept, and waited for the funeral cortege to move past them. Swept along by the crowds and feeling less a member of the media than a mourner among her masses, I had no doubts in my mind that this glorious woman—so adored and admired for her beauty, style, devotion, sense of honor, conviction, and compassion—was deeply and passionately loved by the world. But it wasn't the world's love that she craved. She wanted her Happily Ever After. Like you, like me. Women searching for a sacred partnership in this world whether it comes in flesh and bone or wood and stone.

I knew the only way that I could leave Newton's Chapel was with the surety that I would be coming back. I made an offer to buy it on the spot.

"In literature and art, love is a myth we tell ourselves. By myth I mean not an invention or falsehood but rather a narrative that enfolds our deepest beliefs and longings. Love is the story we place above all others, the one we invest with the most value," Rosemary Sullivan ruminates in her brilliant exploration of women, passion, and romantic obsession, *Labyrinth of Desire*, which I believe should be required reading for every woman upon reaching the age of eighteen. "I have come to believe that falling obsessively in love is one of life's necessary assignments. It cracks us open. We put everything at risk. In the process we discover the dimensions of our appetites and desires. And life, to be lived fully, demands desire," Rosemary tells us. "Falling in love in this way will usually occur at a time of transition. We may not be conscious of it, but something has ended and something new must begin. Romantic obsession is a cataclysm breaking up the empty landscape."

Perhaps when we experience a *coup de foudre*—love at first sight—with a person, place, or project, the question we really should be asking ourselves is *What is it I'm longing for?* Or, *What is so lacking in my life that I need something completely different to externally shift the direction in which I'm going?*

How about money? Although Rosemary Sullivan is meditating on the emotion women feel when they fall in love at first sight with a partner, and I'm the one making the leap to house fever because I've succumbed to both, money is wrapped up in all affairs of the heart. (Did you know that the name of the greatest lover of all time, *Casanova*, means "new house"? It can't be a coincidence!) Money decides and defines the boundaries of both home improvement and passionate flings.

Every relationship we have in our lives is a reflection back to us of the relationship we have with ourselves, especially our relationship with money. Until our relationship with money is healthy and sacred, our relationships with men or lovers can't possibly be so. Nor can it be with our home. How did millions of people succumb to taking out subprime mortgages they knew in their hearts they couldn't easily pay back every month? If that's not an obsession, then I don't know what the word means.

Walk through the rooms of your home and see if you can't use them to access your deepest feelings about food, body image, sex, health, marriage, creativity, parenting, spirituality, and self-nurturance. All these crucial aspects of our lives and beliefs are revealed in each of our rooms. This might be an overwhelming task at the moment, so it's a perfect puzzle to be solved over time with the Comfort Companion. When it comes to uses, it's been my experience that women create spaces for their husbands, partners, and children long before they create one for themselves, until at some point in their lives they realize they're alone and need to live somewhere.

The point worth pondering today: Do we deliberately but unconsciously hurtle ourselves toward the perilous obsession of financial ruin the way we do with romantic disasters? What else would you call being saddled in credit card debt over designer dresses, shoes, and handbags? Only the focus of desire has changed. Suddenly, without warning (or so it seems), the river rises as the convergence of our "random" financial choices surges to a flood.

Could bankruptcy of the heart, the psyche, the body, and the soul as well as the pocketbook be the mystical trigger for the essential, obligatory transformation that terrifies us? To claim and define a life of our own choosing?

When the slight, strange ligaments of fate strip us bare of everything we thought we held dear, when we are cornered to defend what we cherish, when we are forced to say to the world, "Thus far and no farther," this is how we finally create a life based on contentment, sanity, and serenity, even if it comes without a committed relationship, Barbie's dream kitchen, or prodigious funding.

Here's a thought worth holding: No matter what has gone before, no matter who has hurt or betrayed you, no matter how much money you spent or saw squandered by another, at this moment here is your truth. "Nobody can take away your future," Dorothy B. Hughes wrote in her 1945 novel *Dread Journey*, explaining, "Nobody can take away something you don't have yet."

So hold tight to your dreams—they are yours to keep.

The Ledgers of Love

Yours, Mine, Ours

The reasons that so many marriages fail is not that there is too little money in the bank — though that is undoubtedly in many cases a factor — but too little riches of other sorts treasured, laid by, counted over, assured and reckoned with foresight and with honesty and wisdom in the spending of them.

— ANNE BRYAN MCCALL,
WOMAN'S HOME COMPANION, FEBRUARY 1926

Since ancient times, every generation of women have been told by their mothers, aunts, and grandmothers, "It's just as easy to marry a rich man as a poor one."

I beg to differ.

That's because from Jane Austen novels to Lifetime television movies, few women regularly hang out with the wealthier-than-thou, especially these days. One doesn't just show up as a Chalet girl at the World Economic Forum in Davos, Switzerland. Here each January, a gilt-edged guest list of financiers, economists, globalists, royalists, activist film and rock stars, former presidents and prime ministers gather to chat up one another's agendas during the day and party like it's the 1980s at night. Bankers, risk management insurers, and hedge fund honchos used to attend, but after the Great Recession began, it's become unseemly to cavort on taxpayer bailouts, whether the men-in-suits think so or not. Still, propriety wouldn't stop Anita Loos's darling gold digger, Lorelei Lee. "Don't you know that a man being rich is like a girl being pretty?" Marilyn Monroe so succinctly explained in the delightfully screwball 1953 comedy *How to Marry a Millionaire*.

The twentysomething daughter of a friend is madly in love and planning what seems to her mother to be the world's biggest wedding. The bride's face truly lights up whenever she talks about her fellow, and she is filled with wonder and delight about every aspect of him. She knows the little things—the music he likes, his favorite teams, and how he got his middle name—and she knows the big things, too, how many children they want and where he wants to retire.

She knows all the same things we all did when we were head over heels and getting ready to glide down the aisle. But the gaps in their knowledge of each other are also the same as ours were, which is frightening by the time one is old enough to be Mother of the Bride. We also knew the names of our future kids, the kind of house we wanted to buy, the vacations we'd take together, but how many of us have ever really talked about the day-to-day mechanics of how to manage our resources in order to make those dreams come true and stay true with our new husband?

I'm not talking about prenups and retirement plans (more about that later); I'm talking about how most of us have made financial decisions *the hard way* before, during, and after marriage, by denying what we need and hiding what we expect financially until it comes to blows. Women of all ages lack clarity about our needs, wants, and expectations even in the calmest times of our lives, let alone amid the ecstatic and erratic bliss of falling in love and planning a wedding. Still, every Baby Boomer woman I've ever met knows that money is the mystery guest at the back of the church when the minister asks if there is any reason why this couple should not be lawfully joined together. If they've never discussed their feelings about money, then the bride and the groom should be the first ones to answer. Why we choose to be polite and quiet at this crucial moment in our lives is the most cosmic or karmic question about money we'll ever fudge. A friend once confided to me that she was attending a wedding soon and dreading it. She knew both the bride and the groom and how they each handled money and she believed that their marriage would be such a disaster, she felt guilty attending. "How can I drink to their happiness, when I know they will be miserable?"

De profundis. Now I know why there wasn't a dry eye when I married the Englishman. No one wanted to break my heart and confide their misgivings about my misalliance; everyone crossed their fingers and hoped there'd be a happy ending. There was. When the divorce decree was pronounced to grateful and reverential signs of the cross and "Thank you, Jesus," "Amen, Lord." But if anyone had talked to me, I probably wouldn't have listened anyway. I was too busy being happy—or planning to be, at least.

Dramatics aside, few women want to discuss money with a man with whom they're dating, living, engaged, or even married. However, we all know that ever since the world began, men and women size each other up from the first mingling of the pheromones to see if a partnership is a possibility (thanks to Charles Darwin and *On the Origin of Species* for this insight). You are analyzing height, maybe width, often length. You consider the number of times you laugh or roll your eyes. And you assess the size of the wallet or the generosity of spirit, and usually that's determined by whether or not he pays for the cappuccino at Starbucks. You think, *I might have a prince here, I can't let this one get away.* So we keep silent until we are forced to speak up. Well, it's been my painful experience that by the time the money is discussed in this way, it's too late to go home early.

Another friend, who's in the thirty-fifth year of a genuinely happy and enviable marriage, recounts the shock she had when she realized her long-haired beloved, the most liberated and least conventional man she had ever known, struggled fiercely when her career took a major upswing with a raise in pay to match. After a long and bumpy ride, they uncovered his latent conviction that a man should be the main breadwinner; it took a lot of love, work, and internal adjustments for them to get over that hump.

Similarly, over time my friend discovered that she felt an unacknowledged pressure to give her family the "perfect" home, even while working long hours. She found herself particularly annoyed whenever her husband complained about the cost of a new sofa or landscaping bill, even though her paycheck covered it. Didn't he understand those actions were her way of expressing love and satisfying her need to feather their nest? And if she toiled in the office, wasn't it her right to decide how, where, and when the money was spent? It took them awhile to figure out what was going on, and for both of them to shed their Ozzie and Harriet expectations of domestic goddess and breadwinner. Finally they began to "talk it through." The conversation's been going on between them for twenty years, and she says they're not finished yet. But now there is a category in their budgeting for "house and garden."

Needless to say, few young (or not-so-young) lovers are excited to sit down and hash out their money madness when there are hopes and dreams to discuss. But maybe the global financial crisis is just the opportunity we've all needed to stop being economical with the truth. In fact, part of growing up (no matter what your age) and growing together as a couple is figuring out how your expectations fit your reality, which are always changing, or should be. Remember, Darwin taught that it wasn't the biggest or strongest of the species who survived, but the ones most adaptable to change. Evolution is not shortsighted, and neither should be our solvency.

"Shall I marry a poor man?" a young reader named

Susan asked the *Woman's Home Companion* "agony aunt,"
Anne Bryan McCall, in February 1926. "I plan to be married in the fall; yet I'm afraid to, because maybe for a while
we shall have to skimp and save, if my fiancé is to get the
success he is hoping for.

"Already I've spent hours and hours on budgets. I
wonder if anything gets under your skin like being poor.
I know my friends are pitying me and, frankly, I've begun
to pity myself. Maybe that's disloyal of me...So will you
either scold me, or help me to see things clearly?"

"My dear Susan...No one who has ever fully faced
that problem feels very much like scolding about it, I
think...Poverty in marriage, if it is to be met practically,
calls for riches of another sort than those to be put in
the bank...You will need riches of the mind, riches of
the spirit, riches of affection—not imaginary riches, but
very real ones—with which to meet the expense. And your
whole problem, as I see it, and which only you can answer
is, *have you got them?*"

If we work toward achieving these riches of spirit as
well as material solvency, we are putting our best foot forward on the path to financial serenity.

Wedlock Deadlock

Her present life appeared like the dream of a distempered
imagination, or like one of those frightful fictions, in
which the wild genius of the poets sometimes delighted.
Reflection brought only regret, and anticipation terror.

— MRS. ANN WARD RADCLIFFE,
THE MYSTERIES OF UDOLPHO (1794)

Like many women who find themselves processing financial events they never expected, there are moments when I feel baffled, bewildered, even bereft after nearly a year of this resettling. Then there are the furious and feisty days when closets get cleaned and files purged. Some mornings you wake up with a dreadful sigh, the submerged grief swelling up in your chest like a bad cold. You know you should rest—that's what you'd tell your daughter or best friend—but you keep on shuffling; a month later the doctor calls it bronchitis, pneumonia, or a staph infection, and you're forced to rest. But most days, even when the sun is shining and it's quiet on the surface, you ache all over, all the time—anticipatory aches, I've come to call them, muscle spasms from holding yourself so tense, waiting for the next shoe to fall.

So many unexpected personal permutations must be considered when we're attempting forensic accounting, in order to reconcile love, betrayal, passion, and promises expressed through money. Our well-being is intricately connected to our dis-ease about money; wealth and health are intertwined ligaments, and I'd be lying if I tried to convince you otherwise. "The first wealth is health," Ralph Waldo Emerson reminds us, and he didn't just mean whether we could make it through the day by remote control; he was referring to the vitality, energy, enthusiasm, and optimism that are necessary to turn our lives around from any setback. Like money, our emotional moods ebb and flow as we learn to make peace with the past in order to have a future.

So I must deal with the instrument of my current financial undoing: the third husband. A few years ago I married an Englishman, but to my sorrow and dismay, the Englishman married my money. This is the conclusion of a British court and because of "such unreasonable behaviour," I can't be expected to live with this man, but neither can I reclaim all the money and assets that flowed into his possession and control. Because no one knows where the money has gone. So I've got a choice—to move on and create a new life for myself, or to use my time, creative energy, and emotion to wail with rage and dig up the past. The choice seems pretty clear when it's someone else, doesn't it? Move on and make a new life from scratch, SBB. What about you? Are you holding on to a core of wrath that's burning you from the inside out? It doesn't matter how righteous our fury is. It doesn't matter if it's Bernie Madoff, Goldman Sachs, Lehman Brothers, or a charming English roué who professed undying love or having your best interests at heart: If you don't watch your own back and count your own silverware, nobody else does. When it's gone, it's gone.

Now love has filed for bankruptcy; my heart has been forced to sell its assets, shut its doors, and go out of business. To my astonishment, at this writing, everything I've worked for over my entire career is up for grabs in an English court and barristers, solicitors, attorneys, and accountants on both sides of the Atlantic are working on my behalf to prevent this catastrophe. I can't even believe how much this has cost me. I was forced to sell my last wonder-fully extravagant purchase—Marilyn Monroe's furs—to finance ending a marriage with a scoundrel. That could have been the money for my new start and in a way, it was. But this goes a long way toward explaining why I've spent the last year in my pajamas writing this book in the corner of my sister's living room.

Shortly I must return to England for the court hearing on whether or not to recognize our prenuptial agreement, which stated that we each would take out of the marriage what we brought into it. The Englishman brought an umbrella stand, a fire screen, a sketch of himself as a young boy, family photographs, golf clubs, his cricket gear, and the car he drove in through my creamy ivory stone electri-fied gates. I came fully loaded with three beautiful homes, paintings, antiques, investments, pension, and businesses. In a short space of time, most of my lovely assets came under the hammer in the auction rooms of Christie's and Sotheby's, turned into cash at the Englishman's insistence "for our mutual benefit." He was forceful, but I gave my consent, albeit under duress of verbal abuse and emotional battering as I became too afraid to speak up or protest un-til I finally packed up the cat and left.

Now the Respondent (as I have come to call the ex) refers to what's left, including my precious Newton's Chapel, the books I have written in the past, and the one I'm writing now, as well as the career I created over two decades, as his "chattels," harking back to the Dark Ages when a woman had no rights, possessions, or even power over her own life, separate from her husband's whims and pleasures.

"To a generous mind few circumstances are more af-flicting than a discovery of perfidy in those whom we have trusted," the early English novelist Mrs. Ann Ward Rad-cliffe wrote in 1791 in her pioneering Gothic novel *The Romance of the Forest*. Mrs. Radcliffe's heroines were always innocents, "good girls" who trusted strangers too easily, to their regret and ruin. After the malevolence of the mysterious, seedy baronets with dark pasts who swept them off their feet, plundered their fortunes, and locked them in the towers of gloomy castles is revealed, the heroine exchanges her silk gown for chain mail, helmet, and sword to outwit the rake and reclaim her future.

During the nineteenth century, to be "Mrs. Radcliffed" needed no explanation. Her page-turning technique and heart-churning romances inspired generations of women novelists, including Jane Austen, Mary Shelley, Charlotte Brontë, and Daphne du Maurier.

Is there a woman with soul so dead that she never to herself has said, "I'd love to be a heroine in my own Gothic romance"? Be careful what you pray for, dear one. I shudder from the memories of what brought me to my life's Chapter 11, and I'd be very economical with the truth if I didn't admit that I'm sad and scared that these proceedings can even take place. It gives new meaning to my meditation on the nature of the sacredness of money throughout this book.

"Bankruptcy is a sacred state, a condition beyond condition as theologians might say, and attempts to investigate it are necessarily obscene, like spiritualism," John Updike writes of a dark void so many are passing through today because of the economic crisis. "One knows only that he [or she] has passed into it and lives beyond us, in a condition not ours."

It is so heartbreaking when marriages break up, however long they lasted or didn't. It means not only the loss of love, but the loss of our futures and friendships as well as our financial well-being. Very few couples have enough money to allow both parties to maintain the same lifestyle after the breakup, so on top of watching the other aspects of our lives crumble beneath us, we have to deal with the shattering of the most tangible sense of safety for ourselves and our family, especially if there are children of the marriage.

"The last thing a newly single mother in the midst of negotiating a child-support agreement wants to hear is that she should substitute insight for cash," Liz Perle admits in her illuminating memoir *Money: Women, Emotions, and Cash.* "Everyone's divorce is different. But each requires us to put a price on our lives. That means that someone has to assign a value to something that the other spouse has just said they don't want anymore. It's a kind of paradox, one that requires a strong sense of inner worth to lay claim to an outer one."

When I talk to my friends who are also in the middle of messy divorces, they have no doubt that they are justified in whatever tactic they or their lawyers take. But it is just as shocking to be the mouse forced to roar as it is to be the cat finding this previously meek creature threatening him.

However, when I talk to friends who have gotten to the other side of this battle, almost to a woman they regret any additional vindictiveness they exerted in the process of saying "Good riddance." These friends have never regretted the breakup and have landed on their feet in a way that is usually more gratifying than the life they lived before the conjugal crash.

The one regret I do hear after the fact regards any lashings-out over the money. Whether or not it really made a difference in the financial well-being of either partner, the memory of feeling spiteful bothers them more than the memories of the other person's failings. Having to face the external fiasco of their lives was one thing; having to face the denial of the "better angels" of our own nature is another.

But every coin has two sides, and no one goes through such emotional and financial turmoil gracefully all the time. We need to give ourselves permission to rage, stand up for ourselves, shout the world down, and fight for what is just and fair if we are ever to allow ourselves to eventually forgive both the Petitioner and the Respondent in the tearing asunder of what was once so beautiful. When we can accept the entire range of emotions—hidden, present, or future—after love files for bankruptcy, the Divine Receiver gifts us with moments of stunning clarity and unexpected compassion. But Heaven will not be mocked. Or as Mrs. Radcliffe so poetically put it:

> Fate sits on these dark battlements, and frowns;
> And as the portals open to receive me
> Her voice, in sullen echoes, through the courts,
> Tells of a nameless deed...

How to Talk to Your Husband About Money

August 1945: There was a time before the war—it seems in another world. Where has it gone? Am I the writer who wrote Black Narcissus? Has she gone, just as the money has gone?

—RUMER GODDEN

"What Were They Thinking?" is a magazine and newspaper headline often used as a commentary over funny and bizarre photographs. But what I've always wondered, and I suspect you have, too, is what our personal heroines were thinking when they faced the challenges, crossroads, changes, and choices that shaped the trajectory of their lives. How did they recover when sorrow slapped them down? How did they feel after achieving a long-desired dream, only to find that some of their friends were too jealous to share their joy? How did they cope when the golden coach turned into a pumpkin and suddenly their overnight success turned to ashes? Or their private marriage became public fodder? When the diagnosis was devastating, who did they call? When they discovered that all the money was gone, how did they take the news? When they were depressed, scared, anxious, and lonely, what did they do for relief, reassurance, or comfort?

I'm thinking particularly of the Anglo-Indian author Rumer Godden and the moment, in July 1941, when she discovered that all the money she'd entrusted to her stockbroker husband Laurence Foster to invest for her and her family was squandered. Lost. Gambled. More than that, Laurence had borrowed on her future earnings and owed scores of other people huge debts, including his stockbrokerage firm, other brokers, and money lenders. He even raised capital on their life insurance policies without her knowledge. This shocking discovery meant that Rumer's continuing royalties from *Black Narcissus* would have to be used to bail them out of financial ruin, instead of creating a much-desired homestead. Can you imagine having your next creative thought mortgaged to the hilt? Her reaction was unsurprising, according to her biographer, Anne Chisholm, in *Rumer Godden: A Storyteller's Life*: "Shock, anger and anxiety are a powerful mixture and the debacle of July 1941 left Rumer with a permanent sense of shame and injustice."

But Rumer's subsequent dilemma is what rivets me because it's such a typical feminine reaction. She could do nothing publicly during World War II; Laurence was a captain in the army, and as long as they remained married Rumer and their two daughters were eligible for family benefits, which they desperately needed. However, secrets are corrosive to the soul—especially secrets that keep you trapped in anger and deceit. Eventually, after the war, Rumer divorced Laurence and remarried. But the experience shook her to the core of her being. It would be *forty-five years* before she would even broach the shocking trauma in her memoirs. Yet here, between the lines, is a notation full of meaning and one that every woman sorting out her independent financial solvency should consider: "I had kept the full financial prospects of *Black Narcissus* [the film] to myself which made me feel mean, but I was learning wisdom." I believe what she meant was that she learned to keep her own financial counsel instead of always playing Lady Bountiful, a role I know very well. A sudden windfall is a wonderful thing and you immediately want to share it, but keeping your relationship with money intimately private is the beginning of wealth wisdom.

Another rich, famous, and accomplished woman who suffered financial ruin after allowing her husband to manage her career and money was Doris Day. In their fascinating book *The Money Mirror*, Annette Lieberman and Vicki Lindner recount how Doris entrusted her fortune and assets to her third husband, Marty Melcher, "who in turn, entrusted them to an unscrupulous Hollywood shark, Jerry Rosenthal," who "invested" Day's money in mysterious oil wells and other bogus or ill-fated properties. From the beginning Doris had doubts, not about her husband but the type of investments he was making for their future. She felt uncomfortable in high-risk ventures and preferred to invest in art. Had she followed up on her intuition she might have soon realized that Marty knew even less about money management than she did. But anytime she'd bring up the question, it would always boil down to the same explosive retort: "Don't you trust me?"

Doris Day recalled: "Although I didn't like being in oil wells and hotels, there was no question that I did trust Marty."

She should have made it a question.

For after Melcher died, Doris discovered the shocking truth—that she was broke. Marty had even signed her up to do another television series she had not wanted in order to pay his debts.

Lieberman and Lindner address this type of feminine money mismanagement, which they described as money blindness: "Sometimes we use the power of our imagination to manufacture our dreams—in Doris's case, a loving, protective trustworthy man—and close our eyes to the glaring difference between reality and myth. Unfortunately for Doris, money got mixed up with her unresolved emotions."

I was enjoying a girls'-day-out last week when a friend mentioned that she and her husband were going to "talk about money" the next day. The other women laughed, rolled their eyes, and immediately exchanged comedic horror stories about how they hate being called on the financial carpet by their significant others and how they put those talks off as long as possible.

In the midst of general merriment and margaritas, I was struck by how much we sounded like a bunch of schoolgirls who had been called into the principal's office. Clearly we saw ourselves as the person with less power and prestige in our marriages, so we were the ones who had to follow the rules set down by our partners. We saw and accepted our role as having to explain and justify financial choices we have made or want to make.

No wonder we hate those talks! So we put them off, and when we have to deal with them, we think the best way to prepare for the grilling is to either minimize the info that will trigger a confrontation or be prepared to "compare and contrast" our foibles and expenditures with our partner's, making sure we come out looking better by putting him in the wrong.

How do you talk to your husband about money? Every woman at some point in her life has mixed up her heart and her bank account. Some of us do it repeatedly, because we all learn life lessons at our own pace. And I would bet, almost to a reader, that most women don't have an answer because they've never really considered the question. That's because money usually brings up barbed reappraisals: Who's earning what? Who's contributing zilch to the household? Whose spending habits are out of control? Who exercises the power in the relationship by controlling the checkbook?

Rumer Godden never spoke with her husband about money until there wasn't any more money.

Neither did Doris Day.

Neither did I.

What about you?

I've never been able to hold up my end of a conversation about money with any man unless I had my own bank account and could point to it as the answer to all spending questions from anyone. Why was I so defensive about spending? Perhaps because I was never able to finish a conversation about money logically with myself. Certainly this was a lesson I thought I'd learned after my second divorce and during the decade that followed, which brought me much success and money. Clearly I was wrong again.

So I accept the responsibility that I didn't ask for money advice or really hold conversations with anybody about money. I didn't want anyone telling me how not to spend it or suggesting that I spend it their way.

Still, years on your own come with a tax on loneliness. When I met my third husband, much like Doris Day, I wanted someone who could take care of me, emotionally and business-wise, which blinded me to the reality that the Englishman couldn't take care of himself, much less me. Like Marty Melcher, he had many stories about his business acumen in the financial battlefield known as "The City"—the Wall Street of London—but gradually I became aware that the only stream of income into the joint checking account was mine.

When I would bring up the subject of money, he would berate me for not earning more, yell at me for all the spending I did before he arrived on the scene, and behave like an emotional bully. In his eyes I was a "loser" and a "has-been." According to him, I had not one personal friend or professional colleague who cared for me for any reason except the money they could make or take off me. Now, of course, I realize that this was his worldview because this was exactly how the Englishman was "managing" my finances and business, taking it off me as fast as possible. But gradually I succumbed to the barrage of negativity engulfing me, learning to keep my silence and my own counsel in order to keep the peace. Until one day, on our second anniversary, I asked him why he treated me so appallingly. He said simply, "I realized *all* the money was gone."

It would take me another two years to process this information, believe him, and get out.

So here we have three talented women—Rumer Godden, Doris Day, and me—who excelled in the eyes of the world but not in our own, for despite our ability to make money with our creativity, hard work, and moxie, we did not know how to talk to our husbands about our money until we all ended up not having any.

From our Cautionary Tales case analysis, here are a few hints on how to talk to your husband about money:

- With a bank account that's solely in your name and that no one else knows about. This savings account is completely separate from the savings account you have with your husband or partner to handle emergencies. This is your "I'm Out of Here" money, for whatever that phrase might mean to you someday. As Rumer Godden pointed out, you may feel like this is a little "mean," but keeping some money close to your chest is the beginning of financial wisdom. Remember, just as in a partnership, money stays where it's wanted.

- With a joint account to cover all the household needs and with a very clear understanding of who contributes what for the common good.

- With a dedicated pin money stash of cash to which you contribute every week, thanks to the money you save using the cash envelope system.

- On a weekly basis, when you refill your envelopes with cash and the two of you go over how the week's money was spent.

- Without making secret purchases, which undermine your confidence in yourself.

- Without spontaneous purchases, which erode your trust in yourself.

- By keeping track of how you spend, when you spend, and why you spend. What emotions did you experience as you were in this spending cycle?

I've come to understand—and you will, too—that when you feel comfortable about your money, you'll talk to your husband or partner about your finances, coming from a place of quiet strength and power, not submerged hysteria. All of the above hints reinforce your commitment to yourself and to your money.

In her memoir *A Time to Dance, No Time to Weep*, Rumer Godden is frank in remembering the distress and disillusionment caused by her husband Laurence's fiscal philandering, but she recognizes (as must we all) her own naïveté and wishful thinking when she granted him carte blanche over their finances, even though she was the primary wage earner. "Wanting him truly to be head of the house I had left our expenses to him, making over money when he asked [writing checks from her account to cover his debts]...but nothing had been paid. Sometimes I still cannot believe it; Laurence had stood by while I sold the furniture, knowing that he had already sold it twice over to different people. He had sold the car. When I went to the bank to try and cash the children's policies they had already been cashed; our joint account was empty." When she was handed a list of the debts her husband owed his brokerage and was asked by the managing director, "What are you doing to do?" she said, "Pay them."

Of course, that is the first instinct honorable women would have—isn't it? No. The first instinct we need to have is to protect ourselves.

Here is the difficult lesson Rumer Godden shares with us as we come to terms with regaining our clarity, safety, and solvency: "Of all the silly things I have done in my life I expect that was the silliest; it took almost all the *Black Narcissus* money I had saved. In those two words I threw away what would have been some security for myself and the children."

We must never again allow a situation in our lives that would prompt us to write such a chilling admission in our memoirs. Which is why you need to learn to talk to your husband, and if ever I have another one, so will I.

Terms of Endearment

Prenups, Post-Ops, and Oops, You Did It Again

Since marriage isn't forever anymore, real commitment comes after the fact: when you burn the prenup.

—ERICA JONG

In my hopelessly romantic imagination, the two most precious gifts I could give the Englishman—my terms of endearment—were as perfect as I was certain our marriage would be. For a wedding gift, I gave my new husband the Duke of Windsor's private dictionaries—a matching set in dark blue leather with the royal crest, which sat on the duke's desk during his exile after he gave up the English throne in 1936 "for the woman I love." I had purchased them at the famous Sotheby's sale in 1998 and saved them in my Hope Chest for the day I met my soul mate, a man whom I was sure would be willing to give up an entire kingdom for the love he felt for me.

And for our tenth anniversary, I planned to burn our prenuptial agreement, because surely by then all the people who were shaking their heads over our union would see that we were one of the world's great romances. Alas, the marriage didn't make it to the fifth round, and all I can say in between the weeping is "thank you" to the

intuitive cosmic Powers That Be who insisted on nudg-
ing me to get a prenup. I resisted—it's hardly romantic to
prepare for a divorce before the wedding vows—but that
was before I learned that a happy marriage is as much a
partnership in the business of Life as a reverie in domestic
bliss.

"Marriage is about trust, and trust takes you quickly
to the matter of money," Erica Jong wrote in the essay
"Beyond Marriage" (2000). "It is very hard to trust someone and share all your worldly goods with that person, but
the alternative is worse." She describes how ten years after she and her fourth husband were married, they burned
the prenup. "We burned it in a wok at the end of a dinner
party to which we had invited our dearest friends—and
our lawyers. Either that's the most romantic gesture ever
made, or the stupidest. I prefer to see it as romantic." And
so did I, but unfortunately I didn't make it to the wok
burning stage, unless the crash and burn counts. Cover
your head, the cinders are still falling.

As long as there have been marriages, there have
been "marriage settlements," from biblical times up until
the twentieth century when they went out of fashion
except for the very rich. The most famous chronicler
of the inescapable linchpin that held nineteenth-century
English society together was the Victorian author Anthony Trollope, who wrote forty-seven novels on the
subject of courtship and marriage between 1847 and his
death in 1882. During that time, the Married Women's
Property Act (1882) passed, changing English law so
that a woman could continue to be a separate owner and
administrator of her own property after marriage. This
was cataclysmic in its reverberations throughout English
aristocracy and makes it all the more inconceivable that
modern prenuptial agreements still aren't recognized as
law in Great Britain. In the English court system, each
prenup must be argued on its own merits, an experience
that's the emotional and financial equivalent to being tor-

tured on the rack before being dragged to the chopping block.

However, Trollope's fictional characters — both women and men — were constantly finagling ways to con, capture, and keep sums through their cleverness at the marital charades. In his 1864 novel *The Small House at Allington*, the mercenary Adolphus Crosbie sets his sights on Alexandrina, the daughter of an earl, in order to advance in English society. But Alexandrina manages to bind him "hand and foot" in a premarriage settlement. The heart of the settlement rests on insurance policies paid for out of the groom's meager savings. Here are the groom's thoughts on his happy union: "If he would only die the day after his marriage, there would really be a very nice sum for Alexandrina, almost worthy of the acceptance of an earl's daughter." Needless to say, she has similar thoughts. The marriage breaks up within weeks, and she returns to the privileged bosom of her mother. Adolphus was still bound to pay maintenance for his wife, however, as well as those dastardly annual insurance premiums. In this comedy of marital manners and money, his estranged spouse continues to cost him even after he's made a widower; when she dies on the Continent at the health spa at Baden-Baden, he's saddled with expenses he could never have imagined such as "the embalming of her dear remains" and payment for "that horrid, ghastly funeral." The only memento poor Crosbie ends up with is a mourning ring composed of his beloved's hair.

That's what you get when you marry for money, not love.

A decade ago I created an irrevocable family trust that, after my death, protected certain assets for my daughter so that if she married and then divorced, her inheritance couldn't be part of the marital pot to divide. At the time my attorneys wanted me to isolate my own assets in a similar fashion in case my own future marriage had a similar sad ending. I was aghast. I couldn't imagine marrying someone unaware that he was more interested in my money than my love. This confession now confounds me, but a woman in love and getting ready for a later-life marriage is not thinking clearly. I realize now that I stayed married to the Englishman for two more years beyond his chilling confession because I simply could not process or accept the idea that someone would marry me for only my money. Also, there was such a sense of shame. I bought into every one of his lies. I thought if I confided this to my family or close friends, I'd shrivel and die from the humiliation. Now, after therapy and counseling, I realize that fortune hunters always count on isolating their wives with shame, manipulation, lies, and guile. But in tarrying to end a marriage that I knew had become emotionally abusive, I now realize I lost much more than money.

When young women marry for the first time, setting out with their husbands to create a life together that will contain future financial assets, I can understand why they would be reluctant to prepare on paper for the dissolution of those marriages. But after a woman has been married and had a family, she has many more assets than she might at first realize: a family business, prospects of a future inheritance from elderly parents, pensions, an interest in real estate. She also has an obligation to take care of her own children and grandchildren.

As heartbroken as I am over marrying a man who didn't respect or love me, I am so grateful to have had a prenuptial agreement, which I only insisted upon because my circle of intimates bravely would not back down. I was strong in my conviction of true love, but luckily they were stronger in forcing me to be practical. And when the judge made my prenup into an order for a clean-break dissolution, ending the most painful experience I've ever known, my relief at being returned my own life, home, possessions, career, and future was so enormous, I still shudder with gratitude.

Now I'm convinced that the lesson women of all ages need to master is the Million Dollar Baby rule: Always "protect yourself." Self-preservation is the soul's prime directive. We can't take care of anyone if we don't start with ourselves. And when it comes to mixing money and love, the pen is mightier than the kiss.

Part Six

To Begin Again: Creating a Life of Contentment

One day my life will end; and lest
Some whim should prompt you to review it,
Let her who knows the subject best
Tell you the shortest way to do it;
Then say, "Here lies one doubly blest."
Say, "She was happy." Say, "She knew it."

—JAN STRUTHER

Calling All Girls

An Account of Your Own

*I have never written a book that was not born out of a
question I needed to answer for myself.*

— MAY SARTON

Writing about money is both an exercise in peeling an
onion and an exorcism. Without warning, hot,
smarting tears accompany a flash of insight, as I find myself pulling back more layers with each slice than I could
have imagined when I started this process. Nothing about
money is as simple or as straightforward as it might appear
to onlookers, especially if the onlooker is you.

Take my first money anecdote: My parents couldn't
pay the $75 to take me home from the hospital, so my
father got a loan from the bank. Literally from the first
breath I've been living on borrowed money. Early patterns
around money—my nana's quarters, Granny's round numbers, and my parents' beliefs that somehow money will be
there *magically*—set up a perilous obstacle course for me.
But I'm not alone. The entire Baby Boomer generation
was raised on Frosted Flakes and postwar con-
sumerism—from spanking-new three-bedroom suburban
boxes (bought on the GI Bill) to shiny bright appliances,
cars, and backyard grills. Young Americans had survived
the hardships of war and were now celebrating the right
to buy their way to happily ever after on the deferred pay-

ment plan. The first credit card, Diners Club, debuted in 1950, just around the time that television entered America's knotty-pine-paneled living rooms. I can still remember my dad proudly flashing that shiny piece of mystical plastic when the family went out for dinner. Our own children, the Gen Xers and Gen Yers, inherited this magical thinking from us, never really knowing a financial framework without credit and debt.

But back to where our futures began.

For girls growing up in the 1950s, our financial role models began with June Cleaver, Donna Reed, and Margaret Anderson. Black-and-white TV shows with laugh tracks (*Leave It to Beaver*, *The Donna Reed Show*, *Father Knows Best*) recorded these women's domestic bliss of pearls, heels, frilly aprons, and husbands who handled the money. This pleasantly reinforced the stereotype of a stay-at-home mom with a perfectly supportive husband who provided undisclosed sums with which she smoothly ran the household while looking pretty and perky. Sign me up.

However, some of my favorite skewering of money management came from the screwball financial schemes of Lucy Ricardo and Ethel Mertz, as this bit from a 1953 episode of *I Love Lucy* reveals:

> RICKY RICARDO: Fred, how often is Ethel's checking account overdrawn?
> FRED MERTZ: Never.
> RICKY RICARDO: Never? How do you manage that?
> ETHEL MERTZ: It's easy. I never had enough money at one time to open a checking account.

Finally, we have the fabulous Lorelei Lee (Marilyn Monroe) and her two blond chums (Lauren Bacall and Betty Grable), who are nearly broke but put all their cash toward renting a chic but barely furnished penthouse in

New York in the hope of snaring wealthy husbands in the 1953 film *How to Marry a Millionaire.*

So, to recap the female Baby Boomer teen tutorials for fiscal responsibility: Marry a rich man, marry a man who makes you feel rich, or throw your bills up in the air, à la Lucy, and pay whichever ones land on the floor faceup. Most of us did not have a career path when we first needed to grapple with financial concerns. Betty Friedan did not write *The Feminine Mystique* until 1963!

You can see there were some fatal flaws in our financial education. Humongous gaps in connecting the dots, dollars, and sense.

A dear friend told me recently about the time when she was fourteen and asked her father to escort her to the bank to open her first account with her babysitting money. The whole experience was empowering and excitingly ceremonial, and she laughingly confesses she's never felt more grown-up than that moment when she first held her slick dark blue passbook with SAVINGS BOOK imprinted in gold on the cover. Its stately records of deposits and balance of $100 written in perfect blue-black ink gave her an enormous sense of security; for months she would sleep with it underneath her pillow at night and locked in her jewelry case while she was at school. She also found that she increased her babysitting assignments for the sheer pleasure of being able to go to the bank every month to make another deposit and treat herself to an ice cream soda afterward.

There is something wonderful about having your very own money, separate and apart; having a special place to store money reminds you of your power, creativity, and independence. Adding even small amounts can give you a sense of achievement, increase your peace of mind, and motivate you to bigger and better accomplishments and healthier personal relationships. As you become more comfortable with managing larger amounts of money, you open up the potential for your dreams to come true. You

grow in grace, wisdom, and talent, becoming a good stewardess of Divine Providence.

My friend said she took all of this for granted when she
was growing up, but like many of us, the more she became
part of a couple, a family, and a small business, the less she
thought about possessing personal money as an important
safeguard to her individuality and authenticity. When she
did start to think about it, she felt guilty: Wasn't it selfish
to put some of her money aside and not pool it with the
family resources?

No, it's not. Having your own bank account is a statement that you have your own identity, your own dreams,
and your own goals. It is important protection for your
well-being.

Do any of these early money memories spark your
own? How astonishing it was to discover myself on the
page for the first time in my favorite preteen magazine,
Calling All Girls, "the magazine for sub-teens, debs and co-
eds." While I was writing *Simple Abundance*, I remembered
the ragtag remnants of a story I read when I was ten, a
story that held a key to understanding my core belief in
self-improvement. The main character was a young girl
named Posy, who changed her life by giving up her sloppy,
slovenly ways and became the Harvest Queen. Posy was
my first literary dose of self-help. I read her story com-
pulsively, especially the part where she begins to clean
her room. I was astounded by both the act (cleaning your
room voluntarily?) and the notion that pretty, smart, neat,
well-groomed girls—Harvest Queens—weren't born that
way: They were *created*. Why, if Posy could change her life,
I could, too! That was the summer I walked into a revival
tent on the pages of *Calling All Girls* and was baptized in
the Church of Improbable Happy Endings. My faith in aspirational literature sustains me to this day.

Anyone old enough to remember this palm-size
monthly magazine with its redemptive pulp fiction and
cheery how-tos knows what I mean. Although *Calling All*

Girls' cute blond cover girl (drawn by pinup illustrator Freeman Elliott) probably bore little resemblance to its readers—and certainly none to me!—I adored her easy good looks, great outfits, seasonal costumes, and cute dachshund. Unfortunately, when I scoured years' worth of the magazine, I couldn't find one article about budgeting your way to financial happiness.

Sometimes when you travel back to your wonder years, unwelcome memories arrive. Perhaps you were the girl who always felt like an outside because of her hand-me-down clothes; who served punch at the dance rather than taking the floor herself because her family couldn't afford dance lessons; the girl who quickly passed the popular kids' hangout so that no one would suspect she had to work after school to help her family now that her father had abandoned them.

Remember that what you are doing here is neutralizing all the misinformation, neglect, abuse, cruelty, and negative emotions you carry as a "money orphan." In the same loving, patient way that you'd approach teaching a young child learning to count, you will teach yourself money management. The little girl within is fascinated with the process of learning but then after she doesn't get it right quickly becomes frustrated. You as her mother or money mentor must switch her attention to something else and then return the next day to the colorful beads for her to count. Eventually, through great patience, care, love, and direction, she learns and feels a great sense of accomplishment and pride.

This is how you will feel again, once you learn how to be a Good Stewardess of your money. "The well of Providence is deep," Mary Webb wrote in *Ladies' Home Journal* in 1946. "It is the buckets we bring to it that are small." And that largesse extends to both the giving and the receiving of Life's bounty.

The New Home Economics

Counting Our Blessings

*Women must have some one to fight for; something to
fight against, or they fall by the wayside. Nothing keeps
them so much alive as never having quite enough money.*

—PHYLLIS NICHOLSON

In exploring the treasure trove that is women's domestic
literature from 1850 to 1960, it is reassuring to remember that the word *economics*—which we've come to
associate with Wall Street and not the kitchens of subur-
bia—is actually derived from two Greek words: *oikos*
(house) and *nemo* (management). An *economist*, then, as
originally defined, is "one who manages household affairs." What's even more fascinating is that the term
homemaker was coined by *Ladies' Home Journal* in a series of
ads that began running in 1931:

> There is a new word in the English lan-
> guage—Homemaker. It is not yet in dictionaries, but
> when it is, it will be defined like this:
> HOMEMAKER, n. feminine. One who makes a
> home, who manages a household, cares for her chil-
> dren, and promotes the happiness and well-being of
> her family.

Homemaking, one word not two, is a bigger job than housekeeping. It is a bigger job than any man in any business. More money is spent in homemaking, in the aggregate, than in any other human endeavor. And the returns in satisfactions, pleasures and progress, are also greater. The future of America is more dependent upon homemaking than upon all our other industries combined... The homemaker may be a wife and mother. She may be daughter or sister. She may be a widow, businesswoman, she may be young, middle-aged or old. But she must be a manager, for she spends eighty-five percent of the money that goes into all retail trade... To this HOMEMAKER the whole of *Ladies' Home Journal* is dedicated each month.

That's you. And me. I've been both a "working mother" in an office and a stay-at-home "working mother." But I've rarely attended to my home as a business. Do you? After we've dusted, mopped, straightened, vacuumed, made beds, breakfast, lunch, and dinner, either before or after we've commuted two hours, we're exhausted. In this everyday stupor, do we even realize that we manage micro global economies? What if our domestic "futures" —women's natural resources such as time, creative energy, emotion, enterprise, and money—were traded like oil, gas, sugar, corn, cocoa, wheat, or orange juice? Would there be "confidence" in how we would perform in six months or a year from now? What's our volatility index? In fact, how are we performing today? You laugh and so do I, because if we don't, we'll all be crying in our beer.

"Home economics has not fared well at the hands of historians. Until recently women's historians largely dismissed home economics as little more than a conspiracy to keep women in the kitchen," Sarah Stage tells us in the fascinating reconsideration of "women's work" that she edited with Virginia B. Vincenti, *Rethinking Home Eco-*

nomics. "For the generation of women who grew up in the 1950s and 1960s, the words 'home economics' still conjure up memories of junior high school classes in cooking and sewing—hours spent making aprons and white sauce, twin symbols of prescribed middle-class domesticity. The feminists of the 1970s cast off their aprons long before they burned their bras."

And in so doing, they cast their daughters and granddaughters adrift. "Many middle-aged women of today had mothers who were dissatisfied housewives. These mothers taught their daughters not to get trapped but to get their degree and go out into the world and fulfill the mothers' frustrated ambitions. In droves, the daughters did just this—overall, a good thing," Cheryl Mendelson explains in her encyclopedic domestic primer, *Home Comforts: The Art and Science of Keeping House*. "However, many young women have confided to me sadly that they felt sometimes as though they were being driven from things feminine and domestic by mothers who would not let them help cook or teach them anything of the mother's own domestic crafts, no matter how much the daughters wanted to learn them."

But that was then, and this is now. And while there is some truth to the notion that we can't go home again, what we can do is cherish, celebrate, and consecrate our home again to reach a new pride of place, one leftover feast and replaced button at a time. We begin by acknowledging the role that homemaking is *meant* to play in our feminine soul's nurturing by giving thanks that instead of a crisis, what we face each morning is a golden opportunity to redesign our lives and our family's future through our creative choices. Some of the changes that you and I are having to make through necessity are choices that we've long desired, even secretly prayed for, but didn't have the courage to pursue. Perhaps your house has gotten out of hand with clutter. You have to downsize because of the economy and are forced to edit your possessions, sorting between what's meaningful and what's junk. If you can accept the priceless spiritual gift hidden in this season of relinquishment, you will know peace and plenty that the world and all its stock markets cannot take away.

I've learned the hard way that women don't create homes for themselves; we create them for our husbands and our children. If you don't believe me, think about the rooms of your house and how many nooks are yours — is there a comfy chair with a good light for reading? What about next to your bed — do you have an end table large enough to hold all you need (a good reading lamp, stacks of books and magazines, a journal or notebook and pen for those 5 AM brainstorms), bed linens you can't wait to crawl underneath, and something cozy to cuddle? I'm sure that no matter what your financial situation is right now or has been in the past, your self-nurturance in your own home has probably been scant.

And for the opportunity to reverse this anti-home-keeping trend, we give thanksgiving no matter what the season of our life.

The Art of Elegant
Economies

*Domestic novels reveal the textures of women's lives
and the infinite possibilities and permutations of the
domestic space. They also give contemporary women the
chance to reflect that we are fortunate in not being
compelled to live in that way unless we choose to do so,
which makes domesticity a potentially enriching way of
life, not a reductive one.*

— JANE BROCKET

One of the reasons that the Victorian era tugged on my
heart so strongly in my thirties when I was a working
mother with a small child was that during the nineteenth
century, women were not conflicted about their role in the
home. For the Victorians, a happy home was viewed as an
island of stability amid a sea of social change. Mother was
captain of the good ship *Tranquility* or—as Mrs. Isabella
Beeton instructed British homemakers in *The Book of
Household Management*—"the Commander of An Army."
First published in 1861, this 1,112-page compendium of
"tried and tested" recipes as well as advice on matters of
hygiene, etiquette, and family life sold more than sixty
thousand copies in its first year and for generations of
homemakers served as a practical guide to achieving domestic bliss. So comprehensive, authoritative, and

indispensable was Mrs. Beeton's resource that when a young woman married it became a custom for her mother to give her a copy of the Bible and "Mrs. Beeton's." Nothing more, it was assumed, was needed to achieve a happy home.

On the other side of the Atlantic, Mother was considered "the Light of the Home," as the American women's bible, *Godey's Lady's Book*, proclaimed in 1860. Household rituals, family traditions, and seasonal pastimes as organized by Mother celebrating the joys of home and family life were society's moorings. Indeed, during the Victorian era, the pursuit of domestic bliss was elevated as a feminine art form. Cooking, decorating, gardening, handicrafts, and creating family recreational pursuits were considered a woman's most rewarding achievements.

A large number of influential women helped cultivate and promote the cult of domestic bliss. These were the "literary domestics," nineteenth-century women writers who penned and edited an astonishing range of work — domestic manuals, sentimental novels, and advice columns in Victorian ladies' periodicals on both sides of the Atlantic. Literary domesticity took many forms: from the Beecher sisters' *American Woman's Home* to Mrs. Henry Wood's sensational novel of a woman abandoning her child and husband, *East Lynne,* and Louisa May Alcott's sublime evocation of the happy family in *Little Women.* Literary domestics provided middle-class Victorian women with iconic images of what happiness looked like: from white-linen Sunday dinners to blue-gingham-lined holiday picnic hampers.

What is interesting to note, especially with the luxury of a century separating us, is that many of the literary domestics enjoyed much more personal freedom than did their readers. This was due, no doubt, to the financial security and independence their writing provided them. In an era when women did not assume positions of responsibility outside the home, most literary domestics began their careers as a means of supplementing their incomes when the men in their lives—either husbands or fathers—were unable to provide, usually because of illness or death. A number of Victorian women writers—especially those without children—became extremely prolific, often writing two or three novels and numerous magazine articles in one year, all of which were eagerly awaited by both their publishers and their public.

Of course today, the florid prose, famous works, and even best-selling names—such as Mrs. E. D. E. N. Southworth, Catharine Maria Sedgwick, and Mrs. M. E. Sherwood—have long been forgotten; like much nineteenth-century domestic ephemera, they have fallen through the cracks of our American social history. But in their heyday, the commercial success that literary domestics enjoyed caused some of their male rivals, such as Nathaniel Hawthorne, to dismiss them enviously as "that damned mob of scribbling women."

Across the pond, our English cousins were also enjoying success and stirring up trouble with their pens. One of the most interesting literary domestics was Mrs. Elizabeth Gaskell, whose first novel, *Mary Barton*, was a grim and gritty commentary on working conditions in English mills and as far removed from cozy-home-fires women's lit as you could imagine. The novel was controversial but widely acclaimed and brought Mrs. Gaskell to the attention of Charles Dickens, who invited her to write a more genteel column for his magazine *Household Words*, which she did in an eight-part serial written between 1851 and 1853 and called *Cranford*. Although Mrs. Gaskell was enormously popular during her lifetime (1810–1865), her standing is now overshadowed by the Brontë sisters, George Eliot (Mary Anne Evans), and Jane Austen. But during her time, Mrs. Gaskell wrote poetry, ghost stories, and the first biography of her friend Charlotte Brontë in 1857.

Both the daughter and the wife of Unitarian ministers, Elizabeth Cleghorn was born in 1810 in London. Sadly, her mother died when she was a year old, and she was sent to be raised by an aunt in the English countryside village of Knutsford, Cheshire. Although "Cranford" is an imaginary English village, it is based on Elizabeth's childhood experiences and gives the reader glimpses into nineteenth-century village life in England with gentle wit and great sophistication.

To begin with, Victorian Cranford is populated mostly by women—or, as Mrs. Gaskell describes it, "in possession of the Amazons," for "all the holders of houses above a certain rent were women." The feminine residents—single, widows, and spinsters—keep trim gardens without weeds, treat the prized cow as well as a daughter, know the goings-on of everyone in the village, even if strict societal convention dictated that social calls must not be longer than fifteen minutes and only between the hours of noon and 3 PM, and believed that nothing tastes better with tea than plain bread-and-butter sandwiches. They saved rather than spent, and the art of putting by, putting up, and putting away was refined in a perfectly charming feminine way. In other words, the "gentle folks of Cranford were poor...but concealed their smart under a smiling face. We none of us spoke of money." Instead the villagers practiced *"elegant economy."*

Elegant economy, or the art of turning one's ratty red silk petticoat into a magnificent crimson parasol, is at the heart of Mrs. Gaskell's *Cranford*. Beneath the daily round of the women's goings-on, a vibrant tug-of-war between love and longing, denial and delayed gratification, wants and needs is played out in every polite conversation, whether accompanied by bonnet trimming or an exchange of knitting stitches, beauty secrets, apple potpourri recipes, or sponge biscuits. You will be enthralled to discover it.

Elegant economy is an inspiring game, especially in the depths of midwinter. Like finding joyful simplicities, the idea of each day is how to use what's familiar in new and delightful ways—and then stretch and save those pounds, pence, dollars, and cents. Elegant economies transform Frugality (such a mean-spirited word) into the imaginative Thrill of Thrift. But even if you've yet to meet Mrs. Gaskell's Cranford ladies, you can get to know elegant economy. This week, try eating down the pantry before another trip to the supermarket, or going through your closet for items that might be reincarnated—a woolen sweater shrunk in the wash or with thinning elbows can become a charming pillow or tea cozy; a teapot missing a lid can hold daffodil bulbs or a small basil plant. For as Mrs. Gaskell reminds us, "anticipation" is "the soul of enjoyment." And as far as I'm concerned, "elegant economy" is an idea whose time has come again.

The Thrill of Thrift

Morale and New Curtains

Deprivation is a negative state of existence. It puts work and living into reverse... Now it's one thing to tighten the belt and another to go forward with the belt tightened...

—*HOUSE AND GARDEN*, AUGUST 1933

As I write, today is the first day of spring. Instinctually, our eyes turn toward the light, indoors as well as out. "March sunlight comes pouring in revealing the general shabbiness of the life surrounding us," the English country writer Phyllis Nicholson confessed in her Home Front memoir, *Norney Rough* (the name of her Surrey house), published in 1941. "The sun thrusts its glorious yellow face into every nook and cranny of rooms that have been veiled so long in wintry gloom... shells of our working lives reveal their shabbiness with startling clarity." Life's threadbare patches cry out for attention.

"Curtains show where they have been pulled to and fro for nine Aprils," Phyllis laments, surely for most of us. "How tiresome curtains are. They don't die satisfactory deaths like cups and saucers which crash cheerfully into eternity, but merely linger on and become intensely boring. Yards of perfectly sound material can't be discarded merely because they have reached a certain age. That would be like divorcing a wife for the sole reason that she was thirty-five."

And yet...

Still, something must be done. Attention must be paid to what we get used to seeing every day. Living spaces decay before our eyes without our awareness, which is how I've ended up with shreds of what formerly were bright yellow organza café curtains. They were looking a bit dull and dusty, and I should have stopped with the feather duster and the open window. But no, spring fever's gotten hold of me and I thought I'd just give these a gentle hand wash, except that when they slid off the curtain rods they disintegrated, as if they'd been made of paper instead of fabric.

Granted, they were hung a decade ago, so let this be a cautionary tale. Curtains should be taken down annually for cleaning and vacuumed with that nifty little hose attachment you've never quite figured out what to do with, every three months. But really, this does bring up the question of what to do with the thirty-five yards of orange velvet drapes. The Laura Ashley custom-made cottage sprig or the pleated brown-and-pistachio barkcloth tiebacks that never went in your mother's dining room, never mind yours.

Get rid of them. Just because something's been hanging in a room for as long as you can remember or longer doesn't mean it has to be a permanent fixture. I know women who hold on to curtains longer than they do houses or husbands. "Oh, these can be cut down...," they say as they pack them away for a new incarnation somewhere else in the unforeseeable future. Listen, if you know how to sell them on eBay, by all means do; if you don't, then donate them to a charity shop, but for a guaranteed spring tonic, start by taking them all down. Decide which to discard and which should have a reprieve. But only if they make you as happy as the first time you hung them. Or for a change, why not let those windows that can go bare, do so? It may seem like a small thing, but revolutions have begun over trifles such as cake.

"To recover morale one must abandon the uncertainty of the past months and deliberately make what seems a tremendous effort to improve affairs," *House and Garden* magazine editorialized in September 1932 in a plea for the return of joie de vivre, "New Curtains and Morale":

For long enough time we have looked at those moldering curtains. Now they begin to revolt us. We are through with tolerating that shabby rug. We have read the inconsequential books and want no more of them. We have had enough of piously wearing old clothes. We are wearied of apologies and excuses. Let Fate bring whatever consequences it may...the woman who takes pride in her home will want new curtains. Or it may be a new chair...Or new wall paper or a new set of the latest kitchen utensils...Morale is displayed when one goes out and performs some deed without regard to consequences, some deed that requires the best of bravery or taste or intelligence.

So take a deep breath, ladies, and pull those damn curtains down. You'll be surprised and delighted by how expansive is your view. And on a clear day, you might even be able to see tomorrow.

Tuppenny Rice
and Treacle

Half a pound of tuppenny rice,
Half a pound of treacle;
That's the way the money goes;
Pop! Goes the weasel!

—W. R. MANDALE,
NINETEENTH-CENTURY SONG

Glancing at the blank pages of a little ledger I cherish, purchased for $1 in an English flea market, *Ryman's Complete House-Keeping Book, Arranged for Entering Expenses for 52 Weeks and Adapted for Commencing at Any Period of the Year* (circa 1900), I marvel at all the categories nineteenth- and early-twentieth-century homemakers needed to budget for with their housekeeping money:

Baker and Confectioner
Butcher
Fish and Poultry
Fruit and Vegetables
Grocer
Milkman
Wine, Spirits and Beer
Draper and Hosier
Dressmaker and Tailor

House Linen
Laundry
Shoemaker
Coals and Wood
Earthenware and Glass
Ironmongery
Oilman and Window Cleaner
Education and Books
Furniture and Repairs
Medicine and Attendance
Postage and Stamps
Stationery and News
Amusements
Garden Expenses
Gas and Electricity
Gifts, Subscriptions, Clubs
Chapel
Insurance
Motor Expenses
Rent, Rates and Taxes
Telephone
Travelling Expense
WAGES

"Housewives managed, through unstinting work and infinite ingenuity, to create a decent quality of life," Doris E.
Coates tells us in *Tuppenny Rice and Treacle: Cottage Housekeeping 1900–1920.* "Working class mothers were the un-
sung heroines of those days. With little money and no
security they performed miracles of home-making, bringing up their families without envy or self-pity, and cheerfully making the best of their small resources." Using her
grandmother's account books, Doris reveals that "without
health or welfare services, women fed and clothed their
families, cared for them in sickness, kept their houses spot-
less and created happy homes. How did they manage?
Obviously only the minimum basic necessities could be

afforded, and there would be a stark difference between their regular purchases and the items which appear on to-day's list of essentials.

"Of course the shops of those days did not have the bewildering display of packaged, pre-cooked, frozen or exotic goods to which we are accustomed, but they offered many tempting things like ready-made cakes, tinned fruit, canned meats, preserves and sweets, which were beyond their means, except for festive occasions."

When we are in a financial crisis, one of the first things to go from our daily round is any pleasure, beginning with food. Economizing becomes punitive. We stop going to restaurants, ordering takeout, and buying organic meat and vegetables. Instead we stay home, we buy on sale, we make do. But with what? We exchange osso buco at our favorite Italian restaurant for supermarket macaroni and cheese in front of the telly. (Don't get me wrong, I regularly get cravings for hot dogs—with Dijon mustard, grilled onions, and relish, plus a side of macaroni and cheese—but the casserole is homemade, and the hot dogs are turkey and grilled. It's inexpensive, but also filling and nourishing.) It never occurs to us to fulfill our desires by learning to prepare the slow-cooked, family-style stews that happily feed multitudes of Italian bambinos very frugally. Mama Mia, she knows best, especially when she advises leaving on the store shelf (even at a warehouse club) prepared convenience foods full of chemical preservatives that Mother Nature never imagined. Sticking to a household budget, making do, blessing the loaves and the fishes, stretching the leftovers into a feast, growing what they can and gathering in is what generations of women have always done; the kitchen has always been the heart of the home even when the hearth was the back of a cave.

There's a reason that Martha Stewart became a billionaire besides the fact that she was hardworking, clever, creative, savvy, and determined. She was also brilliant at branding feminine yearning for home comforts. Certainly

Martha was blessed to have been taught to cook, sew, clean, and garden at her mother's side—and if you were, too, then so are you! But the majority of my generation of women and our own daughters, including me, have had to homeschool ourselves one pot of stew and one fumbled hem repair at a time. Still, as George Eliot reminds us, "It's never too late to be what you might have been."

And returning home, reclaiming our home, and celebrating our home life is how we're all going to make it through these difficult financial times of uncertainty.

There is something so nourishing and nurturing about the notion of proper pantries and well-stocked larders—a continuing link to all that was good in the past, and the reassurance we need every day, especially now. A century ago, women didn't agonize over food the way we now do. Sadly, women rarely take pleasure in eating anymore, and this emotional flatline is evident in the way we shop for and store our food.

Think of the adored Barefoot Contessa, Ina Garten. I would follow that woman to the ends of the earth if she led a pilgrimage (and in fact she does, to the kitchen every week). Or think of Mrs. Bridges in Masterpiece Theater's *Upstairs, Downstairs*—a big, healthy, hearty, hardworking, handsome woman with a lusty laugh and appetite whose kitchen was certainly a sacred space. At Ina's table, like Mrs. Bridges's, we know that we would be well fed, grateful to be included at the feast, and laughing between every forkful.

Yes, the very rich, upper-class Bellamy family gave Mrs. Bridges carte blanche when stocking her well-ordered shelves, but if you remember, the folks downstairs ate as well as those fortunate enough to be invited to the dining room table. Mrs. Bridges had no ambivalence about enjoying one of life's Divinely appointed blessings—she loved food, she loved to cook, and so her pleasure blessed everyone else in her household. Her simply abundant larder proves that pride can't truly be a sin. Call the vision to mind: A specially designed room off the kitchen groaned with meat, fish, and fowl—not just baked or roasted but potted, brandied, and smoked—cheeses stored on cold slate shelves, freshly churned butter, eggs, and dry ingredients—flour, sugar, salt, rice, oats, and bran—stored in burlap sacks. Her pantry shelves held glistening jars of jams, jellies, conserves, fruited honeys, marmalades, mustards, chutneys, pickles, and nuts, along with herbal marinades and home remedies such as blackberry cordial. There were tins for breads, cakes, pies, scones, and biscuits. Willow baskets held apples, pears, and seasonal fruits like apricots, peaches, and plums, as well as root vegetables with the goodness of the earth still clinging to them. There were sighs, smiles, and good cheer at the table and in the heart.

And there can be and will be again on the *Peace and Plenty* path.

Pocketbook Meals; or, The Art of Using Up

How often do you try a new recipe? This is not a trick question. How often do you avoid experimenting with a new recipe because there's no time in a crunched week or month, and how many times because you're missing half the ingredients? Salt. Pepper. Tomato sauce. Oregano. Don't go getting exotic on me now.

Okay, here's a new culinary challenge. How many times have you thought about dying the unbleached muslin curtains *for the attic* while luncheon cooks? Or even more revealing, how many times have you ever prepared lunch for yourself at home without the children?

I needed a reminder on stocking the larder for our pinched pocketbooks and so cast my mind back to when creating a Fancy Pantry was a passionate delight. It was so reassuring and nurturing to reach into the pantry cupboard and find everything I needed to prepare something wonderful to eat without running to the supermarket before I joined the car pool. I had $250 every two weeks to spend on food and divined what I thought was a brilliant strategy. The secret was that I'd plan a week's worth of meals on Friday, then create my shopping list—divided between the food warehouses and the farmer's market—on Saturday; on Sunday I'd begin the week cooking in a galley-size kitchen. Menus were seasonally based, then I'd try supermarket specials and a repertoire of family favorites—everyone at the table had one night a week when it was their choice. Smiles all around.

When I went back to my storehouse of pleasant kitchen memories, I see that the woman who wrote the *Simple Abundance* reflection on July 13 was inspired by her favorite literary domestic, Nell B. Nichols from *Woman's Home Companion*, who reigned and entertained women about the joys of homemaking in the 1920s, '30s, and '40s. Before America had Martha Stewart, it had Nell. It was Nell who taught me how to plan meals and shop for the week with such a cheerful élan and quiet confidence that "well, you simply must try it, my dear."

And I did. "I think of the house as a ship on the sea of life," wrote Mrs. Nichols in 1926. "Every homemaker is a pilot traveling over calm or troubled waters, steering, exploring, discovering." After a cup of tea with Nell I always want to bob my hair, slip into a simple drop-waist cotton chemise, tie on a checked apron with a bow, and listen to Scott Joplin on the wireless as I dye those unbleached muslin curtains.

And what are we exploring today over the rough seas of money's ebb and flow? Why, the "Art of Using Up" or elevating leftovers from disguising cold meat to appetizing savory suppers, also known as "Ten Cents to Splurge," "How I Used My Drippings," "Pocketbook Meals," and—my favorite category of all—"The Knack of Secondary Meals." Did you know that during the depression of 1893 and the bank panic of 1907, the secondary meal trade became a booming business? Ritzy hotel restaurants would sell their leftovers to thrifty housewives who knew a good thing. Then came World War I and severe rationing, the Crash and bread lines, World War II and Spam, up until Julia Child taught us how to roast a chicken in the 1960s.

Now we face economic uncertainty again and we've forgotten that when there's little joy in the world, at least we need to be comforted and fed at home. There's a reason we describe hard times as "belt tightening." That's because from the first moment we hear of financial distress, our grown-up stomachs start to turn and churn. Good eating is the first thing eliminated.

I'm continually surprised at how much food we waste because of modern perks of refrigeration and convenience foods (keeping in mind that once canned beans were considered extravagant) — and don't I sound like Nell Nichols after the Wall Street Crash of '29? Even if you had all the money in the world, what we surreptitiously throw into the tip is usually enough to tip the food budget back into the black if we just made the connection. However, I'm certainly not the one to chide; we're all working so hard to keep bodies and souls together one pot of chili at a time. But if you're throwing out more blackened bags of "salad" than you're eating in a week, this is a habit that should be broken.

To be perfectly honest, I never had sticker shock over a designer pair of shoes when I could afford them, but I have been flabbergasted to find a pint of Chilean blueberries selling in California for $7.99, especially when I remembered they never tasted as good as Maine blueberries from a roadside stand in August.

However, there's a reason women read cookbooks or watch fantasy food programs in bed: Lying propped up is about the only way we have enough energy to digest the very thought of a new recipe, never mind rethink how we cook, shop, eat, and save money at the same time. Advises Nell: "I have made a list of satisfactory meals planned around only one cooked dish. This list is hung on the door of my kitchen cabinet for reference. When I am lacking in ambition I do not wonder what to have for dinner."

First, let's bring order to the cupboards, refrigerator, and freezer with a proper clear-out. In the cupboard, anything past its *shelf life* (which means it's probably a couple of years old already) is tossed. I know some people argue that we should donate canned foods of any kind to homeless shelters or food banks, but I think this is terrible. Spiritual tradition of every faith tells us to feed the hungry *better* than ourselves. So out go those old tins of bloater paste, and when you purchase a bottle of extra-virgin olive oil or some sea salt for your fancy pantry (on sale), if you're able, buy another to donate. The gratitude of the people working in shelter kitchens for the gift of quality condiments and staples is heart humbling and soul nourishing.

Now, if you are in the line receiving a food parcel, to take the sting out of this blessing, imagine the meals you'll be making in your kitchen to bring back to the community shelter someday soon. What is your family's favorite casserole? See yourself making enough to feed a hundred grateful mouths. Do you want the people you're feeding to feel humbled or happy? There is a Divine circle of completion between sowing and reaping, between giving and receiving. It's part of our spiritual sojourn on earth to learn how to truly receive all the gifts Mother Plenty is bestowing on us every day. I've often wondered during this season of personal relinquishment if I wasn't taken off the front lines of Giving to everybody else in the world, so that I might learn the huge spiritual lessons of Receiving to set me on the journey toward peace and plenty. Women are bountiful givers to others and reluctant receivers. How many times do we say "Oh, you shouldn't have." One of these days Heaven is going to come back with "Okay, we won't."

Just a meditative morsel worth pondering.

Now to the refrigerator: Here we part with the half-eaten remnants of ancient cultures—yes, including the Seville orange marmalade your sister-in-law brought back from Spain a decade ago or the stepson's lavender honey from Provence. If you didn't finish it in a year, trust me, you're not going to get a craving to spread it on your toast now. Personally, I think keeping and consuming anything past its sell-by date is dodgy, whether it has fuzz on it or not. Nell and I agree: If it smells like fish, throw it back. And in the freezer: Speaking of fishy, if you can't remember when you froze that tuna casserole, you know what to do. Ditto anything that's been in there for six months or more. You think I'm kidding? It's tasteless by now, and yes, that matters. No matter what our budget, we need to feed our souls.

Like tracking our spending, our relationships with food, hunger, and money are bound up with conflicting emotions and the tangled skeins of domestic bliss. But paradise lost can so easily be restored again, one muffin crumb or bowl of fettuccine Alfredo at a time. First we notice our pattern of feeding ourselves and our loved ones. Then we look at how we're spending our food money, counting the cost of takeout and prepared food. I don't think many of us hunger for designer kitchens at the moment. Perhaps we just want to appreciate the mixers, grills, fondue pots, and ice cream machines gathering dust. A galley-size kitchen is sacred ground to she who has lost hers through the perfect storm of debt, divorce, disaster, or death. So before you enter yours, take off your shoes and say a blessing for your table. Put on your favorite apron, stir the stockpot, raise a glass of good cheer, and tell me, what's for dinner tonight?

PS: Nell suggests—and I do, too—that you might like to:

- Create a master list of groceries.
- Divide your grocery list into different categories, such as Fresh Produce, Dairy, Meat, Fish, Pantry Staples,

Paper, Household, Pet, and Personal Care Products. No, there is no category for "snacks." You know why. Nell made all her snacks. Delicious additions include quick breads, muffins, biscuits—and bring back desserts. "Home baking is the best home builder."

- Your list serves as your automatic reminders. If you're a clever girl, pop the list on your computer and you can print it out.

- Keep the master list on the fridge with a pencil and instruct helpful family members to add items as they use them up.

- Select your favorite family recipes, including your own. Ask the lodgers in your household their preferences. Include Main Dishes, Side Dishes, Salads, Desserts, Homemade Snacks.

- Basic pantry staples include flour, spelt, rice (wild rice, risotto), pasta and macaroni, oil (olive and vegetable oils), cereal, oats or gluten-free grains, crackers, canned tomatoes, olives, canned or dried beans, peas, lentils, the spices you use regularly such as chili powder or oregano, soy sauce, canned tuna or salmon, chicken, fish, and beef stock, Worcestershire sauce, peanut butter, dry sauce mixes, vinegars, salad dressings, sugar (white and brown or sweetener), molasses, jams, jelly, mustards, horseradish, relish, nuts, raisins, cooking chocolate, baking ingredients. Use your recipes to give you an outline. I like to have a savory cupboard and a baking cupboard. And a wonderful custom is to bring back regional food favorites when you travel—maple syrup from Vermont, wild rice from South Carolina, pralines from Texas...

- Make your pantry (which can start off as just two shelves) pretty, easy to clean, and inviting, using all your vintage bowls, tins, baskets, and pans to organize items. Bask in all the comfort and joy waiting to be simmered, baked, chopped, roasted, and used up with flair and thanksgiving. Blessings, now and forever, on your thrifty fancy pantry feasts.

The Thrill of Thrift

Dream Kitchen Reveries

*The Beautiful is everywhere; perhaps more in an
arrangement of your saucepans on the white walls of your
kitchen than in your eighteenth-century living room or in
the official museums.*

—FERNAND LÉGER, FRENCH CUBIST PAINTER,
1881–1955

If a woman's bedroom is all we need to know about her
sex life, what clues do the other rooms of her house represent? Accept for a moment that your bathroom tells of
your self-nurturance or lack of it, your front hall (or what
substitutes for an entry space) reveals your commitments
and overextension to others, the lack of any personal space
(sewing, crafts, exercise, reading nook, personal desk),
your self-esteem. It takes one to know one, dearest Reader.

So what of the kitchen? Well, when a woman is tired
of her kitchen and what is created in it, she is tired of
life. She's boxed in; she feels she has no choices. Her enthusiasm for life is just as jaded as her taste buds. Is that
how you feel today? If you're ambivalent—you love your
kitchen curtains but hate what you've been cooking—start
investigating dispassionately. After all, the one reason for
this exercise is to make you feel better by the end of it!

So what have you eaten for the last week? How many
of those recipes were new? How many were dearly loved

and delicious? How many were rolled out and onto the table by rote or home delivery from start to finish? How many Lean Cuisine dinners or how many leftovers did you freeze rather than throw away six months ago? Stay calm. Thank God these are only rhetorical questions meant to prime the creative well...or feel for a pulse.

"Ordinarily we do not link pans and pots with the thought of beauty or romance, and yet it is our own fault if we may not, or cannot, do it," Elizabeth Macdonald wrote in the March 1927 *House Beautiful*:

> Only a shallow or a materialistic mind fails to be thrilled by the possibilities resident in pans and pots. Your true romantic walks in a happy trance of imaginary splendors when she wanders through the aisles of a kitchenware department in a huge city store. Out of the piles of twinkling silver aluminum, the gravely decorous rows of ironware, the sturdy blue enamel dishes, and the chaste white ones with their colored rims, she builds dream kitchens in which her imaginary self contentedly presides.

Having spent the last year without a kitchen of my own, I can assure you that the dream kitchen is not a reverie reserved for moments when we have loads of cash to build or renovate. I think that one of the greatest blessings of the *Peace and Plenty* path is that we realize the interior vision is more important than the outward expression, because everything is first created in our imagination—whether we see bill collectors banging down our door, or envision laying vintage French shelf paper in cabinets in apartments or homes we have yet to physically inhabit. Just to show you what I mean, let us return with Mrs. Macdonald to a kitchen imagined almost a century ago:

> Take for instance the white enamel ware on this next counter, with its bewitching vermilion (dark red)

rims. She sees it in a kitchen finished with the new lacquer paint, not the shiny, but the dull sort, a white like the warm tint of jersey milk as she used to see it set in pans upon the buttery shelves at her grandmother's farm. At the windows, her mental hands hang the checked gingham curtains of the cream and vermilion scheme. Instead of a valance, she covers the rod with a doubled ruffled run of the same material. The kitchen cabinet panels have a delicate pattern of bittersweet drawn with Japanese simplicity of pattern. The sink is shining porcelain and the stove has most of its surface enameled to match.

On the imaginary floor is linoleum, not too dark, but picking up the vermilion tone in a neutralized hue. At the window where she will sit while she waits for the psychological moment in her cooking processes, there is a chair low enough to relax in comfortably and built as a chair should be built, with the back of the seat at least two inches lower than the front of it. The chair is of wood, but it has a puffy down cushion covered with the checked gingham and finished with an inviting and impractical little ruffle. Beside the chair is a bookshelf big enough to hold a little sewing basket too, and beneath her feet, as she sits in the chair, lies a braided rug with a broad black band around the outside and stripes of the vermilion mingled with the black for the field. Possibly, also there might be a black cat to purr.

Being the true romantic you are, can you see this kitchen in your mind's eye painted with delightful words and imagination? Maybe not all at once, but use this meditation this week—and if you have a little time to spare for this creative brain-nurturing, cut out pictures to help you bring this dream kitchen forth on paper.

The eternal Law of Attraction responds to our inner vision and conscious creation. Whatever we consistently "see" with our eyes, heart, or imagination must be replaced or replicated in our real world. This is a wonderful imagination-strengthening meditation. Perhaps the last thing on your mind is owning or cooking in a dream kitchen. You have so many other more pressing needs or wants, and probably many of them have to do with money. But if there is a secret to becoming more prosperous when the rest of the world is shouting "lack," it's learning to dwell in contentment thanks to the small touches, the subtle nuances of domestic bliss (even in your imagination!) that every woman loves and needs.

Many years ago when I was in the final waiting stage for *Simple Abundance* to be published (after I finished writing, but before it hit the bookstores), I went antiquing with my sister Maureen, who was visiting. I told her I was searching for a miniature Blue Willow tea set for Katie and I had a feeling I was going to find it soon, much in the same way I "knew" *Simple Abundance* would be on the best-seller lists.

And then I remarked, as if I knew what I was talking about, that it was just as easy to find a Victorian Blue Willow tea set as it was to earn a million dollars. *The creative and spiritual process was the same, and it's the one I'm encouraging you to share with me today.* I had to hold the vision—see Katie and myself having tea parties in the backyard with the Blue Willow tea set, or the replica *New York Times* best-seller list with me at number one. I repeated these daydreams every single day. They felt so good that I made them part of my daily "quiet time." The next year both the tea set and the best-seller list arrived in my life. Recently my sister reminded me of this story because I've been frustrated that a long-held dream was taking too long to manifest. She instantly helped me recharge my focus and vision, and I have no doubt it will pay off.

Elizabeth Macdonald points out that "there is vastly more fun to be had by using creative imagination in the kitchen than even in the living-room. Through its exercise the kitchen becomes not only outwardly beautiful but inwardly satisfying...We may never need to recapture exactly the same sort of vitality that came to the Colonial family from around the fireplace, but we can find new forms of family loyalty and coherence" in the kitchen that's the heart of our hopes, wishes, and dreams. And we first encounter them in our sacred imagination.

Now, anyone for tea? Won't you come into my new kitchen?

Becoming Mrs. Miniver

*Linking our personal story to the great web and patterns
of those who have traveled that path before can
significantly alleviate the aloneness and confusion that
often plague the modern woman. Myths show us what our
stories have in common.*

—SHERYL PAUL NISSINEN

During those terror-heightened months after September 11, I remained in New York until Christmas. Just the thought of being an ocean away from Katie was unbearable. Even after she was allowed to return downtown to her dormitory, a few blocks from Ground Zero, she came home uptown to me on weekends. The apartment on Central Park West became our refuge, our soul shelter, and with every turn of the key our home. But it was very difficult to concentrate, let alone write—and writing was what paid my bills. I became very much a recluse (not that I'm much of a bon vivant now) with a fairly rigid personal schedule. In the morning, I would straighten my drawers and closets and make lists of their contents, as if by ordering my inner world, I could impose order on the outside. In the afternoon I finally used a birthday gift certificate for riding lessons at the Central Park stables, or delivered cases of soft drinks to the volunteers at Ground Zero, or just sat on a park bench. Even the old fallback of shopping couldn't break the pall because everywhere in the city there were makeshift shrines at fire and police stations, and every day more funerals were held than you could ever imagine.

In the evening, at precisely 6 PM, I would prepare a different pasta recipe from the one cookbook I had in New York and decant a decent bottle of red wine. (If you weren't going to start drinking good wine on your own when the world was blowing up, I reasoned, you would never find a time to appreciate it.) Then I arranged a pleasing dinner tray and took it to my bedroom. Once ensconced under my comfy duvet, wearing my favorite Victoria's Secret jersey pajamas and Lands' End gray cashmere sweater robe and socks, I'd eat dinner in bed while watching old black-and-white films, particularly ones with World War II themes. During these post-9/11 days, I soaked up what life was like for women during the Home Front years. These films seemed both appropriate and comforting in this frightening time.

Think of movies as celluloid myths told to a culture sitting not around a campfire, but in front of a screen. "Movies elevate our sights, enlarge our imagination. Film, like poetry, is one of our heart's most subtle agents. It reminds us of what we know, helps us stretch and change," Marsha Sinetar suggests in her fascinating book *Reel Power: Spiritual Growth Through Film*. "Their themes and images can powerfully equip us to see ourselves as we are, at our worst, and at our best, or, to help us invent new scripts about who we hope to be...Certain films—like certain lovely people, glorious works of art or music, and special instances of prayer—seem a grace expressly given for our edification."

I was not alone needing comfort. As America reverberated from the shock of terror on our own shores, I was frequently asked to give advice to other women. I felt so inept. Secretly I needed a woman in my life whom I could emulate; one who possessed "repose of the soul," a grown-up woman to help me remember what mattered most—making a safe haven in a scary and tumultuous world for my daughter and myself just as she had for her own family. I turned to the most frequently viewed movie in my evening ritual, the Oscar-winning 1942 wartime saga *Mrs. Miniver,* starring Greer Garson. Directed by William Wyler, it depicts an English middle-class family's heroic struggle to preserve what was precious in their daily life during the London Blitz before America entered the war.

Kay Miniver was the woman I needed in my life. Many of you already know her from Greer Garson's stunning performance; or maybe you haven't yet made the lady's acquaintance. Do so as soon as possible. You are in for such a treat. But remember that you want to go as far back as you can when retracing steps, whether it's a money choice or a movie's origins. The heart of the matter is always the original source.

Before Greer Garson so beautifully embodied Mrs. Miniver on the screen, she was a figment of British journalist Jan Struther's domestic reveries, written anonymously and featured in the London *Times* between 1937 and 1939. Known for her stylish prose, witty poems, and modern hymns, Jan had been asked by her editor to write "about an ordinary sort of woman who leads an ordinary sort of life—rather like yourself."

Charm makes everyone feel better, and during this time, threats of war were daily headlines in Britain. Mrs. Miniver's contagious zest for dashing "through life at full tilt, with gaiety, energy, and grace" captivated readers' imaginations.

It was lovely, thought Mrs. Miniver, nodding goodbye to the flower-woman and carrying her big sheaf of chrysanthemums down the street with a kind of ceremonious joy, as though it were a cornucopia; it was lovely, this settling down again, the tidying away of the summer into its box, this taking up of the thread of one's life where the holidays (irrelevant interlude) had made one drop it. Not that she didn't enjoy the holidays; but she always felt—and it was, perhaps, a measure of her peculiar happiness—a little relieved when they were over. Her normal life pleased her so well that she was half afraid to step out of the frame in case one day she should find herself unable to get back. The spell might break, the atmosphere be impossible to recapture.

I adore Kay Miniver and you, if you don't know her, will, too: Nothing in her daily round was (or is) too insignificant to become an uplifting source of reflection, revelation, reconnection, and renewal, even money worries. She reminded readers how much they had to be grateful for in the small particulars of our everyday epiphanies: the familiar route to a holiday home; unread library books to look forward to; the comforting feel of the banister beneath your hand as you climb the stairs; having another's hand to hold and eye to catch at a dinner party; the small indentation at the nape of your child's neck, so perfect for a quick kiss; the pang of parting from the old family car; finding the perfect calendar to give pleasure throughout the year; the notches on the nursery door as the children grow; a hat with a floppy bow; the mingling scent of roses and a fire in the hearth; crumpets for tea on a rainy afternoon; choosing beer over wine if you are on a budget.

"Perhaps you might call this the testament of a happy woman," the English writer Christopher Morley wrote in the American Book of the Month Club edition of Jan Struther's essays published in October 1939 (as *Mrs. Miniver*), just after World War II broke out in Europe.

Mrs. Miniver's musings on "eternity wrapped in domesticity" became a best seller on both sides of the Atlantic and a powerful force for popularizing America's entry into the war.

Recently, I went back to *Mrs. Miniver* as channeled by Jan Struther to discover what words of advice and wisdom she might have to offer concerning finances. She did not let me down.

"Economy has been called a habit of mind, and certainly it is not until it has become a habit that it can cease to be irksome. For some natures it never does cease; but for others—and they are not always the naturally prudent ones, either—there is a queer satisfaction to be got out of being in a State of Economy. It is hard to analyze this feeling; the main ingredient, perhaps, is a sense of relief at the sudden simplification of life, at the narrowing of one's field of choice," Mrs. Miniver observes, and isn't that true? "One spends far less time, for instance, in making up one's mind between the equal though differing attractions of sole and herring, wine and beer, silk and gingham; between going out to a film and staying at home with a book; between giving a party and not giving a party; between the excitement of new shoes and the familiarity of old ones.

"Of all the many factors which used to affect one's decision—time, effort, digestibility, chic, comfort and so on—there remains only one: cost. To weigh the alternatives in this balance alone is the work of the moment..."

What a marvelous way to think of budgeting—as our work of the moment. Not forever, but for now. We can do anything for now.

"Like the whiff of a certain perfume wafted from an earlier period of one's life, the thought of Mrs. Miniver brings back a time fifty years ago when the Western world was in the terrible turmoil of World War II," Greer Garson recalled lovingly in 1990. "It was suddenly a world of quiet heroism, compassion, faith, and all the best in the human character—the world, in other words, of Mrs. Miniver—summoned to combat all the worst.

"Mrs. Miniver was typical, I think, of the women of the day. Will we be able to relate to her now, in *our* day? We can hardly imagine the ever present dangers of England during the blitz, yet we know all too well of wars with all their disasters and heartbreaks. For this reason among many others we can surely identify with the spirit of Mrs. Miniver—the spirit that contended with all that unnatural stress and survived."

Whenever I am feeling small and fragile, reaching out to another woman across time and the past restores me in a way that nothing else can. *Mrs. Miniver* is a marvelous way for you to begin your own time-traveling sojourns.

Celluloid Heroines

*The main figure in the Home Front is the woman. It is
she who must make the stand, rally her family around
her like a general, and plant her own feet firmly on the
home ground. Everything depends on her wisdom, her
enthusiasm, her vision of what home can produce, what
home can be.*

—HARPER'S BAZAAR, MAY 1942

W hen a book or movie strikes the same chord in millions of people, it is the work of God, even if it
springs from a human heart, mind, and hands. "Myth is
the revelation of divine life in man [or woman]," the great
Swiss psychologist Carl Jung believed. "It is not we who
invent myth, rather it speaks to us as a Word of God."
Mrs. Miniver was such a Divine inspiration—the embodiment of a sacred archetype of a woman defending her
family and home from all danger through her faith, intelligence, strength, courage, determination, unshakable
optimism, and love. And it is such a powerful myth precisely because each of us can see ourself in that role.
Unfortunately, both women who brought Mrs. Miniver to
life—actress Greer Garson and author Jan Struther—
found their personal lives eclipsed by this myth, at least in
the public's eyes. Although both women tried in vain to
explain that they were not Mrs. Miniver, the world would
not see them otherwise. Nor, alas, could they themselves.

When Spirit intervenes directly in our lives by inviting

us to become a co-creator in something momentous that will change the world—and you may not believe this at the moment, but I'm talking about your co-creation as well as mine—our conditioned response is "Who are you kidding?" or "I'm out of here." So instead of basking in the Light of illumination and inspiration, we're blindsided by it. That's why, thank God, when I started writing *Simple Abundance* I thought I was only writing about eliminating clutter from my life. I was blessed, at that time, by not needing to know the full extent of God's dreams for my "little" creation. Quite frankly, it would have scared me to death and the book would never have been written.

How clearly I remember my shock upon discovering that many of my readers had their own impression of who Sarah Ban Breathnach was, and increasingly the public image of the woman who wrote *Simple Abundance* began to restrict my life in a disturbing way. At book signings some women would seem dismayed that I wore high heels and red nail polish, and they would tell me so. "That's not what I expected you to look like."

One woman went so far as to exclaim: "Oh, you can't be my Sarah. My Sarah doesn't look like you!" I asked her what "her" Sarah looked like and she told me she wore Laura Ashley and Birkenstocks—a fine vision for her, but it certainly didn't describe me.

One wonders how Mrs. Miniver's fans would have reacted if they had known that when she was making the movie, Greer Garson, then thirty-three, was having an affair with Richard Ney, the actor who played her college-age son. Hollywood mogul Louis B. Mayer persuaded both of them to wait until after the movie's first run before getting married, which they did, but it only lasted four years and the turmoil that ensued was the very opposite of Mrs. Miniver's calm reality. Fifty years later at the end of her life, Greer Garson would say, "Graciousness has haunted me my whole life."

Jan Struther's private life was the darkest caricature

of her creation, as different as day and night. Imagine living up to this compliment from the *St. Petersburg (Florida) Times*, found among Jan Struther's personal papers after she died. "Of Mrs. Miniver's philosophy, one can truly say that she has found the true art of living, the art of loving, the art of marriage, the art of family life, the art of happiness. There are no triangular love affairs, not an indecent suggestion. It is a book any granddaughter can safely put in the hands of her grandmother."

But the truth was that by 1939 Jan Struther's marriage was deeply in trouble, for she had fallen in love with a much younger man, a Jewish intellectual who had fled from Nazi-occupied Vienna to live in the United States. Under the cover of bringing her two younger children to safety in America, she followed him to New York, where she would remain during the war, carrying on a clandestine affair with him while her husband was a British POW. After the war ended and her husband returned home, Jan Struther divorced; finally, in 1948, she married Dolf Placzek, her younger man. However, the incalculable strain of the secrecy, stress, and guilt Jan carried, along with the burden of pretending she was the perfect incarnation of saintly womanhood for years, contributed to a nervous breakdown, a five-month stay at a psychiatric sanatorium, and a paralyzing depression before she died of breast cancer in 1953.

"I sometimes imagine the kind of grandmother she might have turned into, if she really had been the 'Mrs. Miniver' of her own creation," her granddaughter Ysenda Maxtone Graham writes in her immensely touching biography, *The Real Mrs. Miniver: Jan Struther's Story*. She recounts that "during the height of *Mrs. Miniver*'s fame and success during the war, Jan toured America as an unofficial ambassadress for Britain, giving hundreds of lectures about Anglo-American relations to enchanted audiences. The public wanted to believe that she was the embodiment of her fictional creation—a sensible, calm, devoted wife and mother. She felt it was her wartime duty not to disappoint them. No one guessed...that she was in fact, living two parallel lives."

As her granddaughter reveals, the tragedy was that Jan Struther "had a remarkable capacity for writing important things down." But after the words were written, after the inspiration pierced the heart of the reader, after the inspiration became an icon, Jan Struther paid a price for accepting the mantle of martyrdom and the duty of self-sacrifice. God did not ask her to be anything but herself, flawed, imperfect, but a woman with a gift for knowing what matters most. But by ignoring and denying what her granddaughter calls her "thorn-sharp" needs—the love, lusts, and longings that are every woman's sacred hungers—hers was a short life that ended sorrowfully in "shudders and sighs."

As we learn about other women whom we admire, we can pick and choose aspects of their lives in the creation of our own magical, mystical portrait—our personal myth—and live our own Happily Ever After, whatever that may mean.

The Thrill of Thrift

Pre-Caution Closets

*It is seldom in life that one knows that a coming event is
to be of crucial importance.*

— ANYA SETON

Whether you observe Candlemas or Groundhog Day
on February 2, the two share a similar theme: Are
you prepared for another six weeks of winter? Both sides of
the Atlantic have suffered record snows lately, and last
night the cupboard at one woman's domain was completely
bare. Let me just say that when you share the last tin of tuna
with the cat and the budget pizza exhumed from the back of
the freezer resembles a mouthful of wallpaper paste, it's
time to rethink how you prepare for an emergency.

"Better to be safe than sorry is an old adage which
we may well take to heart in war time," *Closet Close-Ups*
(*House and Garden*, 1942) reminds us. "Have you an Air
Raid closet where all the supplies that pertain to this emergency are kept together? It may be only a cupboard but it
should be intelligently planned."

And do we? Well, we all know now that every day
women around the world must rise to the occasion and
cope with perfect storms. Having a fully stocked Emergency Cupboard would endow a sense of peace and plenty,
serenity, infinite confidence, and gratitude if we outfitted
one in the following way:

First-aid kit; lanterns, flashlights, batteries; candles, practical candlesticks or votive candle holders; battery-operated radio; blankets; collapsible camp stools; toilet necessities (toilet paper, baby wipes, hygienic hand gel, diapers, tampons); bottles of water for drinking and washing; canned food supplies for three days; long-life milk and juice boxes, instant coffee, tea bags; camp stove; saucepan; plastic garbage bags and paper towels; assorted snacks in a plastic tub with top; toys for children (only used in emergency situations so they will be amusing), games for grown-ups, including travel editions and playing cards; books for all ages and inclinations, one per person; pet supplies, including leash for dogs and pet carrier (a separate one from the one lost somewhere in the garage); kitty litter and rock salt stored in a bucket with an ice scraper and small shovel; a change of clothing for each family member, labeled and kept in clear plastic tub containers with tops; a set of color-coded towels for each family member; pocket-size personal toiletries, including travel toothbrush; extra prescription medications (ask your family doctor about a special prescription for this) and regularly used over-the-counter drugs; a file with copies of important documents; and finally, half a dozen bottles of the homeopathic Rescue Remedy, because if you need this closet, you also need to keep your wits about you, and nothing does it for me better than my little yellow box of the Bach's Rescue Remedy and my framed KEEP CALM AND CARRY ON reminder.

Oh yes, and smelling salts for my gentle Reader, who's swooning from the very thought of this activity.

Of course you see that if you did have this closet, neatly outfitted, labeled, *in clear plastic stacking boxes with lids*, ready to be thrown into the car should, God forbid, you have to evacuate your home due to fire, flood, earthquake, or anything else that "happens to other people," you *could* keep calm and carry on. If you were stranded in your house without electricity, in the cold and dark, you'd know that everything you needed was in one place, praise Providence, and you could grope your way there, too, on your knees if you had to, which isn't a bad way to start or end any day, let alone an emergency.

The other benefit of this project is that the time that you spend "preparing" to handle any contingency is not time you waste worrying about money. And I'm not suggesting you run out and buy everything new. You probably have half of these items strewn around the house in various places, except the batteries. Nobody ever has enough batteries.

Now, you may be thinking to yourself at this point, *Wow, SBB's really been in crisis mode lately, because this is a list of a woman who's dramatically been caught out at one point or another without this or that item and vowed she'd never be caught out again,* and fair enough, you'd be right. But you'd also be right in thinking that my "Pre-Caution Closet" has been not only influenced by Scarlett O'Hara and Mrs. Miniver, but also inspired by the Bible's description of God's perfect woman in Proverbs 31:10–31, particularly verse 21: "She is not afraid of snow for her household."

Sheconomics

Sighs, Sorrows, Subterfuge, and Self-Sabotage

*Drained of emotion, money is nothing. It has no power
except the power we give it. And what we give it
determines what it gives back to us.*

—GRAINNE O'MALLEY

A close friend jokes that she loves the television series
Hoarders on A&E because she's relieved that at least a
few people have more secrets stashed away than she does.

She then tells me about the years when she had a
huge basement closet filled with unopened sets of porcelain china tea sets that she found absolutely irresistible.
She had many times more than she could ever use and she
lived in fear that someone would stumble onto her hoard.
For a couple of years, every Christmas she would gift her
circle of intimates with gorgeous tea services. While it was
extravagant, it was also a little weird. Now the nieces are
getting tea sets for their weddings.

Many of us have goodies stashed away in the back
of the closet, in the trunk of the car, or even in another
friend's case, in a storage unit. We think we are hiding this
from our friends and family, but maybe we're also trying
to hide it from ourselves.

We hope that by keeping these money mistakes out of

sight they're out of mind. But are they? What about the resulting bills? The eBay strikes? Is our discomfort hidden truly? Is it worth the submerged shame or the guilt?

What is hoarding all about?

Fear. False evidence appearing real. Fear that there won't be enough. But enough of what? Bedsheets? Gucci bags? Jimmy Choo shoes? Wedgwood? Dove Beauty Moisture Bath? Campbell's Chunky Chicken soup? Believe it or not, I have another close friend who stockpiles the soup that eats like a meal in gigantic quantities. She picks up two cans every time she goes to the supermarket; that's four cans a week. Can you imagine how many cans end up on her shelves within a year? But then last Thanksgiving, I created a similar hoard with Libby's canned pumpkin. There'd been some minor news report that the year's pumpkin supply was down because of the bad weather and there "might" be a shortage. Well, Heaven preserve us if I didn't rush out the next day to three different supermarkets and stock up on Libby. Then I had Thanksgiving at my daughter's house and she bought a pumpkin pie from Whole Foods. But come this year, I will make pumpkin pie aplenty. I'd better check the sell-by dates.

So the question that our interest in hoarding begs: Whither doest thou push our emotional buttons? We're afraid, yes. But of what? We're afraid that there won't be enough money, not that we'll run out of canned pumpkin. We're afraid that we'll be abandoned and next year's Thanksgiving dinner will be at a homeless shelter.

We need to be very gentle with ourselves. We're so fragile right now. It's no wonder the back bedroom is filled to the rafters. If only it would stop there. Often we try to address these issues by going cold turkey. We try to ignore the urge, deny the hunger we feel, and impose an external white-knuckle discipline that rarely, if ever, works. Then to make ourselves feel better, we take a shopping trip to a warehouse outlet that only sells in bulk in order to save money.

However, if we realize these hoarding urges are speaking to something very important, even crucial to us—financial security—then we will respect our desires to be safe, but channel them differently. We can explore what it feels like to feel safe, such as holding on to our cash instead of stocking Noah's Ark.

The mistake we are making is not about having these hoarding urges, but indulging them without exploring the emotions behind them and the skewed belief that a hundred cans of pumpkin pie puree (or bedsheets, shoes, bags, bath gel, soup, matching china cups and saucers) will fill the vast emptiness that being short of money triggers. As with any addictive trigger, we need to teach ourselves to slow down when approaching the intersection of impulse spending and action for the yellow (caution) traffic light, and then stop at the red light for a breather and a rethink.

I know this sounds elementary, but I've taught myself to say "Yellow…Red" before making a purchase, especially on eBay where you're only a click away from bankruptcy. I've got it written on a Post-it note on the computer and also wrapped around my debit card and cash envelope. It's a miraculous prompt for slowing me down before impulse buys. I only wish I'd learned this while I still had plenty of disposable income, but I am much better prepared to take care of money now and plan on having a passionate relationship with money again, if only so I can revel in the rewards of being a Good Stewardess of my talents.

"How we feel about money is crucial to how we manage it," Karen Pine and Simonne Gnessen tell us in their book *Sheconomics: Add Power to Your Purse with the Ultimate Money Makeover.* "Money management might not be top of your list of wildly exciting things to do but, once you understand money, you'll discover the thrill of earning it, managing it, not worrying about it, as well as spending it."

The path to peace and plenty is one of patience, prudence, perseverance, and pride. It may be a small thing to others, but if you've been an impulse spender and hoarder, going three days without buying can feel exciting—but frightening, too, because it's new behavior.

"For most people, money is more than just notes and coins. It signifies power, status, comfort, confidence, happiness—indeed a whole array of emotionally loaded stuff," Karen and Simonne reassure us. "As women we play our deepest fears and desires in the way we behave with money... Emotional management is where financial management begins."

The Shoe Made Me Do It

Understanding the Emotions of Spending

We get a deal o' useless things about us, only because we've got the money to spend.

— GEORGE ELIOT

What's your most pleasurable spending experience? It could be as frivolous as a pair of designer shoes, or as momentous as the down payment for your first home, being able to send a child to college, or taking your mother on a much-desired vacation.

Some of my most wonderful shopping memories revolve around window-shopping, a splendid tradition that—like layaway, Christmas Clubs, and Vacation Clubs—is on my thrift fun list and should be on yours. As a young working woman, dressing up on a Saturday in white gloves and my pink Pappagallo shoes with hot pink tassels and my lime-green and pink floral Bermuda bag with a wooden handle, I'd meander through the Georgetown district of Washington, DC.

Up and down Wisconsin Avenue I'd stroll, very rarely going into the expensive shops, but certainly enjoying a visual feast of creative display and then occasionally going into the shop to "just look." This ritual would be practiced for a couple of months until the end of the season, when that much-desired sweater, scarf, or hat (rarely an entire outfit) went on sale. I'd always ask ahead of time when the price would be the lowest so I could be there when the shop opened, crossing fingers and closing the deal with cash saved just for this purchase. Oh, the pride I'd feel as it was wrapped in tissue paper and placed in a lovely shopping bag. I then walked out with the heady feeling of delight only a longed-for treasure at a good price can bring. Next, I'd treat myself to lunch at a nearby French café: delicious onion soup, salad, and a glass of red wine. It was Heaven, and I learned to appreciate the luxurious pleasure that only delayed gratification can bestow.

At the opposite end of the money scale, I won't kid you, having enough commas to walk into virtually any store and buy something without looking at the price tag, especially gifts for family and friends, is pretty amazing. But behind the buying was the *knowing* your card would not be turned down, that you had no credit limit. If you've ever slunk away in shame because your card was denied and you had no alternative payment, well, I can feel the blood rushing to my cheeks as I write. But when you have money in the bank, you ask to speak to whoever is on the other end of the telephone saying no and in the nicest possible way, tell them to check again. They do. Boy, is that fun.

The sense of being "entitled" to shop at Neiman Marcus, Bergdorf, or Harrods was exhilarating. But here's what I found incredibly fascinating: In the beginning I still dressed up to go shopping, and so did Kate when we shopped together. Not quite white gloves, but at least makeup and carefully planned attire. We kept noticing, however, that other people shopping at Prada or Barneys looked like ragamuffins, in their torn-at-the-knees $500 pairs of jeans. Somehow this didn't seem right or feel proper, and we would discuss the psychology of the rich and famous. They did seem different from us, because they didn't give a damn.

Then on one occasion I had to find something to wear for an unexpected event. Not having a closet full of evening clothes, I dashed into Neiman with Kate to find something. We were decidedly dressed down. She pointed out that we didn't look like we could shop at Neiman, and I said to her, "It's fine. We *know* we can shop here," as I quickly gathered up evening dresses to try on in the locked dressing room. I knew I could pay the tab. Because I knew that, I felt entitled to be on the fourth floor, where the couture designers were displayed. In just a few months my attitude had shifted completely from my pre-money stance.

Feeling *entitled* was the secret to feeling rich. Not being rich, but feeling rich. I had emotional and financial permission to be there. But who grants this permission? Who awards this cosmic Pass Go and collect your $850 pair of Christian Louboutin silk pumps?

Is there any way we can give ourselves this security at a lower price point?

Ponder this: How much of the joy of shopping is connected to the sense of anticipation, imagination, instant gratification, and fulfillment? And how much is the permission, the benediction to buy, to treat or indulge ourselves?

This is not to say that our heels should poke out and become blistered before we buy a pair of tennis socks.

But maybe we should realize that the positive emotions of shopping have much more to do with allowing ourselves to experience pleasure, rather than obtaining the final purchase. And then we can plot and plan our pleasures with more well-chosen and well-spent moments that trigger serenity rather than shame, such as dressing up on a Saturday afternoon, going window-shopping, and finding a fabulous French café for lunch.

Table for one, please.

Guilty Pleasures,
Buyer's Remorse

*If you have made mistakes, even serious ones, there is
always another chance for you. What we call failure is
not the falling down, but the staying down.*

— MARY PICKFORD

I t's hard to believe in a world economy without eBay, but
this relatively young company has only been around
since 1995. The triumph of eBay was demonstrating the
international truth that one man's junk was indeed another's treasure. Think of this for a moment: The first
offering on eBay (then known as AuctionWeb) was a broken laser pointer, which sold for $14.83. By the time eBay
went public in 1998, the founders were billionaires.
Clearly they were thinking and growing rich at the same
time.

What did we do back then with the junk we accumu-
lated in the spare bedroom, garage, attic, basement, and
closets? Left it there and pack-ratted some more. Think
of all the entrepreneurial spirit that went unfocused and
unchanneled before we learned how to hit the BID NOW
button.

A friend has neighbors who have become masters of
the eBay universe. They started slowly, picking up odds
and ends at flea markets and selling them online in their

free time. They've gotten so good at it that they have both left their former full-time jobs and now live very well off the profits of their eBay sales. They are passionate about their new jobs, explaining the perks as the easy and immediate cash flow, good profits, being their own bosses, and their ability to set their own work schedule.

My last couple of years living in England, as things got tight, I confessed to my friend my cash-flow situation and the fact that I had an entire closet full of Manolo Blahniks that I couldn't wear anymore because of an injured knee. I wish to Heaven I had been able to give them to my daughter, but my foot's smaller; close friends could have inherited some pairs but, again, the shoe didn't fit. My friend told me she was so inspired by her neighbors that she allowed herself to be recruited; she started her own little eBay boutique. This friend is a college professor, known for her razor-sharp intellect. I had imagined her too erudite to care for this highly commercial exchange.

"I mean no offense but...," I told her when she offered to help me turn shoes into cash. "I never would have expected you to sell on eBay?"

"Well, I'd never have thought you'd be selling your Manolos, no offense, either."

Fair enough. No offense taken. We've been good friends for more than thirty years. Then we got to talking about the dynamics of eBay, the furtive aspect of it all, having to pop away from the dinner table or bed to make sure that you're not outbid for whatever it is that you'll just die if you don't get. Another pair of Manolos and you won't believe the price!

Do you remember the episode in *Sex and the City* when thirtysomething Carrie Bradshaw cannot buy her apartment because she maxed out her credit cards on a closetful of Manolo Blahniks worth $40,000, becoming "literally the woman who lived in a shoe." Oh, how we laughed on the night that episode aired.

However, after a few laughs, my friend and I got to

wrestling with the issues just beneath the surface of so many women's lives. Our need for a "secret stash" of possessions instead of cash. Shoes. Designer handbags. Depression glass ice cream soda glasses. Scrapbooks (that's mine). Vintage women's periodicals (for my work, you understand). Scottish tartan pillboxes. Lusterware teapots. Another woman's unfinished needlepoint canvas of a golden retriever (when you're a cat woman). Collectibles of all kinds.

Hoarding. Buyer's remorse. Guilty pleasure. Addictive behavior. Gambling. Drugs. Overeating. Alcohol. Out-of-control spending. And the added bonus of PayPal private accounts, which never show your financial information to anyone, not even you, Babe.

You do it alone; you don't share your eBay triumphs or traumas, unless your husband finds you sobbing by the light of your computer screen at 5 AM because somebody beat you by one cent. Let's make something clear: eBay is not a girls'-night-out activity. It is secret. You might call it personal. Call it what it is: It's secret. Secrets of any kind are toxic to our soul. Rather like ingesting a wee bit of liquid mercury every time you sign in. We concluded for some women, ourselves included, that our attachment to eBay is as misunderstood and as potentially destructive as Internet sex addiction. Men have porn. Women have eBay. Either activity pushes the button of our partners, endangers our relationships, and should be raising red flags.

Then we took a test to see if we were shopaholics. Join in, your secret's safe with me:

> My closet (trunk of the car or other secret hiding places) has unopened shopping bags in it.
> I buy things I don't need.
> I buy things that I didn't plan to buy.
> I consider myself an impulse buyer.
> My favorite activity is shopping.
> My family, friends, or co-workers have made

cutting remarks about the number of pack-
ages that arrive for me.

I regularly pay more than I intended to for eBay
items.

I have maxed my credit card out on eBay purchases and have had to turn to alternative
funding, such as "borrowing" money from my
401(k).

I have been given eBay strikes because I bid for
things I could not pay for when the bill came
due.

How'd you do? Well, you're not alone.

We both had basements and crawl spaces in our homes
filled with boxes and piles and closets full of items we've
purchased over the years that we'd never used or weren't
using anymore. But let's look on the sunny side of things:
We had *inventory*. So with both sides of the Atlantic covered, we jumped into our new project: to redeem our past
spendthrift hoarding—by selling.

Then we ran into an identical snag. Every time we
tried to figure out how to price an item, we both felt overwhelmed with a variety of conflicting feelings. Ashamed
that we'd ever purchased it in the beginning and frustrated
because we knew all too well that the price that would
make it sellable on eBay would mean we had to take huge
losses compared with the full retail price we'd paid. This
triggered an implosion of remorse.

Maybe the worst sensation I felt was panic: What if I
sold all my Manolos and then was suddenly thrust back
into a life that demanded toe décolletage, not rubber
Wellington boots? Within a few minutes, I was on a roller
coaster of fraught emotion. Next, I was grieving for the
death of my career, and then my marriage. Five years before, I'd thought I was marrying a partner who would
shoulder the financial responsibilities with me, not make
me take over the economic care of his children from a for-

mer marriage, but instead he'd made me carry the entire financial load by myself, even if that meant resorting to selling my designer clothes and shoes.

I've said it before, but here is a significant benefit of retracing our steps: It allows us to be glaringly honest with ourselves. You are your own lie detector. During this spiritual process, there are plenty of shudders and heart palpitations, but equally there will be redeeming sighs and tears of relief. Keep going, but know that you must take it slowly. Wrap a tapestry of compassion, not recriminations, around the shoulder of your shopping self. What if I said to that haunted little face now looking back at me over her shoulder, dazed and confused as she was fleeing from her home for the last time, with the cat in his carrier: "Sweetie, they're only shoes."

Maybe those Manolos were a part of my downfall, but what's done and lost can be ransomed back with deliberation, compassion, and kindness.

Our authentic truth opens up the cage door, and we see for the first time that it's been locked from the inside. We've always had the key. But now the difficult part comes. We have to be willing to walk away from our self-imprisonment, and some of us have become so damaged that we don't realize we have the power to change our behavior with just one choice. To get up after we've fallen down.

I never got around to becoming an eBay seller—it all seemed way too complicated for me. So I've still got a great collection of Manolo Blahniks stored in my English closet waiting for their return engagement. On the other hand, I could always use them to be my eBay fallback savings plan. One thing's certain: Instead of cursing myself for having bought them foolishly, I bless them for becoming a real life lesson.

The Thrill of Thrift

Every Woman's True Passion — Cupboards and Closets

Not very many women expect to attain mansions. All that most of us ask of Providence, husbands and architects is a house just big enough for our families, properly arranged to make good housekeeping possible. All women want to be good housekeepers.

—*HOUSE BEAUTIFUL*, FEBRUARY 1932

Is there a woman alive with as much storage space as she really needs, or as many closets as she truly wants? Of course not.

"'I don't want a lot of rooms in my house,' they tell each other over their tea and cucumber sandwiches. 'I want a few nice rooms, and about fifty closets,'" the *House Beautiful* architectural editor wrote in 1932, pleading for "long-suffering but hopeful Housekeepers" across the country:

The housewife may straighten and put in order from dawn until dusk, yet the moment a child runs from school and deposits his roller skates in the middle of the living-room floor, or her husband comes in from a post-business game of tennis and parks his racket on the mantel, the whole house is out of order.

Each member of the family has a certain number of possessions. He, or she, will be only too delighted to join in the good-housekeeping policy of a place for everything and everything in its place, provided such a place exists. It is just as annoying for the small daughter of the house not to be able to find the jacks and ball that she had somewhere last autumn as it is for the housekeeper to have everyone's traps strung around all over her neat rooms. The ideal house would be one in which there actually was a place for everything, so that to put away one's possessions, where one could easily find them again, without referring to a busy and perhaps irritable mother, would not be so much a duty as a right to be indulged in with pleasure, as a matter of self-protection.

Clothes closets have, in the past few years, become something of an art. In the large cities shops exist which make a business of tacking glazed-chintz frills on the edges of shelves, of building a complicated edifice which reminds one, somehow, of a dovecote, to house the innumerable hats, shoes, and frocks of milady's wardrobe. Of course, for most of us, these closets exist only in advertisements or in magazine articles.

How extraordinary that in seventy-eight years, little has changed in the cozy home circle. A few years ago Notley Abbey, the home of Sir Laurence Olivier and Vivien Leigh, was up for sale in England. I went to take a look at the shambled wreck it had become since their highly celebrated romance and marriage, which began in 1937 and lasted until their divorce in 1960. You could see the former beauty in the bones of the house, and it was easy to imagine restoring Notley to its passionate past. As I wandered from public rooms to the private part of the abbey, I couldn't ignore a distinctly unsettling feeling. Then I entered Vivien Leigh's bedroom suite, and I was stunned to discover she didn't have a decent closet to her name! According to her biographers, Vivien spent many long periods confined to bed suffering from cyclic manic depression and the tuberculosis she would die from at fifty-three. Her intimate surroundings could not have contributed to her well-being. No woman, especially one who is ill, whether it's with a bad cold or a chronic debilitating condition, can ever hope to find respite or recover in a cluttered bedroom.

Just as our emotions trigger our spending patterns, our storage space determines our ability to keep house or — more important — create a home for ourselves.

It's funny what weird personal prompts can set off a panic attack, especially when you're trying to suppress your money fears. The thought of the exquisite Vivien Leigh (not to mention Scarlett O'Hara) without a decent closet triggered such a visceral reaction in me.

The English estate agent explained that Vivien Leigh probably had a huge armoire to hold her negligees, day dresses, and evening gowns (remember, women dressed up in the 1930s, '40s, and '50s), but it couldn't assuage my dismay at this domestic horror. Where did the shoes go, and the hats, the handbags and gloves? When in emotional crisis about money, seeing piles of clothes strewn all around the room can only make things seem worse. I'm very serious about this. A woman's home goes a long way toward alleviating her discomfort. Closets are the first step toward recovering a sense of inner equilibrium, especially when the financial woes of the world impinge on our personal dreams.

So it would seem that no matter how rich and famous a woman might be, if her husband picks out the house (and Notley was Sir Larry's first love), she's bound to come up short in the closet and cupboard department. Regrettably, for you, me, and Vivien Leigh, the closets women still lust after only exist on the pages of glossy shelter magazines and in closet stores. Most of us are still making do with the minimal space we've got.

After all, and this is vital to remember, no matter what your house looks like today, no matter how much money you have in your checking account, no woman—and that includes both of us—wants (or sets out) to be a bad home-maker. It just happens when you don't have space in which to put everything. I know.

"There is nothing like fixing up closets to give you a feeling of complete satisfaction," Henrietta Ripperger wrote in *A Home of Your Own, and How to Run It*, published in 1940. Likewise, few things are as frustrating as searching for something you know should be in there and not finding it because it shares a hanger with something else. "The real waste in clothing comes not in the buying, but in not using it," Mrs. Ripperger reminds us, and we know she speaks the truth.

So, let's do our best. Realistically, it takes about three hours to clean and reorganize one closet, which I've come to view as a sixty-minute investment each for mind, body, and spirit. Cleaning out closets sounds simple, but unless you want to end up just "straightening" the confusion, you have to come prepared with determination to sort, sift, and say farewell, so you'll need lots of large trash bags.

Start with an easy task by taking everything out of the closet and sorting it all into two piles—the immediately wearable and the not.

Let's look at the second pile first. You'll be amazed at how much of your wardrobe is not being worn because pieces are irrevocably torn, stained, or have broken zippers. Now, unless something has such sentimental value that you'd grab it in case of fire, toss it. (And if it were that important, you would have repaired it years ago.) I once kept a green satin evening suit from the 1940s that was two sizes too small and zipperless. I'd held on to it for more than a decade because it represented both a memory and a fantasy—the babe I'd been in my twenties when I'd lived and written about fashion in Paris, and the spirit of the woman I wanted to become again, including learning dressmaking skills. As soon as I made the connection, I gave it away to a friend who wore it with glee as soon as she replaced the zipper, which she did in about a week. She looks fabulous in it, and her gratefulness is enduring.

Now evaluate the importance of the wearable clothing by asking each piece these four questions:

1. When were you last used or worn?
2. Did I feel beautiful or comfortable in you?
3. When and how could you be used or worn in the future?
4. If I were moving instead of cleaning, would I take you with me?

This last question, in particular, elicits your true feelings.

There are bound to be items of clothing that you haven't worn because they don't physically fit anymore (and don't fool yourself into thinking that losing a few extra inches or pounds will make a difference, because we both know it won't). But do the clothes hanging in your closet fit your present lifestyle, or has it changed without your closet catching up with you? Do the clothes you reach for every day fit your daily round? Or the becoming reflection you yearn for in the mirror? Perhaps you traded in working in an office and now work from home. Or hiking has become your new passion instead of golf. If the shoe continues to fit, wear it, but if not, recycle.

We think that it's dresses, skirts, and pants hanging in our closets, but really it's our past, for most items of clothing are associated, for good or ill, with people, places, and periods in our lives. I can't even look at the cover of a Laura Ashley catalog without "seeing" the wife and daughter of a small-town mayor, identically dressed in white sailor dresses, red-ribbon straw boaters, and parasols for the annual Independence Day parade. It doesn't matter how far removed either Laura Ashley (who tragically died in 1985) or I have become from her first cottage sprig print—women get embalmed in emotional memory. What's worse is that we persist in wearing our shrouds in order to be "practical."

And while it's true that the past asks only to be remembered, that doesn't mean you need to entomb your regrets. I once fell in love with a black lace cocktail dress that cost me more than I ever thought I'd earn, but I envisioned wearing it for a special, hopefully romantic occasion and I was willing to pay the price for both fantasies. I may have looked gorgeous in that dress (and luckily I have the photographs to prove it), but that didn't alleviate the distress that accompanied the evening, foreshadowing what turned out to be a romantic disaster. Long after I parted from the man, the dress remained on its black-lace-padded hanger. Every time I cleaned the closet, I convinced myself that it had cost too much money to give away. But what was really so hard to abandon was all the pent-up emotion, the disappointment and anger that I hadn't been able to express all those many years ago.

Finally, Heaven helped me and yes, I do believe a stuffed closet and living in chaos are within the reach of prayer. Eventually I reached a point in my life when I truly was ready to move on, but the fancy threads were binding me to a part of my past best left behind. So I decided to create a ritual romantic exorcism. Once again, I got all dolled up in the dress, poured myself a glass of champagne, and sat down at the dining room table for a little uncensored conversation with the greatest love I never had. It was very therapeutic. Now another good friend of mine looks terrific in my former misery; in fact, it's become her "lucky in love" outfit. Go figure, although I did bless it and have it dry-cleaned before passing it on!

It's easier for us to get rid of clothes we've physically outgrown than the ones we've spent a lot of money on or invested with our hopes. But severing the emotional threads that bind us, whether they're silk, wool, gossamer, or regret, requires unconditional commitment to our future happiness, and sometimes that desire takes longer than we think it should to make its way down to the soul level. But trust me, when the soul divests for the heart, you'll wonder, in amazement and true gratitude, why it took you so long to clean out that closet.

Dorothy Parker and the Darling Millionairess Club

Take care of the luxuries and the necessities will take care of themselves.

— DOROTHY PARKER

I knew that the smart, sassy literary icon Dorothy Parker was my kind of gal the moment I learned of her famous retort to a ringing phone: "What fresh hell is this?"

A lot of women feel a special kinship to the Jazz Age's delightful Mrs. Parker—she was a trailblazing journalist, poet, screenwriter, and outrageous libertine. Her sparkling wit, coy self-deprecating charm, and keen psychological perceptions into the battle between the sexes are legendary. Among her many accomplishments, she was a founding (and sole female) member of the group called the Algonquin Round Table, along with humorist Robert Benchley, Harold Ross, editor of the *New Yorker*, and playwright Robert Sherwood. The cabal, who met every day for lunch at the Algonquin Hotel, was also known as "the Vicious Circle" because of their alcohol-fueled barbs, sarcasm, and withering wisecracks about one another's work and sexual peccadilloes.

Born in 1893, during the last golden decade of the Victorian era, Dottie Rothschild came from an upper-middle-class family, but her childhood was very lonely and sad. By the time she was sixteen, her sense of family was fractured: Her mother died when she was just a tot of four; her stepmother cruelly banished her to the nursery; her older brother vanished without a trace; her favorite uncle Martin, a first-class passenger on the *Titanic,* perished in 1912; and her father died the following year. In an era when most women never considered working outside the house, Dottie had to fend for herself. She embraced a shocking Bohemian artist lifestyle with fervor, bobbing her hair, ringing her eyes with kohl, abandoning her corsets for fetching cloche hats, silk flapper dresses, stockings, and garters. She became a celebrated conversationalist and insightful writer who went for the jugular in between the lines of her poems, theater criticism, witticisms, and short stories. She was successful at a very early age: a *Vogue* staffer in 1916 for two years, then a theater critic at *Vanity Fair.* In 1917 she married a young stockbroker, Edwin Pond Parker, just before he shipped overseas toward the end of World War I. While he was gone, Dorothy created both a brilliant career and a fulfilling life of her own. They divorced in 1928.

Over the years she enjoyed tremendous accolades and success, becoming one of the most famous women in America as part of "the Smart Set," an exclusive group of legendary talents in the entertainment industry who enjoyed tremendous wealth and luxurious living despite the Great Depression. The entertainment industry was booming during the 1930s, and Dorothy Parker headed to Hollywood. There she married the Southern actor and writer Alan Campbell in 1934, and together they formed a lucrative screenwriting company for Paramount Pictures, working on such films as the 1937 Oscar-winning blockbuster *A Star Is Born* and Alfred Hitchcock's 1942 film *Saboteur*, for which she received a second Academy Award nomination.

Parker had fairly disastrous relationships with men but an even worse one with money. I identify with her and so might you, as I'm realizing that for many women, including me, money and men don't mix.

Money flowed in and out of Dorothy's pocketbook like sand through a sieve. On the surface she was very flippant about it: "I'd like to have money. And I'd like to be a good writer. These two can come together and I hope they will, but if that's too adorable, then I'd rather have money." Which is why it's particularly poignant that money was rarely something Mrs. Parker could hold on to. Perhaps it was because she wanted to be considered an "artist," and from time immemorial the prevalent myth of the great artist held that in order to create art, you must be broke, suffering, starving, alcoholic or drug-addicted, working on a gallery's scant commission or private patron's pittance, and living in a five-story cold-water garret with great views of the stars...and a bucket on the floor to catch the raindrops. Don't forget the fingerless mittens.

It didn't help that Dorothy Parker was born female and received conflicting messages about women and money from the cradle to the grave. She was raised in a Victorian world where men controlled the purse strings, then had to earn a living for herself when she was barely out of her teens. Like so many of us did, she no doubt expected that the wage-earning period of her life would quickly pass when she met and married a handsome, dashing chap, maybe a stockbroker, to take care of her (and her money). Then one day she realized, like so many of us, that he didn't. We are the sole caretakers. Or maybe he helps for a little while, but after a few years we realize to our growing horror that Mr. Feckless might charm the world but he's useless insofar as earning money is concerned, so we divorce him and marry another man (sometimes the same one twice, as Parker did), eyes closed, fingers crossed, hoping against experience that this time we'll be surprised: supported, loved, protected, cherished, coddled, and reassured not to worry our pretty little heads about such mundane concerns as rent, electricity, heat, water, telephone, food, booze, and taxes.

Which is how we, too, end up sitting in the dark, cursing the candle and rattling the tin cup of gruel. Don't forget the fingerless mittens.

Doesn't this sound miserable? No wonder Dorothy Parker's tongue was sharp and cynical. Yes, she became an alcoholic, had endless abusive love affairs with married men, and survived several suicide attempts. But I don't think that's why she became a ghost haunting her own life. I think it was because, as she said, "the two loveliest words in the English language are 'check enclosed.'"

Although she allowed herself a few small luxuries, in general she lived a rather shabby and threadbare lifestyle until her death, always one paycheck away from the next fresh hell. In her later years when fans asked her what inspired her to write, she'd respond, "Need of money, dear." And if you've ever taken any kind of work just for the money, you'll know it becomes menial, even if your face is on the cover of a glossy magazine. Parker was always motivated by the gnawing need for money, day in, day out, and never did anything to take control of her financial life. So it controlled her.

If anything, she took a purposely passive position toward money, which—as I know from my own experience—only makes a situation worse. She never saved a dime and rarely paid her bills. She was infamous for never having cash on her so that friends would pay for whatever taxis, drinks, or daily expenses came up when she was gadding about with them.

But she always made them laugh.

Once someone asked how it felt to be a millionaire. Her retort was, "Well, I've never been a millionaire, but I'm sure I'd be a darling one." However, would she have been? Probably not. If she was so uncomfortable with the

modest financial choices of her daily existence, those pressures would only have grown along with the size of her
bank balance.

There is no reason on the face of the earth that
Dorothy Parker should have become down and out on
Broadway or Hollywood and Vine, because she was much
in demand as a writer for *Vogue*, *Vanity Fair*, the *New Yorker*,
and the studios. When people were on bread lines, she was
earning a whopping $5,200 a week—an enormous sum in
the Depression. But she could never hold on to it; the slippery slope came while she was still in her dressing gown,
nursing a hangover. Inevitably she became the author of
her own misfortune by joining the Communist Party in the
1930s, which led to her being blacklisted in the 1950s during the McCarthy era. The work dried up.

I feel a genuine pang for Dottie Parker because her
throwing away or "losing" her fortune seems more than
a bit careless, and perhaps that's how my story reads as
well to outsiders. Maybe even to you. However, in Mrs.
Parker's and my defense, may I say that the charming-
husbands dilemma—being at the mercy of men who play
at being managers of their wives' careers and their wives'
money—is a terribly uncomfortable state, and very difficult to extricate yourself from. So it's not really fair to
make a sweeping statement about Dorothy Parker's
squandering her fortune, because all our individual money
stories bear poignant scars of shame, as well as moments
of truth. Although it's hard to imagine another woman
with as much bravado and independence, it was all for
show—done with smoke and mirrors—and having become a master illusionist in that regard, I can assure you
that it is a feminine art form that takes studied practice.

But in the deepest recesses of my psyche what really
rankles, like an inflamed thorn embedded in the soft tissue
of regret, is Dorothy Parker's marvelous quip about becoming a "darling millionaire." It was misleading advice,
and I took it to heart. Yes, a darling millionairess can cut

$50,000 checks to charities, bring a group of friends and family on an Italian vacation, always be the one to pick up any tab, remember holiday and birthdays with extravagant gifts, pay for the exclusive golf club membership and classic sports car, the stepchildren's private schools and ski vacations, always have a car on call, the preferred table without reservations or a couture dressmaker to "run a little something up," never mind commuting between London and New York on the Concorde as if it were a Metrorail. But there's nothing very "darling" about fingerless gloves, even if they're being donned by Charles Dickens's darling debtors' prison heroine, Little Dorrit.

I just wish Mrs. Parker could have taken me aside and over the tinkle of ice cubes whispered a few words of wisdom, or at least been frank in some candid essay somewhere: *Listen, Babe, a darling millionaire takes care of her darling self first. That's what makes and keeps you darling and not needy or dependent. So here's the deal. Pay yourself first—a tenth of your check. You'll be amazed at how quickly it grows. Personally, I like to keep mine in big fat rolls tucked behind baby blue satin garters with pink rosebuds over the black-seamed stockings. Brevity might be the soul of lingerie, but contentment comes from paying your own way.*

Amelia Earhart

Hands to Work, Heart to Flight

I have learned from pleasant experience that at the most despairing crisis, when all looked sour beyond words, some delightful "break" was apt to lurk just around the corner.

— AMELIA EARHART

It's been said that Fortune favors the brave, but Providence also attends the well prepared. Some of the most prepared women I know — women who truly possess repose of the soul — have discovered that a well-stocked sewing box is excellent training for adventures close to home as well as far-flung fantasies.

This was the message that pioneering aviatrix Amelia Earhart encouraged in an interview for the popular women's home arts magazine *Needlecraft* in May 1930, at a time when America was reeling from the Wall Street crash six months earlier that had plunged Main Street as well as the money men into the Great Depression. With everyone's nerves shaken and overwrought, America's newest heroine spoke out about the connection between needlework and flying. She wanted American women to realize that their dreams might be curtailed or detoured by the economy, but some of the best dreams begin at the kitchen table while darning socks, or continue in chairs by the fire while hooking a hearth rug. Just make sure you have a copy of *Modern Aviation* stashed next to the sewing basket. For when a woman's hands are busy, her mind is free to dream in a focused manner.

"An interest in needlework doesn't exclude an interest in aviation," Amelia reminded readers who were thrilled to know that she always packed "her little housewife, a small black box filled with a wonderful, large collections of all kinds, of threads, a few needles and scissors," on all her flights. You rarely knew the delights of downtime if you weren't prepared for them.

The creative artistry of handcrafts has been a part of women's domestic daily rounds for centuries. It's only in the last fifty years that what was once esteemed has been demeaned, as crafts have been demoted from being every woman's accomplishment to the personal pursuit of some sane and lucky few. It would appear that handwork, with the serenity it brings, has fallen through the cracks of frazzled modern living. Now that more expensive leisure activities must be scaled back, however, we've arrived at the perfect time to discover for ourselves the alchemy of needles and thread.

Handwork in all its varieties was high art for Victorian women, and their sewing training began at an early age. For Amelia Mary Earhart, born in Kansas in 1897 and part of the last generation of young Victorian women as well as the first generation of "modern girls," life's rich tapestry meant learning to excel at many pursuits. The intimate and intricate soulcraft of handwork gave artistic expression to countless women who often felt straitjacketed by the expectations of a rigid society. In their weaving, basketry, bead craft, needlecraft (embroidery, tatting, cross-stitch, lace making, smocking), sewing, knitting, crocheting, quilting, rug hooking, and leather craft, they found harmony, confidence, and self-determination. When you peruse magazines from the 1930s, you discover that handcrafts also extended to pottery, stained glass, ribbon craft, paper craft (découpage, collage, marbling, paper cutting, scrapbooking), bookbinding, framing, and carpentry. But there were benefits to handcrafting even beyond peace of mind. Women were wise to realize that meditative handwork enabled them to create and maintain boundaries for their own serenity, and they were enterprising enough to create ladies' gift guilds to sell their wares, bringing in much-needed income when times were very tough and money was tight. The contemporary website www.etsy.com continues this venerable tradition as artists of the everyday make and sell their exquisite creations.

"The woman who can create her own job is the woman who will win fame and fortune," Amelia Earhart reminded them as she went from aviation history to the lucrative business of product endorsements and franchising of shoes, clothing, luggage, airplanes, and automobile branding.

I think the great secret that needleworkers know is that when other people see that our hands are busy, they often give us a few moments' grace from their requests. We are granted the pause that refreshes and restores. What the rest of the world doesn't realize (and we shall never tell) is that when our hands are busy, our minds can rest.

Amelia Earhart believed, "Courage is the price that Life extracts for granting peace. The soul that knows it not, knows no release from little things." And for "modern" women who don't realize that courage is best nurtured in small snatches of contentment, we might be missing out on some of the best adventure training possible, not to mention the wisdom of the ages. The next time the fabric of real life seems to unravel before your eyes, turn away from the nightly news and get busy with your hands, so that your mind can serenely sort out where your heart wishes to pick up the next stitch.

The Thrill of Thrift

Creating Your Little Housewife

Between threading a needle and raving insanity is the smallest eye in creation.

—CAITLIN THOMAS

More accurately, raving insanity is triggered when you can't find a needle despite a frantic search through every drawer in your house. Nor can you lay your hands on the thread, scissors, and button for the blouse that pulls apart at your décolletage and you've got an important meeting in an hour. We've all heard the old adage "A stitch in time saves nine," so why is it we only think about that as our hem is unraveling on the way to the office? Our recommitment to the notion of being prepared for anything only occurs for a fleeting moment as the button pops off our jacket or our pants. How have we traveled this far through life without our own "little housewife," or sewing box?

How have we bequeathed to the newest generation of twentysomethings the idea that a sewing box consists of some double-sided tape and a stapler?

I'm afraid that I never thought about the impact of a sewing box on my daughter's self-esteem, resiliency, or sense of accomplishment as a young girl growing up. Luckily she has mastered those issues as an adult, but think of all the young women who have not. Could a needle and thread really impact their lives? I believe the answer to that is yes, when we look at the big picture. As a child in the 1960s, I still took home economics, where I was taught to sew, cook a meal, and bake. When faced with a torn seam, I had the ability to whip out my needle and thread and handle the issue without going to anyone for help. While Kate was being raised, all items in need of repair went to the tailor at our dry cleaner.

It seems the state of a woman's sewing box really mirrors the phases in her life:

- **Early twenties to thirties:** Convenience dominates our busy lives, so we depend on spools of white, beige, red, navy blue, and black thread and a packet of needles, assorted safety pins, and easy iron-on hemming tape.
- **Early thirties to early forties:** Domesticity reigns during our child-rearing and homemaking days. Our sewing kits now contain all the primary colors and neutrals, plus patches and buttons. If we've taken up quilting, the box contains a rainbow assortment of colored threads.
- **Midforties to early fifties:** Our nest is empty, and so is our sewing box. Gone is the hope of a beautiful quilt or nursery layette, so we are back to black and white with a touch of natural. Really it's beige, but beige is so boring we can't face the truth.
- **Midfifties and beyond:** Life begins anew for many of us through our grandchildren. Bring back the colors of the rainbow and beyond. We can teach a new generation that knowing how to sew on a button is a fabulous skill and maybe, just maybe, ripped jeans aren't really a sign of being fashionable.

Now that I'm starting from scratch, I want to be prepared with both a tool chest and a proper sewing box. We can create little islands of serenity in our life designed to slow

us down and give us the chance to reconnect with our being. Designing a new sewing box or basket, no matter our
stage of life, and learning how to sew is a way to emotional
serenity. Here are some of the basics of the sewing basket
that should prime the creative well:

- Needles. Arm yourself with a package of needles that
  come with various-size eyes, designed for different
  types of sewing.
- A needle threader. Because you never know when you'll
  need it.
- A seam ripper is a small and useful tool in repairing
  clothing.
- A thimble. It's nature's protection against stuck fingers.
- A pincushion. Keep those pins at bay when they escape
  from the box of their own volition.
- Pins, straight and ball-headed. They come in a plastic
  box, so put a rubber band around it. Straight pins are
  cheaper, but easily lost. I use just ball-headed these
  days.
- Spools of thread. Start with the basics: black, white,
  beige; the primary colors of red, blue, and green; and
  the complementary colors: yellow, violet, orange. Then
  stock up on shades of those colors.
- Scissors. Start with a six-inch pair that fits neatly in
  your basket, but really the size you like to use is best.
  Tie a ribbon on the handle so you can find your pair easily. Pinking shears as you can afford to add them.
- Tape measure. You know you need it.
- Buttons. A visit to your local fabric shop will inspire
  you. Select some basics and collect all the buttons that
  came with the blouses you have purchased. Also save
  the threads that come with woolens. Now you have a
  place to put them.

It's time to pick a project, be it a quilt or a pillow. You can
find a book to teach you any type of sewing, so you will be

able to find something that fits your fancy.

I have a theory about feeling protected and prepared. We assign money that job, and obviously it does it well. When money isn't what we've got to exchange, however, we need the currency of ingenuity and planning. Every day we need to be prepared in small ways as well as large, and every day we find new wants and needs that can be satisfied through our creativity and organization. The key to a happy life can be found in the sewing box of a woman. Think about the chaos of your junk drawer where your needles and thread reside, and then move them to a saner and quieter place in your sewing box or basket. It is never too late to learn the basic skills, or to go beyond your wildest imagination into embroidery or needlepoint. Fill your life with colors of the deepest hues, or shades of pink that rival nature. Just be sure your embroidery needles have the biggest eye available; today, it is as hard for me to thread a needle as it is for the camel to go through it.

After you've assembled your goodies, look for a pretty lidded basket that can be moved easily. Or use a clear drawer divider for stationery to keep your items in clear view. A place for everything and everything in its place certainly applies to "the little housewife," who is happiest when she's well sorted.

Charm School Confessions

*Every woman wants to get the best from life and make
the most of her opportunities, appearance and abilities.
I believe that Charm is the magic key
to happiness and success.
And I believe that every woman has the seeds of charm
within her. She has only to liberate it.*

— EILEEN ASCROFT (1938)

As long as women have existed, we've been seeking advice from one another. In England advice columnists are called "agony aunts," and in 1938 a hugely popular serial began in London's *Daily Mirror* by Mrs. Eileen Ascroft called "Charm School." Like her Victorian literary domestic counterpart Mrs. Beeton, Mrs. Ascroft filled her column with all the personal tips on feminine wiles that any young woman might need.

Charm schools, books, serials, and mail-order courses have always been with us in one form or another, but their heyday seems to have been between the 1920s and 1960s. In 1919, England woke up after the nightmare of the Great War and realized that an entire generation of men had been lost on the battlefield. Millions of English women who'd grown up believing marriage to be their birthright discovered that there were, quite simply, not enough men to go around. The tabloid press ran alarming stories about the "Problem of the Surplus Women—Two Million who can never become Wives...," and a new niche industry came into being: teaching women to be charming and, hence, marriageable.

Many writers have tried to describe charm, which is about as easy as describing the color pink. The playwright J. M. Barrie described it in his 1919 stage play, *What Every Woman Knows*, as "a sort of bloom on a woman. If you have it, you don't need to have anything else; and if you don't have it, it doesn't much matter what else you have."

When I was in my wonder years, I read that Enid Haupt, the famous editor of *Seventeen* magazine, described charm in this manner: "A charming person is never petty or petulant—rather one who is genuinely interested in people and activities. Charm gives an automatic radiance that magnetizes and, to my way of thinking, is the true essence of beauty. Instead of fading with the passage of time, the charm of a personality grows with the years. One could even call charm a self-developed talent, for it reflects individuality, intelligence and warmth of spirit. Almost anyone can achieve charm—its ingredients are really only self-discipline and thoughtfulness."

And I thought, *I can do that.* So can you.

I've always been a serious student of charm courses—the original self-help movement—because they are so authentically upbeat. In her introduction to the recently reprinted collection of Mrs. Ascroft's columns, *The Magic Key to Charm: Instructions for a Delightful Life*, the amazing actress Joanna Lumley describes how in the Swinging Sixties, when the feminist movement was just catching steam, London's Lucie Clayton school offered only two courses for women: Modeling and Charm. Lumley took modeling but confesses she's always wondered what it was about their charm school curriculum that set up a woman for life: Was it just to appreciate paintings, arrange flowers, lay a table for a dinner party, serve vegetables from the left, and learn how to get out of an E-type Jaguar without revealing one's scanties?

And while Mrs. Ascroft does tackle the importance of keeping one's curls brushed and tied back in a pretty ribbon, painting one's toenails, practicing one's smile in a mirror, and wearing gaily checked gingham overalls in the house, there is much more beneath the surface of charm than crisp white pull-on gloves. Today Mrs. Ascroft might be called a life coach, for she gets at the essence of charm: being happy with who you are. Never is this concept more important than when you're feeling pinched about money.

"To be charming you must be at peace with the world, and still more important with yourself. For no woman who is at peace with herself will ever feel inferior or superior or self-conscious or affected in the presence of others... Charm is something that does not radiate from without to within, but something that glows from within... The knowledge that Charm is no mystery, that it is something within the grasp of every woman."

Charm is literally currency to get others to do what you wish in a win-win situation. Now, because charm and financial serenity are so closely linked in my mind, let's just replace the word *charm* with *prosperity* and see what we come up with.

> To be prosperous you must be at peace with the world, and still more important with yourself. For no woman who is at peace with herself will ever feel inferior or superior or self-conscious or affected in the presence of others... Prosperity is something that does not radiate from without to within, but something that glows from within... The knowledge that Prosperity is no mystery, that it is something within the grasp of every woman.

Isn't that fabulous?

"Charm might be described as enlightened self-interest, a development of one's best self," the actress Arlene Francis wrote in her primer *That Certain Something: The Magic of Charm*, published in 1960. "There must be a spiritual element in charm."

Let's try our experiment again.

> Prosperity might be described as enlightened self-interest, a development of one's best self. There must be a spiritual element in Prosperity.

The hope and truth offered here are so strong, I'm forced to smile even in confronting debts that would otherwise be panic-inducing. Miss Francis was once described as a woman who acts as if life were the best party she ever attended, and in her book she offers her twenty "short cuts" to boost your charm or prosperity quotient. They are so fantastic, it's a joy to pass them on:

1. *Get Up Happy. Every day by some quirk of nature happens to be a new one. If you wreck it at the start, you've already set yourself back and may never recover.* **SBB:** I find that if I say to myself upon awakening, "Thank you for the gift of this wonderful, prosperous day. Today is a day of promise and possibility," I've got a jump on my moods about money.

2. *Get Organized. A great many of us try to plan too much for the day, and as a result get completely frustrated when we do not finish what we start out to do. It is better to realistically complete a small number of things than to nibble away at a large number of uncompleted jobs.* **SBB:** The Secret of the Ages. Use this tip by planning to do one money task a day. Don't overwhelm yourself.

3. *Make Sure You're Well Groomed. No one can be serene and confident feeling scratchy and ill-clad. Your whole attack on the day is improved by the feeling of well-being that good grooming brings to you. It's much more than a surface thing, much deeper than fashion. It's not a question of lace on your*

bloomers or bows on your bonnet; it's a question of being well tailored, well buffed and well-turned. **SBB:** You simply feel better when you're well turned out, and every little edge helps.

4. *Face the Day Without Fear. All of us have small nagging fears when we get ready to start the day. Most of them are groundless and the result of anxiety patterns we've let ourselves get into over the years. Whether your fears are justified or not, you owe it to yourself to take a deep breath and say to hell with them. As long as you are doing the best you can, you have nothing to fear.* **SBB:** Jotting down one entry into your *Peace and Plenty Journal of Well-Spent Moments* shifts your perception, as does praying for a day of financial grace. I promise you, this prayer never fails to cancel out the fear. There is nothing that you and the Mother of Plenty cannot handle together!

5. *Forget Past Recriminations. Many of us have vague and ill-defined shadows from the past which rumble through our minds during the day. There are things we meant to do, the things we feel we ought to do. All that these emotional distractions can do for us is to set us back from the jobs at hand and spoil our present accomplishments.* **SBB:** Try this affirmation: "The past has enabled my future and I'm blessed beyond measure. And today holds only peace and plenty for me and mine."

6. *Do One Special Thing for Someone Else as a Surprise. In doing this, you'll be a lot happier.* **SBB:** Can you be a prosperity blessing for someone else today?

7. *Become a Sunday Specialist—in Just One Subject. Too many of us fail to enjoy the broadening powers of a single, narrow interest in which we can become an expert. It doesn't matter whether it's gardening, sewing, cooking, collecting Civil War books, buttons, or bottle tops. A hobby or interest requiring your disciplined concentration gets you out of yourself and into a world of activity that will add an extra dimension to your whole outlook.* **SBB:** Having something that we're curious about and study for just twenty minutes can save

a whole day from going downhill with worries about money. And you never know when new hobbies can turn into new opportunities for income.

8. *Break Down Your Work into Small Bits. No matter how brilliant we are, it is impossible for us to accomplish more than one thing at a time.* **SBB:** Amen.

9. *Do One Thing a Day to Make Your Home More Pleasant. Your home is the most important part of your life. Unless it is charming and creative, it remains nothing more than a shelter. A gracious atmosphere in your home makes you feel radiant and happy. A dull one pushes you into a depression. Plan to do one small thing a day, so that your improvement never stops. A new lamp for the bedroom. A touch of paint on the bathroom cabinets. An experimental recipe for dinner. A few new flowers for your garden or your table. The reward for doing this will snowball in direct proportion to the thought you put in to it.* **SBB:** This is especially true if you're staying somewhere temporarily. Make sure your area is picked up, and it will pick up your spirit.

10. *Wipe Out a Prejudice a Day. All of us have prejudices that are not only uncharming but often self-destructive…make a conscious effort to get rid of them. They'll never do you any good, and they'll surely drag you down.* **SBB:** This is a great time to deal with your unconscious prejudices about money. Money is not the root of all evil; it's the lack of money that causes sorrow. Making money is your ability to serve God in this world. Try this affirmation: "Money is a blessing in my life and I share this blessing with others."

11. *Force Yourself to Do One Thing You've Been Embarrassed to Do in the Past. We often have to press ourselves to overcome shyness and embarrassment…Perhaps you've been meaning to call on a new neighbor, but you've felt just a little shy about it. Do it in spite of yourself. Things that seem hard to do often dissolve when you do them. Don't let imaginary barriers fence you in.* **SBB:** I've adapted this hint to calling creditors, or making a small payment when I'm embarrassed that it's not enough. Guess what? It always is.

12. *Read Something Worth-While for at Least Fifteen Minutes Each Day. Books are the best companions you can have. They are never obtrusive, they never bother you when you don't want them to, and the good ones enrich each shining hour.* **SBB:** You might want to start reading the books in the selected bibliography. All the books listed have helped me, and they will bless you as well.

13. *Think About Someone You Dislike—and Wish Him or Her Well Even If It Kills You. Our own pettiness and hatreds detract from charm much more seriously than we're inclined to think. When I get letters that tell me I make the viewer sick and why don't I drop dead, I envision the mean, tight, little mind and soul that would prompt such an unpleasant attack, and know what a miserable life such a person must lead. To constantly slander those whom you dislike is to eat away at your own spirit. Inner harmony has for its outward expression grace and felicity, and while that may sound a little Pollyanna at a picnic, it's a darned sight easier to live with than that which Lord Byron so succinctly called "the madness of the heart."* **SBB:** There really is no competition in the spiritual world. God is waiting to bless all of us with increased abundance. Bless the woman who drives you crazy. Jealousy over wealth disappears when you wish someone well-being and abundance.

14. *Practice Looking at a Person Directly in the Eye and Concentrating Wholly on What He is Saying. This is one of the most important attributes of charm—and often the one most disregarded. Very few of us are good listeners.* **SBB:** Use this suggestion for all the financial transactions you'll have during the day—at the checkout counter, the parking lot, the bank. Smile at strangers and wish them well. You'll set in motion a cycle of blessings coming back to you. It's been my wonderful discovery that people seem kinder to one another now and really want to help in small ways. So pass the smiles along.

15. *Spend Five Minutes Analyzing Your Guilts and Fears and Check Them for Reality. Most of our guilts and fears are*

totally unjustified and are hang-overs from the distant past...attic-collector items from our childhood. **SBB:** I'm using this suggestion to help me forgive myself for not watching over my money and my talents. Forgiving ourselves is the hardest job we'll ever have in coming to financial serenity. It's so important.

16. *Clean Up One Job That You've Been Putting Off Doing for a Long Time. All of us have little nagging chores that we've allowed to pile up and are almost afraid to face. These can have a corrosive effect on us unconsciously from day to day. Don't plan to do them all at once; instead, tackle one a day and you'll be surprised how quickly the pile disappears. Try it.* **SBB:** This is a perfect prompt to get your envelope system set up.

17. *Have Faith in a Power Beyond Yourself. Change the things you can change and make the best of those you can't. To do this fully you must be able to release yourself to a Higher Power—whatever you believe in.* **SBB:** I'm calling on the Mother of Plenty during this transformation toward financial solvency.

18. *Resolve to Hold Your Temper Completely for Just One Day Only. For one complete day make a full resolve, that regardless of circumstances, you will hold your temper in check. You might find this so rewarding that you'll want to extend it for another day—and another—and another.* **SBB:** I use this suggestion to practice not spending, just for one day. It doesn't matter what bad habit we're trying to eliminate, the power to change is trusting that each day's effort accrues spiritual interest for us.

19. *Practice Laughing at Your Own Mistakes. Try not to defend your mistakes to others. Admit them graciously and apologize for them if the situation demands it. Laugh at them if you can and you won't have to be afraid of others laughing at you.* **SBB:** I use this one for recalling wild spending and then forgive myself. I'm constantly amazed at how long I can hold a grudge toward myself. What about you?

20. *Practice Forgetting Yourself Completely. It's the only way. It's*

a must. Begin doing this now. **SBB:** Use this prompt to forgive and forget your debts for a day. Once you've set in motion your return to solvency, you've done all you can do for that day. Give yourself a free pass to the *Peace and Plenty* serenity spa for a day.

The only real thing that I can add to this charming financial serenity curriculum is making sure you list all your day's blessings in your *Peace and Plenty Journal of Well-Spent Moments*, because if we follow Arlene Francis's fabulous suggestions, we'll be going to bed with a smile on our faces.

"I believe that charm is one of the strongest things in the world," Eileen Ascroft tells us. "A woman with charm is armed with a magic armour against all the hurtful, sordid things of the world. It is not that she becomes smug or self-satisfied, but simply that she knows how to keep herself pure and untouched by the ugly things of life, and to look for beauty in everything...Go out into the world now, and spread the gospel of charm."

Making Ends Meet...
in a Graceful Bow

Waiting, done at really high speeds, will frequently look like something else.

—CARRIE FISHER

So what pleasures have you planned so far today? Probably not much if you're still worried about money. You're waiting until things get better because you're still using the calculation that personal pleasure has to cost money. Actually what's happening is that you're stuck, and when we are stuck in lack, we don't believe anything good can ever happen again. There's a charming English expression: "Ends meet in a graceful bow, when first we plan instead of know."

How about the "spring cleaning" we'll all be so happily engaged in next month? Nah. It's still wintry and miserable, you say. Yes, the weather is far too blustery for spring cleaning for most of us just yet. I'm of the housekeeping tradition that says, if you can't do it with the doors and windows open, put it off until you can. But since it's going to take at least a good week for us to actually "bottom out" our homes (cleaning from the top to the bottom), the first step is breaking down the time to fit the tasks. In this way the whole adventure in housekeeping becomes not just manageable, but enjoyable and, most important, doable.

This would be the perfect time for you to take a look at your calendar and set aside blocks of time over a month dedicated to the Spring Clean. Here's how I'm planning to do it.

Block out a weekend to Clear Out. This means walking through every room of the house or apartment with garbage bags and boxes to shift, sort, sift, and store. That's all. You will need to throw away with gusto. Already, I begin to feel better at the thought; that's the power of planning. You see it in your mind, figuring out all the steps you must take to get there...and then you take them, accomplishing all with ease. So by the time you actually get to physically do whatever it is you have planned, the hard work is done. You'll find you have unexpected reserves of physical, emotional, and psychic energy at your disposal.

The following four Saturdays, the Order of Works will commence. I'll have prepared the Housekeeping Tray with old-fashioned potions, put a new vacuum bag in, donned the oilcloth pinny and the rubber gloves for scrubbing. Trust me, it takes this long to get up a full tank of steam. When I approach a homemaking project this way, it feels like play; I have so much fun to look forward to, and planning becomes a well-spent interlude—a contentment pursuit of the highest order.

Any project becomes more fun with planning and dreaming, because it's infused with a hopeful energy. "Without leaps of imagination, or dreaming, we lose the excitement of possibilities," Gloria Steinem reminds us. "Dreaming, after all is a form of planning."

I think we've collectively forgotten the fun of planning. We're so used to being rushed off our feet, then pushed onto a hamster wheel in the cage to meet other people's expectations at home or at work, that we're finished off before we even begin. And to be fair, these recent years of financial reversals, shocks, and jolts may have completely derailed many of your cherished "plans"—for that dream vacation, a child's education, starting a new business, a workshop you would have adored taking, the renovations on the house. Perhaps you've lost your job or your savings and you're trying to figure out what to do next. The last thing you feel like doing is "planning." So you automatically default to the flip side of planning, which is "waiting." You wait to see what happens. You advise yourself and others to wait it out. Wait for the tide to turn. Wait until things calm down. Wait to get out of Dodge. Which is how you get stuck in the psychic purgatory of "the Waiting Place," as Dr. Seuss so aptly called the limbo where all the inmates are depressed.

All my life, I've shared the poet T. S. Eliot's approach to waiting: "Hurry up please it's time."

But it never *is* time for the waiting to be over, until it's time. No matter how much wringing of hands, crying, begging, or bargaining we do (and trust me I've done them all, sometimes simultaneously), the waiting will continue until it's damn good and ready, which is rarely soon enough.

It's been my excruciating experience—over and over—that the torture of waiting ceases only when you're no longer consciously aware that you're waiting. You stop jumping every time the phone rings, stop checking your e-mail every half hour, stop pacing up and down until the mail arrives. Exhausted, you loosen your grip on the situation. Why? Because you've given up, that's why. Lost hope. Let go. Licked your wounds and moved on. Call it what you will, you've detached yourself from the final outcome, as the enlightened would say. But what malarkey that sounds like when you're driven half mad with worry and/or desire.

The only thing to be said about waiting, and I hate to be the one to say it, is that it affords you time, if you are willing to work at changing the waiting time to the planning stage. Planning is the soul of the Divine Scheme of Things, and waiting can be transformed from passive to passionate. Heaven and earth may pass away while we're waiting, so we better learn to deal.

What waiting is not: Waiting is not punishment, bad karma, or lousy luck, although at any wretched moment while you're waiting, it feels that way.

The truth is that waiting is when the magic happens. Waiting is the mystical space between dreaming the dream and its coming true. And planning is the eureka inter-section—the alchemy of inspiration and creativity. By George, we get it! The penny drops and the lightbulb flashes because the spiritual electricity switch has been flipped.

What we need to do is remember all those times in our lives when waiting felt full, rather than empty. When a woman is pregnant (with either a child or a creative project), planning a wedding, her garden, a dream vaca-tion, a girls' road trip, or a new decorating project, waiting feels like a state of grace. Luxurious. Fabulous. Indulgent. Over the top and over before you know it. We're willing to wait because, to be quite frank, we're fairly certain we know what the outcome will be, although John Lennon probably put it best when he observed that "life is what happens while you're busy making other plans."

So clearly, it's not the waiting that's the problem, but our slant on the situation—which is skewed. And when women don't have a clue what's going to happen in life, money, love, or redecorating, that's when we go crazy. So let's realize that uncertainty, not waiting, is the enemy within. And the only way I can help you recognize the potential of this productive period is to suggest you take out a pencil with an eraser, a notepad, and your calendar, make yourself a cup of something cheerful, and start plan-ning something to look forward to. A spring cleaning ex-travaganza. A long weekend in Paris to celebrate your thirty-fifth, fortieth, fiftieth, sixty-second, or seventy-fifth birthday, especially if you don't think you can swing it. Planning is very powerful mystically, and what stands in the way of our dreams is figuring out the schematics. How about a sexy weekend with your husband or an overnight with your daughter? How about planning next week's meals before you go to the grocery store? Revamping the laundry room to be as fetching as it is efficient. An adult ed course in something you've never done before, like sewing fundamentals or watercolor painting. Devising an exercise plan that you really want to do—tennis, golf, horseback riding, or fencing—you'll figure it out once you start planning.

Remember, where there's a will, there's a way. Where there's a way, there's a plan. Where there's a plan, there's a pulse.

Upon Finishing
This Book

Life itself is a story and we have to tell it in stories;
that is the way it falls. I have told the truth and
nothing but the truth, yet not the whole truth, because
that would be impossible.

— RUMER GODDEN

Have you ever wondered how books come into being?
"There are four ways to write a woman's life," the
distinguished author and critic Carolyn G. Heilbrun explains in *Writing a Woman's Life*: "The woman herself may
tell it, in what she chooses to call an autobiography; she
may tell it in what she chooses to call fiction; a biographer,
woman or man, may write the woman's life in what is
called a biography; or the woman may write her own life in
advance of living it, unconsciously and without recogniz-
ing or naming the process."

With all of my books, I have unconsciously opted for
the last way, hurling myself out there, completely naked
on the page, not realizing the deep crevices of truth that
I've fallen into and will need to write myself out of so that
I may heal until I find myself living the book sometime in
the future. So, too, was the creative process of *Peace and
Plenty*, which was not meant to be a book at all, when I

started praying on the page as my life fell around me; more a cri de coeur. And then, as the rubble kept falling and my outstretched arms could no longer push the unvarnished knowledge away or keep the searing betrayal at bay, as I followed the money to where it had been earned, mishandled, and spent by me, lost to good works or siphoned by bad business mistakes, then stolen and usurped by someone I loved and trusted, I ran for my life to the only place I knew: the shelter in between the lines of this book. I had reached a point on the compass where I no longer had a place of my own, nor could I recognize the latitude and longitude of the next step.

Newton's Chapel is for sale. I've been waiting until the very end before I had to reveal the anguish of this reality. My English rural idyll of stone cottage and lambs in fields is done and dusted. I have to dig myself out from under the harrowing debt my disastrous marriage and divorce has left behind, among the flotsam and jetsam of my wrecked finances. In a few days, as soon as I turn this manuscript in, or as soon as my long-suffering editor can wrestle it from my hands, I'll move from the benediction of my sister's love and caring one door down to a small apartment six blocks from the Pacific Ocean. It is unlike any of my other moves in that I barely have anything to move at all. A friend was comforting me the other day when I was bemoaning the fact that it would be months before I could pay for bringing over my wonderful things, my still-life paintings, vintage linen, and china stored in England. Remember Meryl Streep in *Out of Africa* as Karen Blixen and how she gets all misty over her "beautiful things," especially her Limoges porcelain? I don't have any Limoges, but I do have a set of Tiffany Christmas china that I began collecting after *Simple Abundance* became a best seller, one place setting at a time. This year I will be really *celebrating* Christmas once again with my daughter. I visualize the waves beating against the shore, the smell of gingerbread, palm trees, and white twinkle lights, my Christmas dishes and our smiles.

My friend told me that concerning possessions Gandhi believed all one needed was a blanket and a bowl. "And did Mrs. Gandhi agree?" I asked her and we both had a good, galloping roar of laughter the way you do when something is so absurd as to be ridiculous.

For my new apartment I have a beautiful new rug, a new television, a brand-new bed, and two rosebushes for the patio. All paid for with cash from my envelopes. I'm good on teapots; every friend I have wanted to make sure I had a real teapot. Two bookshelves hold all the books I've used or referred to in writing *Peace and Plenty*. Three dining room chairs from my daughter. I'll use her discarded black Crate & Barrel desk as a table. I have an old printer's file and a graphic artist's desk with cubbies for my collection of vintage magazine articles and art. I have an easel. I've never had a proper artist's studio before, anywhere, so I'm going to arrange everything as if I'm an artist—and I am, just like you, an Artist of the Everyday. It is a role I'm looking forward to inhabiting in this new life of mine.

I have four closets and art deco French shelving paper! I'm going to have a scented linen closet, a Fancy Pantry, and a Pre-Caution Cupboard. I'll take pictures.

Alas, I don't have a couch. I'm still reeling from learning that in the last few weeks of being able to still live in my home—with grace and favor, an old English expression for "free"—the Englishman sold my gorgeous red leather Chesterfield couch, which I adored. *Sold the furniture* I temporarily left behind so that he could have a semblance of civility as he made plans for his new chapter in chicanery. Do you remember that story I told you about Rumer Godden's cad of a husband, who sold her *furniture* (twice!) while she was away trying to earn money to keep the family together? It wasn't enough that he had pilfered every penny to her name, left her smothered in his shameful debts, and mortgaged her future royalties; he also pinched the furniture! I remember when I wrote that essay being beside myself with rage and thinking, *Well, this is a bit extreme, but women don't lie about things like this, especially in their own memoirs after forty-five years. But what kind of a lowlife would do such a thing?* Careful now, there may be children in the room where you're reading.

God bless Rumer Godden. I don't know how many times the undertow would have pulled me down if it hadn't been for the lifeline of her words. I am mesmerized by how she lived with such determination, fortitude, and grace, nurturing her family and creating so many soul shelters all over the world—while writing fifty-seven books, including novels for both children and adults, nonfiction, short-story collections, poetry, and memoirs. The secret she shares is that no matter where we actually keep house, we must daily dwell in the House of Spirit: "There is an Indian proverb or axiom that says that everyone is a house with four rooms, a physical, an emotional, a mental and a spiritual. Most of us tend to live in one room most of the time, but unless we go into every room every day, even if only to keep it aired, we are not a complete person... I have tried to go most days into them all—each has its riches."

So here we are again. At the end of a book and the beginning of the rest of our lives.

It's time to start over. "I believe that when life brings a devastating change, leaving one alone and desolate, one *can* start over. For I have done just that, three different times, two of them for bitterly unhappy reasons," the glorious Marjorie Hillis Roulston wrote in her 1951 best seller, *You Can Start All Over*:

> You can still recapture that feeling that you are a very special person, which was a secret excitement within you when you were young. It may have waned with the years, and you almost certainly lost it when you found that sorrow could hurt you, as it did everyone else, and you felt alone and unwanted... You were sure, once upon a time, that you were going to do big things or do small ones better than anyone else... All

you have lost as a person—all that matters—is faith and courage, and you can get both back with a little trying. You can be the very special person you once dreamed of being—if you have the will and the enterprise to Start All Over.

Marjorie Hillis was an editor of *Vogue* for many years and one of the first really successful self-help writers with a string of best-selling books from the 1930s through the 1960s inspired by her own chapters in life. As a single career woman in 1936, she wrote her first best seller, *Live Alone and Like It*, which became a bible for women who were, for whatever reason, living on their own. This was followed up in 1937 by *Orchids on Your Budget, or Live Smartly on What Have You*, coming when everyone was downtrodden by nearly a decade of the Great Depression. "Well, who isn't poor?" she asked her readers. "An astonishing number of the people you know, probably including yourself, insist that they have to do a lot of economizing...This isn't because of the size of their incomes or the lack of size; it's because they haven't as much money as they wish they had, which would be true no matter what their incomes. They have a dream of the way they'd like to live, but it's always just ahead of them, and by the time they've covered the distance, it's moved a little farther on. Their ships are eternally on the horizon and never come in."

We've covered a lot of ground together on these pages, and the journey hasn't been without its tears of relief, smiles of recognition, some funny cautionary tales, as well as some scary and sacred moments, which at least we've learned can be one and the same. This is the eleventh book I've written, but something has just occurred to me—at the end of the book we don't reach a destination. Heaven help us, it's true what all the bumper stickers tell us—it's the journey in life that matters, not where we end up, because where we end up is continually changing.

Well, darling Reader, I think this is where we part ways, but only for a little while. I've got brown boxes to unpack and a new life to create. So do you. It's the fresh start I promised us for which I'm very grateful. There is room in my new home and my life for the angels to spread their wings while they nudge me in my new direction, and there will be for you as well, a bounty of well-spent moments waiting to be discovered, embraced, and cherished.

But you know me too well to think that there won't be another book telling us just exactly how we start over again. So let's just say we'll meet back here on the page in a year or so.

Remember, protect yourself first. Have a bank account in your name only. Always count your money, so your money can count on you. Know exactly how much you have and how much you owe. When given an opportunity to spend or save, you know what to do. Keep a pin money stash; it grows quickly and will reward you with a feeling of financial serenity. Solvency feels better than anything you can spend money on. The envelope system really works. Give it and the other insight tools, the *Peace and Plenty Journal of Well-Spent Moments*, the Contentment Chest, and the Comfort Companion, a fair chance, and you'll enjoy the journey.

Blessings on your courage! And may Peace and Plenty always be your portion.

Dearest Love,

Sarah Ban Breathnach

With Thanks and Appreciation

If the only prayer you ever say in your entire life is
"Thank you," it will be enough.

— MEISTER ECKHART

ooks. Damned if I know how they come into being other than miraculous inception. But I've got to confess, the hardest part to write of any book isn't the beginning or the ending but the appreciations. For in between "It was a dark and stormy night" and "The End," the "Book" is a collaborative art. Your name might be on the cover, but you know the talents of many others contributed like thousands of angels on a pinhead—a choir of seraphim and cherubim—just when you, or the Book, needed them.

Firstfold beatitudes to my Divine editor, Caryn Karmatz-Rudy. Caryn and I began our publishing collaboration when she was my co-editor on *Simple Abundance* in 1995, and then she became my editor on *Something More*, as well as many other publishing projects over the past fifteen years. Bless you, Caryn, for helping me craft a very personal experience onto the public page. Over the years I doubt if we've ever disagreed on anything with the exception of whether or not *Peace and Plenty* really required a ninety-page treatise on John Milton to get us all off to a rousing start. You see who won that round. Caryn is now trading in her editor's blue pencil for a literary agent's pen, but I think this is merely an ironic coincidence. Just as I was so blessed in calling her my editor, now others will call her their agent. To much success and potloads of peace and plenty, dearest Editor.

What used to be my home at Warner Books in 1995 has now become Grand Central Publishing. How grateful I am that well-loved and familiar faces still shepherd my work through the labyrinth of time, space, budget meetings, and production schedules. Gratitudes continue with production editor Leah Tracosas, and the always reassuring Thom Whatley, the perfect man for any crisis, as well as Antoinette Marotta and Giraud Lorber. Thanks also to Amanda Englander, who always made me feel connected to GCP no matter when or from where I was calling.

They say you can't step into the river at the same spot twice, but I'm not so sure, especially since I'm so blessed that vice president of publicity Jennifer Romanello is still brilliantly brainstorming with me, and for Elly Weisenberg Kelly, who keeps me in the public loop with a smile. In Sales and Marketing, thank you, Karen Torres, Martha Otis, and Bruce Paonessa for your great enthusiasm for my work, as well as Kelly Leonard in online marketing. To my dear collaborator in Sub-Rights, Nancy Wiese—every book with you is a five-star trip around the world. Thank you. The wonderful and gifted artist Diane Luger—your name is in lights as far as I'm concerned. Bless you for creating an iconic pink vision for *Simple Abundance*, and then topping yourself with a scrumptious cover for *Peace and Plenty*. I jubilantly bask in my books' being judged by your covers. The wonderful editor Emi Battaglia has graciously taken me under her savvy wing as I make my return into publishing's brave new electronic world, and she only had to gently wrench the quill from my quivering fist; now I have two hands to applaud her for all she does for me behind the scenes. Copy editor Laura Jorstad: Thank you for so beautifully perpetuating the illusion that I have command of the English language. Andrea Shallcross, vice president and executive director of contracts: my abiding thanks for your part in my future. Enormous gratitude to executive vice president and GCP publisher, Jamie Raab, for warmly welcoming me in from the cold and never missing a beat or a hug. I'm so happy to be back.

Every woman who wrestles with the terrors of debt, divorce, death, bankruptcy and starting over personally and in business knows the blessing of being advised by lawyers who listen first, then offer advice. I was graced with extraordinary legal counsel on both sides of the Atlantic during the writing of *Peace and Plenty*. Thank you to my English solicitors, Benussi & Co., who are specialists in matrimonial and family law, especially Diane Benussi, Sylvie Sarabia, and Lucy Taylor. Sylvie patiently taught me that emotion and money must be separated and the wisdom that patience and procedure must be applied in equal measures for success. It's a hard lesson but one that I'll continue to write about. My gratitude extends to barrister Robin Rowland of No. 5 Chambers for his expert advice on English matrimonial law regarding prenuptial agreements. In the United States, many thanks to Jerry Miller of Joseph Greenwald and Laake, LLC, in Maryland for keeping me and Simple Abundance, Inc., out of harm's way and to Ned Himmelrich, of Baltimore's Gordon, Feinblatt, Rothman, Hoffberger & Hollander, who are my intellectual property attorneys and always watching my back as well as Simple Abundance, Inc.'s copyrights and trademarks counsel. Bless you, Ned, and your partners for distinguishing between billable hours and extraordinary circumstances. I am forever spiritually in your debt, but to paraphrase Mark Twain, there's a speaking tour with your name on it.

And to Doug White, CPA, of Polan, White and Associates in Rockville, Maryland, when I think of how much gratitude I feel toward you for protecting me and Simple Abundance, Inc., I wonder about Meister Eckhart's opinion that "thank you" is enough. Bless you all.

After two thousand miles down a dead-end road, the enormity of the message of this book loomed so large in my heart and mind while my deadline was so brief that my dearest creative collaborator and close friend, Dona Cooper, helped me shape other women's money woes into graceful and lucid observations. Thank you so much.

My cherished friends Dawne and Tom Winter fed me and poured the wine as I poured out my heart after returning to live in the United States. In England, Elaine and Richard Lees were my sounding boards as I went through the confusing maze of concluding a life's turbulent chapter in England. Thank you to them all.

My beloved pal Mary Jane Brant organized more novenas in Pennsylvania than any book or friend has ever received. If faith is the substance of things hoped for and the evidence of things not yet seen, MJ read this book, and then laughed and wept with me long before ink appeared on the page. She always knew it had a happy ending.

My dearest friend and counselor Anne Windsor, thank you for untangling the snarled skeins of love, loss, money, regret, and destiny with devotion, wisdom, and enormous respect so that I could write another day. In this book's extraordinary journey to being, everywhere I look, all I can see is Amazing Grace. Blessed am I among women.

To my adored daughter, Kate Sharp: You did for me what I could not do alone; you helped me save my life. There are no words to convey my gratitude and love.

And finally I've saved the deepest gratitude for my beloved sister, Maureen Rose Crean. The depth and breadth of your contribution can barely be expressed, never mind returned. When suddenly all was lost and forsaken, it was on your doorstep two weary travelers landed. As you welcomed a bewildered, bedraggled woman and her precious, aged cat across your threshold, there were no words necessary. Thank you for leaving the living room light on, burning all night. Thank you that I didn't have to be strong. Bless you that I didn't have to pack, or look back. Thank you for the key under the mat.

For over a year, Mikey and I slept in her bed and shared her bathroom; I wrote in her living room, he dozed safe and warm on her sun porch, we feasted at her delicious table, and the three of us snuggled safely on her couch watching good triumph over evil in reruns of crime dramas on cable television.

But there's more to thank you for: Every Wednesday and Saturday you drove us to the vet's until our last sorrowful journey. Mikey's little soul managed to stay with me until the morning I finished *Peace and Plenty*. But Sister, without the refuge of your love, God knows, as do I, that we wouldn't have lasted one day on our own.

John Milton in the morning, *CSI* at night, and the care of Dr. Steve Leibl and the compassion of everyone at Hermosa Beach Animal Hospital twice a week. More miracles are wrought of prayer than the world will ever know, and each contributed to the completion of *Peace and Plenty*.

For as long as I've known my sister, the plight of homeless women has been her passionate cause, beginning with all the homeless bride dolls or headless Barbies tucked in safely after their travails (usually at the hands of the evil older sister). Sadly, at no time has her work been more needed than now. Women find themselves and those they love in unspeakable terror unexpectedly and through no fault of their own. Physical, emotional abuse and peril are only a paycheck at bay. May you never know this nightmare personally. But many women have, including me. Being a best-selling self-help author didn't help me find the courage to change my circumstances, but the love of my sister and friends did.

How marvelous that Heaven's dreams for us are larger, more expansive, and unexpected than we could conceive on our own. Toward my sister's dream, it's a privilege to dedicate a tithe from *Peace and Plenty* proceeds to A Bed of My Own through the work of the Simple Abundance Charitable Fund. May it be the fresh start and a safe passage to a better tomorrow for so many women hurting today.

I only pray that all those mentioned who blessed me in creating this book may read the love and gratitude I feel for each of them in between the lines.

More than words can say,

Sarah Ban Breathnach

August 6, 2010

Selected Bibliography

My soulful sustenance and searches for quotes have been many and varied. Collecting the pithy and the profound has been a passion of mine for more than thirty years, and I gather and glean from many sources: books, magazine articles, reviews, newspaper features, television broadcasts, plays, and films. Most of the vintage source materials for *Peace and Plenty* have come from my personal collection of women's magazines circa World War I, the Great Depression, and the Home Front years of World War II.

For the best compilation of New Thought (1880–1939) books on prosperity, I recommend *The Prosperity Bible: The Greatest Writings of All Time on the Secrets to Wealth and Prosperity* (New York: Jeremy P. Tarcher/Penguin, 2007), which contains nineteen classic books, including Napoleon Hill's original *Think and Grow Rich* (1937) and Wallace C. Wattle's *The Science of Getting Rich* (1910).

Ackerman, Diane. *A Slender Thread: Rediscovering Hope at the Heart of Crisis*. New York: Vintage, 1998.

Ascroft, Eileen. *The Magic Key to Charm: Instructions for a Delightful Life*. London: Random House, 2008.

Atwood, Margaret. *Payback: Debt and the Shadow Side of Wealth*. London: Bloomsbury, 2008.

Azar-Rucquoi, Adele. *Money As Sacrament: Finding the Sa-*

cred in Money. Berkeley: Celestial Arts, 2002.

Baldwin, Christina. *Life's Companion: Journal Writing as a Spiritual Quest*. New York: Bantam Books, 1991.

Ban Breathnach, Sarah. *Simple Abundance*. New York: Grand Central Publishing, 2009.

———. *Something More*. New York: Grand Central Publishing, 2009.

Black, Hilary (Editor). *The Secret Currency of Love: The Unabashed Truth About Women, Money and Relationships*. New York: William Morrow, 2009.

Bourke, Angela. *Maeve Brennan: Homesick at The New Yorker*. London: Jonathan Cape, 2004.

Bracco, Lorraine. *On the Couch*. New York: Berkley Books, 2007.

Bradley, Susan (and Mary Martin, PhD). *Sudden Money: Managing a Financial Windfall*. New York: John Wiley & Sons, Inc., 2000.

Bridges, William. *Transitions: Making Sense of Life's Changes*. Cambridge, Massachusetts: Da Capo/Perseus Books, 2004.

Brockett, Jane. *The Gentle Art of Domesticity: Stitching, Baking, Nature, Art & the Comforts of Home*. New York: Stewart, Tabori & Chang, 2008.

Butterworth, Eric. *Spiritual Economics: The Principles and Process of True Prosperity*. Unity Village, Missouri: Unity House, 1998.

Cameron, Julia. *Faith and Will: Weathering the Storms in Our Spiritual Lives*. New York: Jeremy P. Tarcher/Penguin, 2009.

Cameron, Julia, and Mark Bryan. *Money Drunk, Money Sober: 90 Days to Financial Freedom*. New York: Wellspring/Ballantine, 1992.

Campbell, Alexandra. *Remember This*. London: Penguin Books Ltd., 2005.

Chatzky, Jean. *The Ten Commandments of Financial Happiness: Feel Richer with What You've Got*. New York: Portfolio (Penguin Group), 2003.

_____. *Money 911: Your Most Pressing Money Questions Answered, Your Money Emergencies Solved.* New York: Harper, 2010.

Chrisholm, Anne. *Rumer Godden: A Storyteller's Life.* London: Macmillan, 1998.

Coates, Doris E. *Tuppeny Rice and Treacle: Cottage Housekeeping 1900–1920.* London: David and Charles, 1975.

Du Maurier, Daphne. *Rebecca.* London: Victor Gollancz Ltd., 1938.

Emmons, Robert A., and Michael E. McCullough. *The Psychology of Gratitude.* New York: Oxford University Press, 2004.

Francis, Arlene. *That Certain Something: The Magic of Charm.* New York: Julian Messner, 1960.

Fraser, Kennedy. *Ornament and Silence: Essays on Women's Lives from Edith Wharton to Germaine Greer.* New York: Alfred A. Knopf, 1996.

Gaskell, Elizabeth. *The Cranford Chronicles.* London: Vintage Books, 2007.

Godden, Rumer. *A Time to Dance, No Time to Weep.* London: Macmillan Ltd., 1987.

———. *A House with Four Rooms.* London: Macmillan Ltd., 1989.

Goodwin, Daisy. *101 Poems That Could Save Your Life: An Anthology of Emotional First Aid.* New York: HarperCollins, 2002.

———. *101 Poems to Keep You Sane.* New York: HarperCollins, 2001.

———. *101 Poems to Get You Through the Day (and Night).* New York: HarperCollins, 2003.

Graham, Ysenda Maxtone. *The Real Mrs. Miniver: Jan Struther's Story.* London: John Murray, 2001.

Heilbrun, Carolyn G. *Writing a Woman's Life.* New York: W. W. Norton & Company, 1988.

Lamoth, Jeanine. *Victoria's The Romance of Hats.* New York: Hearst Books, 2002.

Lieberman, Annette, and Vicki Lindner. *The Money Mirror:*

How Money Reflects Women's Dreams, Fears, and Desires. New York: Allworth Press. 1996.

Mairs, Nancy. *Ordinary Time: Cycles in Marriage, Faith and Renewal.* Boston: Beacon Press, 1994.

McCabe, Kevin. *The Lucy Maud Montgomery Album*, edited by Alexandra Heilbron. Toronto: Fitzhenry & Whiteside, 1999.

McGinley, Phyllis. *Sixpence in Her Shoe.* New York: Dell Publishing, 1964.

Mendelson, Cheryl. *Home Comforts: The Art and Science of Keeping House.* New York: Scribner, 1999.

Mitchell, Margaret. *Gone with the Wind.* New York: Scribner, 1936.

Nicholson, Phyllis. *Norney Rough.* London: John Murray, 1941.

————. *Country Bouquet.* London: John Murray, 1947.

Oliver, Mary. *New and Selected Poems, Volume One.* Boston: Beacon Books, 2005.

————. *A Poetry Handbook.* Boston: Mariner Books, 1994.

Orman, Suze. *The Courage to Be Rich.* New York: Riverhead Books, 1999.

Penney, Alexandra. *The Bag Lady Papers: The Priceless Experience of Losing It All.* New York: Voice/Hyperion, 2010.

Perle, Liz. *Money: Women, Emotions, and Cash.* New York: Picador/Henry Holt and Company, 2006.

Piggy, Miss, as told to Henry Beard. *Miss Piggy's Guide to Life.* New York: Muppet Press/Alfred A. Knopf, 1983.

Pine, Karen J., and Simonne Gnessen. *Sheconomics: Add Power to Your Purse with the Ultimate Money Makeover.* London: Headline, 2009.

Price, John Randolph. *The Abundance Book.* Carlsbad, California: Hay House, Inc., 1987, 1996.

Ripperger, Henrietta. *A Home of Your Own, and How to Run It.* New York: Simon & Schuster, 1940.

Roulston, Marjorie Hillis. *You Can Start All Over.* New York: Harper, 1951.

Sinetar, Marsha. *Reel Power: Spiritual Growth Through Film.*

Ligouri, Missouri: Triumph Books, 1993.

Stage, Sarah, and Virginia B. Vincenti. *Rethinking Home Economics*. Ithaca, New York: Cornell University Press, 1997.

Steindl-Rast, Brother David. *Gratefulness, the Heart of Prayer: An Approach to Life in Fullness*. New York/Ramsey, New Jersey: Paulist Press, 1984.

Struther, Jan. *Mrs. Miniver*. London: Virago Press, 1989.

———. *Try Anything Twice*. London: Virago Press, 1990.

Sullivan, Rosemary. *Labyrinth of Desire: Women, Passion and Romantic Obsession*. Washington, DC: Counterpoint, 2001.

Trollope, Anthony. *The Small House at Allington*. London: 1864.

Von Arnim, Elizabeth. *Elizabeth and Her German Garden*. London, 1898.

Warren, Elizabeth, and Amelia Warren Tyagi. *All Your Worth: The Ultimate Lifetime Money Plan*. Free Press, 2005.

West, Mae. *Goodness Had Nothing to Do With It*. New York: Avon, 1959.

Wilson, Margery. *How to Live Beyond Your Means*. New York: J. B. Lippincott Company, 1945.

About the Author

Sarah Ban Breathnach (pronounced "Bon Brannock") celebrates quiet joys, simple pleasures, well-spent moments, and everyday epiphanies. She is the author of twelve books, including the two #1 *New York Times* best-selling titles, *Simple Abundance* and *Something More*.

Simple Abundance was named one of the top ten best-selling books in the United States during the 1990s, according to *USA Today*.

Sarah Ban Breathnach was named one of America's "most fascinating women of power and influence," and she is the founder of the Simple Abundance Charitable Fund (SACF), a nonprofit bridge group between charitable causes and the public. The fund is dedicated to increasing awareness that "doing good" and "living the good life" are inseparable. Since 1995, the SACF has supported the vision of more than 100 nonprofit organizations by awarding over $1 million in financial support. The SACF is underwritten with proceeds from Sarah's speaking engagements, royalties, and product sales.

Sarah Ban Breathnach would love to hear from you! Her new address is:

Peace and Plenty
Simple Abundance, Inc.
PO Box 4246
Redondo Beach, CA 90277

Or visit her website at www.simpleabundance.com.

For information about the Simple Abundance Charitable Fund or "A Bed of My Own," please write to us at SACF@ simpleabundance.com.